Judy Lochner
946-4588
24.95

W9-AUI-719

Easy Low Carb Creations

More than 200 Low Carb Recipes

by
Jackie Bible
and
Lori Overmyer

Dreams and **Motivation** *Publishing, Inc.*
Wabash, Indiana

 Published by Dreams and Motivation Publishing, Inc., 135 W. SR 124, Wabash, Indiana 46992. 260-563-6531.
www.dreamsandmotivationpublishing.com

Visit the author's web site at *www.easylowcarbcreations.com*.

Bible, Jackie
Easy low carb creations: more than 200 low carb recipes / by Jackie Bible and Lori Overmyer. Wabash, Indiana: Dreams and Motivation Publishing, Inc., c2004.
256p.
Includes index and appendices.
ISBN 0-974967-0-1
1. Low carbohydrate diet – Recipes. 2. Cookery. I. Title.
RM237.73 2004
641.56383 2004091064

Note: Every effort has been made to provide an accurate nutritional analysis of every ingredient, recipe and menu in this book. However, since nutritional content varies for different brands of ingredients and other variables impact nutritive value of foods, nutritive contents in this book are approximate. The authors and publisher are in no way liable for food allergies or other medical problems incurred as a result of using recipes in this book.

Specific brand names mentioned as utilized in testing of recipes are recommended and are copyrighted by those companies.

Acknowledgements

We would like to thank the following family and friends for their support and sacrifice for allowing our **Easy Low Carb Creations** dream to become a reality.

First, we truly appreciate our husbands, Doug and Mark, for their love, encouragement and willingness to try any food we've prepared. In the beginning, none of us realized how time-consuming this project would become. Thank you for supporting our efforts.

Next, we are grateful to the rest of our family members who provided recipes, graciously prepared recipes, and sampled our creations. Thank you Natalie, Nichole, Blake, Joni, Jayme, Jessica, Mom and Dad Bishop, Mom Fulton, Mom and Dad Bible and Mom and Dad Overmyer. We know **Easy Low Carb Creations** has meant less time for us to spend with you, and we appreciate your love, understanding and support. Nichole, we especially value your "final eye" on the book before it went to press.

Also, our card club members enjoyed tasting parties and provided valuable feedback. We are especially appreciative of Sue for preparing recipes as well as proofreading the final document.

We are thankful for the support from our school community. Mr. Westerlund and his Entrepreneurship class researched cookbook publishing and small business start-up procedures. Miss Hughes encouraged us to go after our dream, and our students couldn't wait to see the final product. We also want to thank Mrs. Forrester for her library expertise, Mrs. Oswalt for her artistic eye and Mr. Barkey for his computer knowledge and help.

Finally, Adam.

Perhaps the most important acknowledgement is the value of friendship. Working together many hours (weekends and after school, often until midnight) could destroy a friendship, but instead the friendship has allowed creativity to flourish and respect for one another to prosper.

Introduction

Welcome to **Easy Low Carb Creations**, a cookbook designed for our friends who had changed to a healthier, low-carb eating style and were bored with eating eggs, meat and cheese.

We made a commitment from the beginning to make this cookbook easy to follow by giving concise, step-by-step instructions and to be sure every ingredient is available at a local grocery store (and we live in a small town). We are proud to have met this goal and know you will appreciate the convenience and savings over prices in health food and specialty stores.

After many months of altering and testing our favorite recipes, many from family members generations before us, we are confident you will enjoy the delicious recipes from within. From Jackie's mom's Vegetable Soup, to her daughter's recipe for Nichole's Stuffed Mushrooms, to Lori's grandma's Foodles (Pork Barbeque) and her sister's recipe for Joni's Chicken Salad; we have included good, home-cooked foods for your family to enjoy. We know you will find our Spiced Pecans, Pickle Pick-Ups and Strawberry White Chocolate Mousse to be some of your "new favorite foods."

You will enjoy having meal plans provided with the carb counts done for you. Great efforts were made to assure you these food combinations (meal plans) are delicious, attractive and include a variety of colors, textures and temperatures, all elements of an enjoyable meal. Each meal plan includes 20 carbs or fewer for the entire meal!

We have included information for food equivilants (such as 2 medium boneless, skinless chicken breasts, cooked = 1 1/2 cups cubed). Also included are substitutions for commonly used ingredients, net carb contents of dairy products and nuts and a recommended list of fresh fruits and vegetables. Be sure to read the Tips for using **Easy Low Carb Creations**; it will make your "creating" easier.

With the support of many family members, friends and students (thanks for cheering us on) our mission is accomplished; Easy Low Carb Creations is complete! We welcome you all to enjoy the recipes we compiled for you, our friends. Good-luck with your low carb lifestyle, and please share our last page **order information** with a friend and visit our web site at **www.easylowcarbcreations.com**.

Table of Contents

Tips for Using This Cookbook 6-7
Whipped Cream, Hard-Cooked Eggs
and Toasted Nuts and Seeds 8
Nut Crusts 9-11
Appetizers and Snacks 12-39
Beef Main Dishes 40-48
Breakfast Main Dishes 49-56
Casseroles 57-72
Chicken and Turkey Main Dishes 73-85
Desserts 86-115
Main Dish Salads 116-129
Pork Main Dishes 130-139
Salads 140-159
Sauces and Dressings 160-168
Seafood Main Dishes 169-176
Side Dishes 177-205
Skillet Dinners 206-215
Slow Cooker Main Dishes 216-225
Soups 226-236
Menus (20 net carbs or less) 237-242
Net Carb Counts 243-246
Equivalents and Substitutions 247-249
Index 250-254
Still Hungry? and Order Information 255

Important! Please read... Tips for Using Easy Low Carb Creations

- nutrient information in this book has been rounded to the nearest whole number.

- "net carbs" are calculated by subtracting grams of fiber from total carbohydrates.

- "prepared" dish or pan means to coat with non-stick cooking spray.

- "sugar substitute*" in recipes is any brand of artificial sweetener that measures the same as granulated sugar. Our recipes were tested with Splenda™.

- "brown sugar substitute, equivalent measure" is any brand of artificial brown sugar that measures the same as brown sugar. Our recipes were tested with Brown Sugar Twin™.

- boneless, skinless chicken breast refers to an indvidually quick-frozen breast, which is really half of a breast.

- "vegetable oil" is listed as the ingredient when flavor of the oil is not an issue for flavor in the recipe. Our recipes were tested with canola oil.

- "herbs" listed in recipes assume the use of dried herbs because they are often more readily available. Since fresh herbs usually better enhance the flavor of foods, utilize the information on page 200 to substitute fresh. When "fresh" herbs are indicated in a recipe, it is strongly recommended that fresh herbs be used.

- imitation crabmeat (surimi) may be substituted for crabmeat in recipes, but it adds 3 carbs per ounce.

- finely chopped nuts, onions or cooked bacon are best prepared by using a 1 or 2 cup electric food chopper to yield desired results.

- "mayonnaise" and "salad dressing" are interchangeable in most recipes; however, nutrient information is based on the first ingredient listed. In recipes listing only one or the other, desired results were achieved during testing with ingredient listed. Let your preference and the following net carb count for a 1 tablespoon serving be your guide:

  Hellman's™ Mayonnaise .1
  Kraft™ Mayonnaise 0
  Kraft™ Light Mayonnaise 1.3
  Miracle Whip™ 3.5
  Miracle Whip Light™ 1

- pan sizes of equal volume may be substituted by utilizing the following chart:

6 cups ingredients

1 1/2 quart casserole dish
8-inch x 2-inch round
9-inch x 1 1/2-inch round
8-inch x 8-inch x 1 1/2-inch square
11-inch x 7-inch x 2-inch rectangular
8 1/2-inch x 4 1/2-inch x 2 1/2-inch loaf

8 cups ingredients

2 quart casserole dish
9-inch x 5-inch x 3-inch loaf
9-inch x 2-inch round
8-inch x 8-inch x 2-inch square
9-inch x 9-inch x 1 1/2-inch square

10 cups ingredients

2 1/2 quart casserole dish
9-inch x 9-inch x 2-inch square

15 cups ingredients

3 quart casserole dish
13-inch x 9-inch x 2-inch rectangular

Note: We are busy women who like to cook once and eat twice (or 3 times). The large number of servings for appetizers and snacks typically starts as part of a meal and then becomes snacks for several days. We also like to cook for the freezer as we prepare lasagna in 2 8-inch pans (eat 1 and freeze 1). Meatballs, vegetable soup and many other recipes are great to have on hand to defrost, reheat and have home-cooked food after working late.

However, if you choose to change the desired yield of a recipe, use the following formula:

Desired yield divided by regular yield equals number by which you multiply each ingredient.

Whipped Topping

- A carton of non-dairy whipped topping has been used when the stability of homemade whipping cream or canned pasteurized whipped cream is inadequate for the structure of the dessert, although it is higher in carbs.

- Canned pasteurized sweetened whipped cream is recommended for desserts requiring topping just before serving, because it is less than 1 net carb per 2 tablespoon serving. Check out the carb counts and variety of flavors available in your local grocery store.

- Real whipping cream has a great flavor. Two cups is made by whipping 1 cup heavy cream until thickened and beating in 2 tablespoons sugar substitute*.

Hard-Cooked Eggs

- Hard-cooked eggs (sometimes called boiled eggs) are properly made by placing eggs in saucepan and covering with water to 1-inch above eggs. Bring water to boil. Boil 5 minutes; cover. Remove from heat; let sit 20 minutes for hard-cooked eggs and 10 minutes for soft-cooked. Pour off hot water; cover with cold water to cool.

- Following this procedure will result in a tender egg white (not rubbery) and will eliminate green ring which sometimes forms around yolk.

Toasted Nuts and Seeds

- "Toasted" almonds, walnuts or sesame seeds are prepared by placing nuts or seeds in a small skillet over medium heat, stirring frequently until lightly browned. No added oil required.

8-Inch Nut Crust

Makes 8 servings

3 tablespoons butter, melted
1 1/2 cups nuts, very finely chopped
1 1/2 tablespoons sugar substitute*

Directions

1. Preheat oven to 350 degrees.
2. In medium bowl, add all ingredients and stir well.
3. Into 8-inch pie pan, press mixture to form crust.
4. Bake 12 minutes or until lightly browned.

Crust volume is sufficient for a deep-dish pie.

The nutritional information below has already been included in any recipe requiring a nut crust.

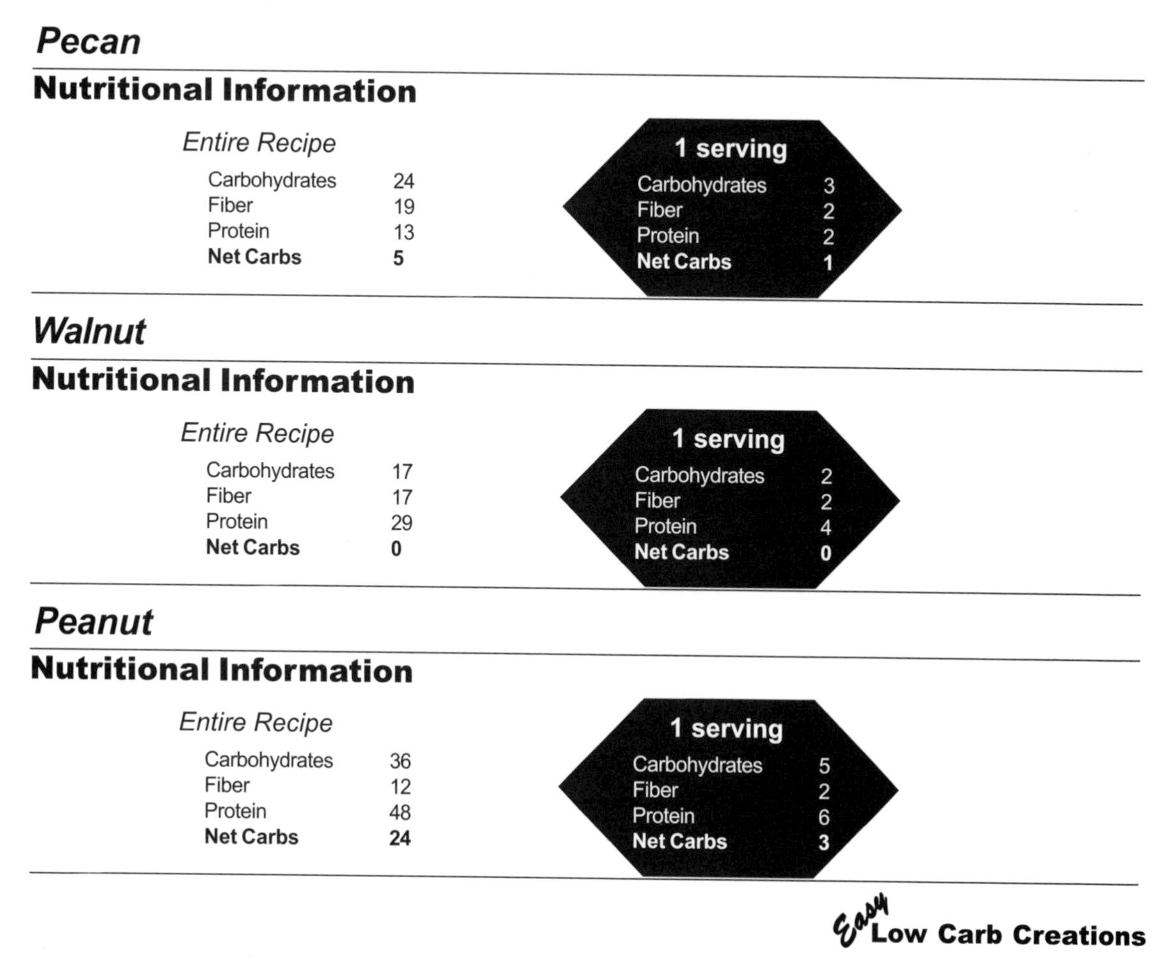

Pecan

Nutritional Information

Entire Recipe		1 serving	
Carbohydrates	24	Carbohydrates	3
Fiber	19	Fiber	2
Protein	13	Protein	2
Net Carbs	**5**	**Net Carbs**	**1**

Walnut

Nutritional Information

Entire Recipe		1 serving	
Carbohydrates	17	Carbohydrates	2
Fiber	17	Fiber	2
Protein	29	Protein	4
Net Carbs	**0**	**Net Carbs**	**0**

Peanut

Nutritional Information

Entire Recipe		1 serving	
Carbohydrates	36	Carbohydrates	5
Fiber	12	Fiber	2
Protein	48	Protein	6
Net Carbs	**24**	**Net Carbs**	**3**

9-Inch Nut Crust

Makes 12 servings

4 tablespoons butter, melted
2 cups nuts, very finely chopped
2 tablespoons sugar substitute*

Directions

1. Preheat oven to 350 degrees.
2. In medium bowl, add all ingredients and stir well.
3. Into 9-inch pie pan, press mixture to form crust.
4. Bake 12 minutes or until lightly browned.

Crust volume is sufficient for a deep-dish pie.

The nutritional information below has already been included in any recipe requiring a nut crust.

Pecan

Nutritional Information

Entire Recipe		1 serving	
Carbohydrates	31	Carbohydrates	3
Fiber	25	Fiber	2
Protein	17	Protein	1
Net Carbs	**6**	**Net Carbs**	**1**

Walnut

Nutritional Information

Entire Recipe		1 serving	
Carbohydrates	23	Carbohydrates	2
Fiber	23	Fiber	2
Protein	38	Protein	3
Net Carbs	**0**	**Net Carbs**	**0**

Peanut

Nutritional Information

Entire Recipe		1 serving	
Carbohydrates	48	Carbohydrates	4
Fiber	16	Fiber	1
Protein	64	Protein	5
Net Carbs	**32**	**Net Carbs**	**3**

9 x 13-Inch Nut Crust

Makes 18 servings

6 tablespoons butter, melted
3 cups nuts, very finely chopped
3 tablespoons sugar substitute*

Directions

1. Preheat oven to 350 degrees.
2. In medium bowl, add all ingredients and stir well.
3. Into 9 x 13-inch baking dish, press mixture to form crust.
4. Bake 12 minutes or until lightly browned.

The nutritional information below has already been included in any recipe requiring a nut crust.

Pecan

Nutritional Information

Entire Recipe		1 serving	
Carbohydrates	47	Carbohydrates	3
Fiber	37	Fiber	2
Protein	26	Protein	1
Net Carbs	**10**	**Net Carbs**	**1**

Walnut

Nutritional Information

Entire Recipe		1 serving	
Carbohydrates	34	Carbohydrates	2
Fiber	34	Fiber	2
Protein	57	Protein	3
Net Carbs	**0**	**Net Carbs**	**0**

Peanut

Nutritional Information

Entire Recipe		1 serving	
Carbohydrates	72	Carbohydrates	4
Fiber	24	Fiber	1
Protein	96	Protein	5
Net Carbs	**48**	**Net Carbs**	**3**

Appetizers and Snacks

Net Carbs	Recipe	Page
3	Bacon Horseradish Dip	13
4	Bacon Wrapped Shrimp	14
7	Bacon Wraps	15
3	Beef Jerky	16
3	Beef Stuffed Mushrooms	17
2	Bleu Cheese Ball	18
2	Bleu Cheese Dip	19
3	Cheese Dip	20
2	Chicken Balls	21
1	Chicken Drumettes	22
1	Chilled Ham Ball	23
1	Dill Dip	24
2	Dried Beef Dip	25
1	Favorite Cheese Ball	26
0	Guacamole Dip	27
2	Ham and Cheese Nut Balls	28
1	Hot Brats	29
5	Nichole's Stuffed Mushrooms	30
2	Party Beef Balls	31
2	Peanut Pineapple Bites	32
2	Pepperoni-Cheese-Spinach Mini Cups	33
1	Pickle Pick-Ups	34
3	Pineapple Cheese Ball	35
2	Spiced Pecans	36
1	Stuffed Cherry Tomatoes	37
2	Stuffed Mushrooms with Bacon	38
1	Stuffed Mushrooms with Parmesan Cheese	39

Bacon Horseradish Dip

Makes approximately 24 tablespoons / 12 servings

1/2 pound bacon, cut into 1/2-inch pieces

1 8-ounce package cream cheese, softened
2-3 tablespoons milk

2 tablespoons prepared horseradish
1/8 teaspoon garlic powder

Directions

1. In skillet over medium-high heat, cook bacon until crisp; drain.
2. In small bowl, beat cream cheese and milk until creamy.
3. To same bowl, add remaining ingredients including cooked bacon; beat well.
4. Cover and chill 2 hours.
5. Serve with raw vegetables or on cooked vegetables or meat.

Nutritional Information

Entire Recipe

Carbohydrates	35
Fiber	0
Protein	38
Net Carbs	**35**

1 tablespoon

Carbohydrates	1
Fiber	0
Protein	1
Net Carbs	**1**

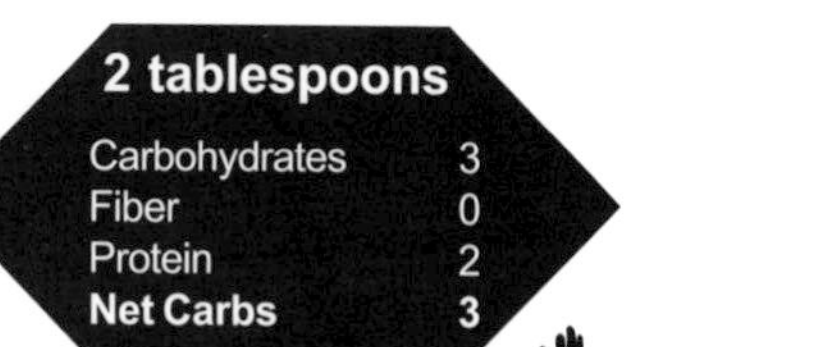

2 tablespoons

Carbohydrates	3
Fiber	0
Protein	2
Net Carbs	**3**

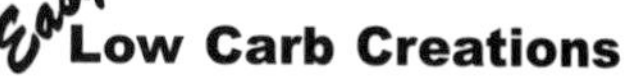

Bacon Wrapped Shrimp

Makes 42 pieces / 21 servings

1 cup chili sauce
1 teaspoon minced garlic

40 peeled and deveined, cooked cocktail shrimp

1 pound bacon, slices cut in half
40 toothpicks

Directions

1. In medium bowl, combine first 2 ingredients.
2. To same bowl, add shrimp and stir to coat; cover and chill.
3. Preheat oven to 400 degrees.
4. Wrap 1/2 bacon slice around each shrimp and secure with toothpick. In prepared 8 x 8-inch baking dish, place shrimp.
5. Bake 30 minutes or until bacon is crisp.

Nutritional Information

Entire Recipe		*1 piece*		**2 pieces**	
Carbohydrates	81	Carbohydrates	2	Carbohydrates	4
Fiber	0	Fiber	0	Fiber	0
Protein	88	Protein	2	Protein	4
Net Carbs	**81**	**Net Carbs**	**2**	**Net Carbs**	**4**

Net Carbs 7

Appetizers and Snacks

Bacon Wraps

Makes 42 pieces / 21 servings

1 pound bacon, slices cut in half
2 8-ounce cans whole water chestnuts, drained
42 toothpicks

1/4 cup brown sugar
1/4 cup brown sugar substitute, equivalent measure
1 cup ketchup

Directions

1. Preheat oven to 400 degrees.
2. Wrap 1/2 bacon slice around each water chestnut; secure with toothpick.
3. In prepared 8 x 8-inch baking dish, place bacon wraps.
4. Repeat until all bacon is used.
5. Bake Bacon Wraps 40 minutes; pour off bacon grease and discard it.
6. In small bowl, mix remaining ingredients.
7. Over Bacon Wraps, evenly pour ketchup mixture; bake additional 40 minutes.

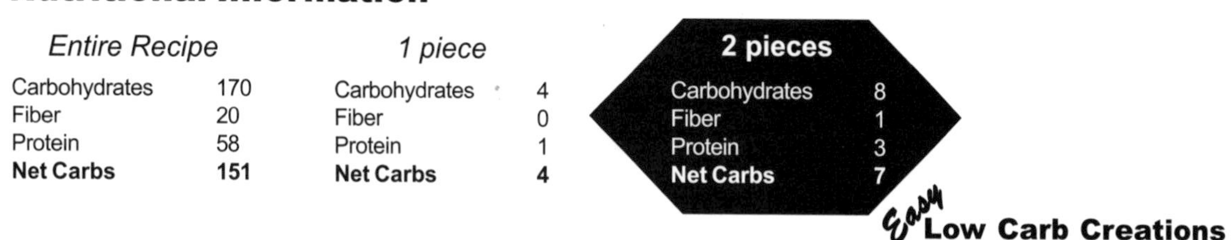

Nutritional Information

Entire Recipe		*1 piece*		**2 pieces**	
Carbohydrates	170	Carbohydrates	4	Carbohydrates	8
Fiber	20	Fiber	0	Fiber	1
Protein	58	Protein	1	Protein	3
Net Carbs	**151**	**Net Carbs**	**4**	**Net Carbs**	**7**

Beef Jerky

Makes approximately 60 slices / 30 servings

5 pounds beef sirloin tip, sliced paper thin by butcher

1 cup soy sauce
1 cup Worcestershire sauce
5 tablespoons ketchup
1 teaspoon garlic powder
1 teaspoon pepper

Directions

1. In large bowl, place meat.
2. In small bowl, combine remaining ingredients. Pour over meat and chill 8 hours.
3. On prepared food dehydrator racks, arrange meat.
4. Follow directions for your dehydrator for cooking time and temperature.

Nutritional Information

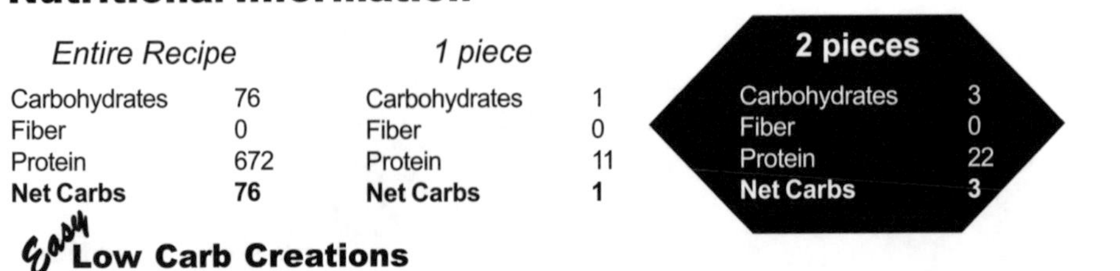

Entire Recipe		*1 piece*		**2 pieces**	
Carbohydrates	76	Carbohydrates	1	Carbohydrates	3
Fiber	0	Fiber	0	Fiber	0
Protein	672	Protein	11	Protein	22
Net Carbs	**76**	**Net Carbs**	**1**	**Net Carbs**	**3**

Beef Stuffed Mushrooms

Makes approximately 24 pieces / 12 servings

1 small onion, finely chopped
1/4 pound ground beef

1 3-ounce package thin-sliced ham, finely chopped
1/4 cup cooking sherry

4 saltine crackers, crushed
1/2 teaspoon garlic powder
1/4 teaspoon pepper

1 16-ounce package fresh mushrooms, stems removed
1/2 cup grated Parmesan cheese

Directions

1. Preheat oven to 350 degrees.
2. In skillet over medium-high heat, cook ground beef and onion, stirring until brown and crumbly; drain.
3. To beef in skillet, add ham and sherry; cook 5 minutes. Remove from heat.
4. To same skillet, add next 3 ingredients; mix well.
5. In prepared 9 x 13-inch baking dish, place mushroom caps.
6. Stuff mushroom caps with meat mixture; sprinkle with Parmesan cheese.
7. Bake 30 minutes or until mushrooms are tender.

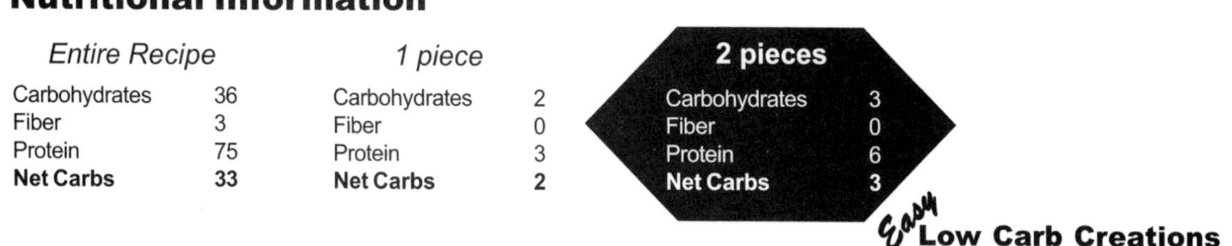

Nutritional Information

Entire Recipe	
Carbohydrates	36
Fiber	3
Protein	75
Net Carbs	**33**

1 piece	
Carbohydrates	2
Fiber	0
Protein	3
Net Carbs	**2**

2 pieces	
Carbohydrates	3
Fiber	0
Protein	6
Net Carbs	**3**

Bleu Cheese Ball

Makes approximately 32 tablespoons / 16 servings

1 8-ounce package cream cheese, softened
4 ounces crumbled bleu cheese

1/4 cup green onions, finely chopped
1 teaspoon lemon juice
1/2 teaspooon minced garlic
1/4 teaspoon pepper
1/4 teaspoon salt

1/2 cup fresh parsley, finely chopped

Directions

1. In medium bowl, beat first 2 ingredients until creamy.
2. To same bowl, add next 5 ingredients; mix well.
3. Form mixture into ball; roll in chopped parsley; cover and chill.

Nutritional Information

Entire Recipe	
Carbohydrates	35
Fiber	0
Protein	41
Net Carbs	**35**

1 tablespoon	
Carbohydrates	1
Fiber	0
Protein	1
Net Carbs	**1**

2 tablespoons	
Carbohydrates	2
Fiber	0
Protein	3
Net Carbs	**2**

Bleu Cheese Dip

Makes approximately 40 tablespoons / 20 servings

1 8-ounce package cream cheese, softened
4 ounces crumbled bleu cheese

1/2 cup half-and-half
3 tablespoons chopped pimiento
1/3 cup green peppers, chopped
1/4 teaspoon garlic salt

Directions

1. In medium bowl, beat first 2 ingredients until creamy.
2. To same bowl, add remaining ingredients and mix well.
3. Cover and chill until 1/2 hour before serving.
4. Serve with celery or on top of grilled chicken.

Nutritional Information

Entire Recipe	
Carbohydrates	46
Fiber	1
Protein	47
Net Carbs	**45**

1 tablespoon	
Carbohydrates	1
Fiber	0
Protein	1
Net Carbs	**1**

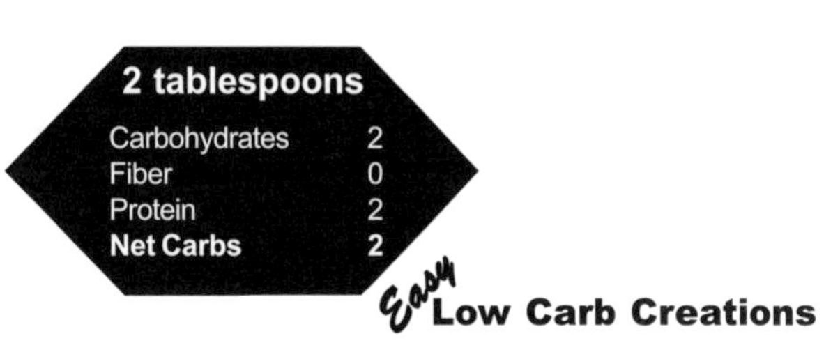

Cheese Dip

Makes approximately 28 tablespoons / 14 servings

1 8-ounce package cream cheese, softened
2 tablespoons butter, softened
1/8 teaspoon onion salt
1/8 teaspoon garlic salt
1 5-ounce jar pasteurized process cheese spread, Old English Style™

Directions

1. In medium bowl, beat all ingredients until smooth.
2. Cover and chill.
3. Serve with celery or on cooked vegetables or meat.

Nutritional Information

Entire Recipe

Carbohydrates	47
Fiber	0
Protein	41
Net Carbs	**47**

1 tablespoon

Carbohydrates	2
Fiber	0
Protein	1
Net Carbs	**2**

2 tablespoons

Carbohydrates	3
Fiber	0
Protein	3
Net Carbs	**3**

Chicken Balls

Makes approximately 40 balls / 20 servings

1 pound boneless, skinless chicken breast, uncooked
3 tablespoons onion
10 water chestnuts
1 4-ounce can mushrooms, drained

2 tablespoons cornstarch
1/2 teaspoon salt
2 tablespoons soy sauce
1 tablespoon sherry
2 egg whites, stiffly beaten

Directions

1. Into medium bowl, grind together first 4 ingredients using food grinder, processor, or chopper.
2. To same bowl, stir in remaining ingredients; form into small, 1-inch balls.
3. In hot fat, deep-fry chicken balls until done.
4. Drain; serve with toothpicks.

Nutritional Information

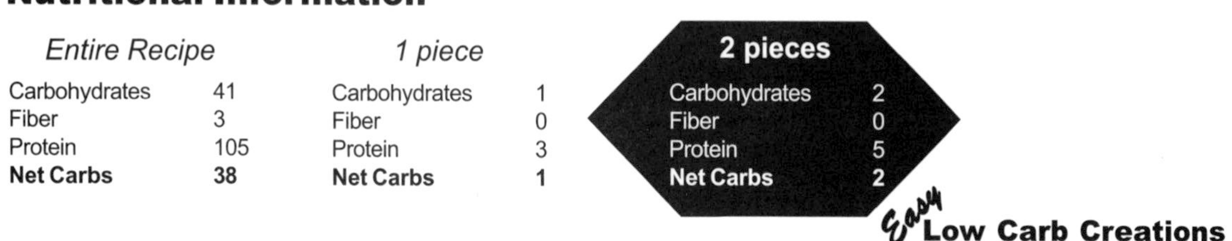

Entire Recipe		*1 piece*		**2 pieces**	
Carbohydrates	41	Carbohydrates	1	Carbohydrates	2
Fiber	3	Fiber	0	Fiber	0
Protein	105	Protein	3	Protein	5
Net Carbs	**38**	**Net Carbs**	**1**	**Net Carbs**	**2**

Chicken Drumettes

Makes 40 pieces / 20 servings

1/2 cup lemon juice
1/2 cup vegetable oil
3/4 teaspoon ginger
1/2 cup ketchup
1/2 cup soy sauce
1/4 teaspoon garlic powder

40 chicken drumettes (5 pound bag)

Directions

1. In large bowl, combine first 6 ingredients to make marinade.
2. To same bowl, add chicken; stir to coat with marinade. Cover and chill 4 hours, turning several times.
3. Preheat oven to 375 degrees.
4. In foil-lined pan, place chicken.
5. Bake 30 minutes; brush with reserved marinade.
6. Turn chicken; brush with marinade and bake additional 30 minutes.

Nutritional Information

Entire Recipe

Carbohydrates	20
Fiber	0
Protein	195
Net Carbs	**20**

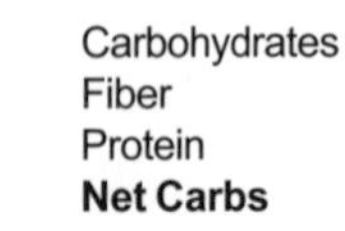

1 piece

Carbohydrates	1
Fiber	0
Protein	5
Net Carbs	**1**

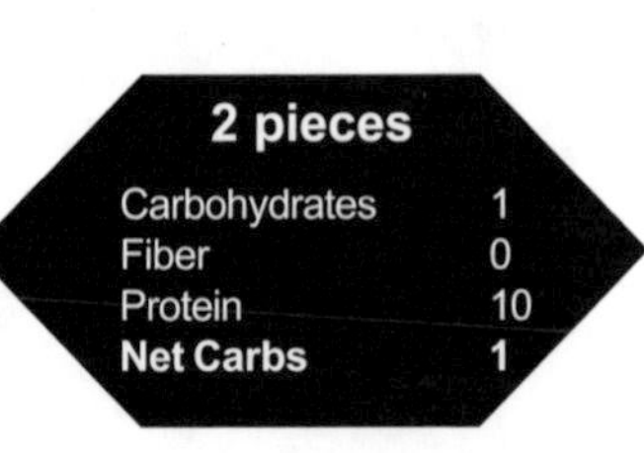

2 pieces

Carbohydrates	1
Fiber	0
Protein	10
Net Carbs	**1**

Chilled Ham Ball

Makes approximately 26 tablespoons / 13 servings

2 4.25-ounce cans deviled ham
3 tablespoons stuffed green olives, chopped
1 teaspoon mustard
1/2 teaspoon sugar substitute*
Hot sauce to taste

1 3-ounce package cream cheese, softened
2 teaspoons milk

Directions

1. In medium bowl, combine first 5 ingredients; shape into ball. Cover and chill until firm.
2. In medium bowl, beat cream cheese and milk.
3. Frost ball with cream cheese mixture; cover and chill.
4. Serve on celery sticks.

Nutritional Information

Entire Recipe

Carbohydrates	12
Fiber	0
Protein	43
Net Carbs	**12**

1 tablespoon

Carbohydrates	0
Fiber	0
Protein	2
Net Carbs	**0**

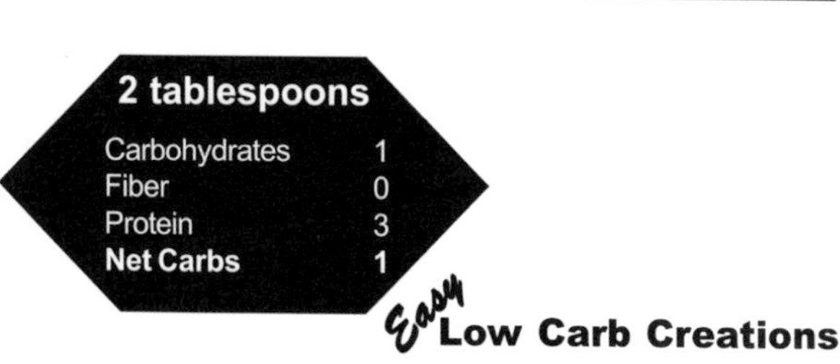

2 tablespoons

Carbohydrates	1
Fiber	0
Protein	3
Net Carbs	**1**

Dill Dip

Makes approximately 34 tablespoons / 17 servings

1 cup mayonnaise
1 cup sour cream
2 tablespoons dill weed
1 teaspoon garlic salt
1/2 teaspoon onion powder

Directions

1. In medium bowl, combine all ingredients.
2. Cover and chill 2 hours.
3. Serve with fresh vegetables or pour over cooked vegetables or meat.

Nutritional Information

Entire Recipe

Carbohydrates	18
Fiber	0
Protein	8
Net Carbs	**18**

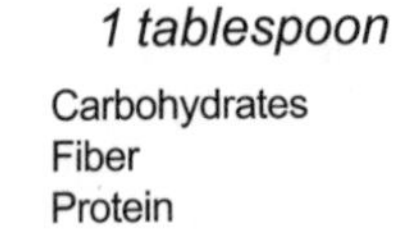

1 tablespoon

Carbohydrates	1
Fiber	0
Protein	0
Net Carbs	**1**

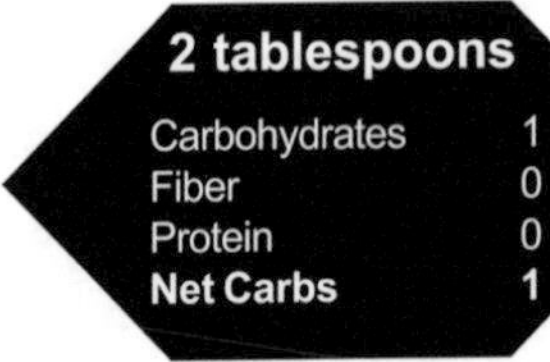

2 tablespoons

Carbohydrates	1
Fiber	0
Protein	0
Net Carbs	**1**

Dried Beef Dip

Makes approximately 50 tablespoons / 25 servings

1 8-ounce package cream cheese, softened

1 cup sour cream
1/2 cup green pepper, finely chopped
2 tablespoons onion, finely chopped
1 4-ounce package dried beef, chopped
1/2 teaspoon garlic salt

Directions

1. In medium bowl, beat cream cheese.
2. To same bowl, add remaining ingredients; beat until well blended.
3. Cover and chill 2 hours.
4. Serve on celery sticks.

Nutritional Information

Entire Recipe

Carbohydrates	49
Fiber	1
Protein	55
Net Carbs	**48**

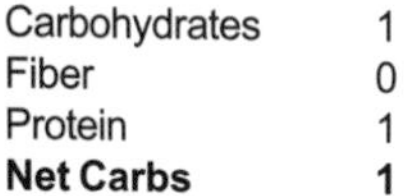

1 tablespoon

Carbohydrates	1
Fiber	0
Protein	1
Net Carbs	**1**

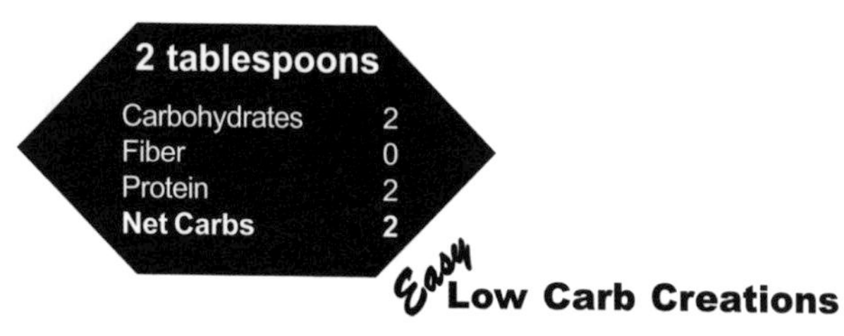

2 tablespoons

Carbohydrates	2
Fiber	0
Protein	2
Net Carbs	**2**

Favorite Cheese Ball

Makes approximately 50 tablespoons / 25 servings

2 cups shredded sharp cheddar cheese
1 8-ounce package cream cheese, softened
1 tablespoon Worcestershire sauce
1/4 cup onion, finely chopped
1/8 teaspoon garlic powder

1 4-ounce package dried beef, cut into small pieces

Directions

1. In large freezer bag, combine first 5 ingredients, kneading until well-blended.
2. Form mixture into one large or two small balls.
3. Place chipped beef on waxed paper; roll cheese ball in beef until well-coated.
4. Cover and chill. Remove from refrigerator 1/2 hour before serving.

Nutritional Information

Entire Recipe	
Carbohydrates	37
Fiber	1
Protein	98
Net Carbs	**36**

1 tablespoon	
Carbohydrates	1
Fiber	0
Protein	2
Net Carbs	**1**

2 tablespoons	
Carbohydrates	1
Fiber	0
Protein	4
Net Carbs	**1**

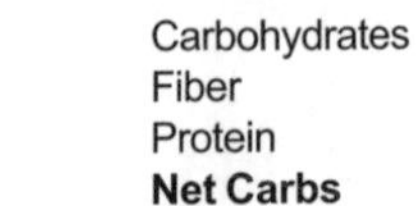

Guacamole Dip

Makes approximately 40 tablespoons / 20 servings

4 avocados, peeled, pit removed

1 1/2 teaspoons lime juice
1/4 teaspoon garlic powder

1/4 cup salsa
2 tablespoons sour cream

Directions

1. Dice 1 avocado; set aside.
2. In medium bowl with electric mixer, mash 3 avocados.
3. To same bowl, beat in next 2 ingredients.
4. To avocado mixture, stir in diced avocado and salsa; fold in sour cream.
5. Serve with fresh vegetables, on salads or on Taco Soup (see recipe page 235).

Nutritional Information

Entire Recipe	
Carbohydrates	7
Fiber	0
Protein	1
Net Carbs	**7**

1 tablespoon	
Carbohydrates	0
Fiber	0
Protein	0
Net Carbs	**0**

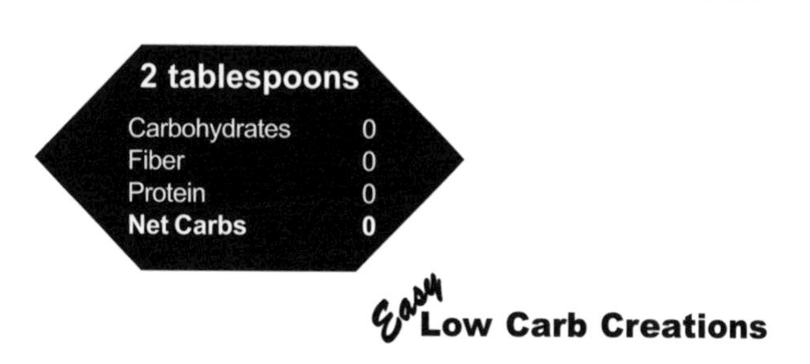

2 tablespoons	
Carbohydrates	0
Fiber	0
Protein	0
Net Carbs	**0**

Ham and Cheese Nut Balls

Makes approximately 50 tablespoons / 25 servings

1 8-ounce package cream cheese, softened
1/4 cup mayonnaise or salad dressing

1 8-ounce can flaked ham
2 teaspoons parsley
1 tablespoon green onion, finely chopped
1/2 teaspoon mustard
1/4 teaspoon hot sauce

1 cup pecan pieces

Directions

1. In medium bowl, beat first 2 ingredients until smooth.
2. To same bowl, stir in next 5 ingredients; cover and chill 2 hours.
3. Shape cheese mixture into 2 balls; roll each in chopped nuts.
4. Serve on celery sticks, green pepper wedges or cucumber slices.

Nutritional Information

Entire Recipe	
Carbohydrates	47
Fiber	11
Protein	61
Net Carbs	**36**

1 tablespoon	
Carbohydrates	1
Fiber	0
Protein	1
Net Carbs	**1**

2 tablespoons	
Carbohydrates	2
Fiber	0
Protein	2
Net Carbs	**2**

Hot Brats

Makes approximately 80 1-inch pieces / 40 servings

2 pounds bratwursts or smoked sausages, cut into 1-inch rounds
2 tablespoons vegetable oil

1 cup beer

1/4 cup brown sugar substitute, equivalent measure
4 teaspoons cornstarch

1/4 cup vinegar
1/4 cup mustard
4 teaspoons prepared horseradish

Directions

1. In large skillet over medium-high heat, add oil and sausage pieces; cook 6 to 8 minutes or until browned; drain.
2. To same skillet, add beer to sausages; cover and simmer 10 minutes.
3. Meanwhile, in small bowl, combine brown sugar substitute and cornstarch.
4. To same bowl, blend in remaining ingredients.
5. To sausages in skillet, add cornstarch mixture; cook and stir until thick and bubbly.

Nutritional Information

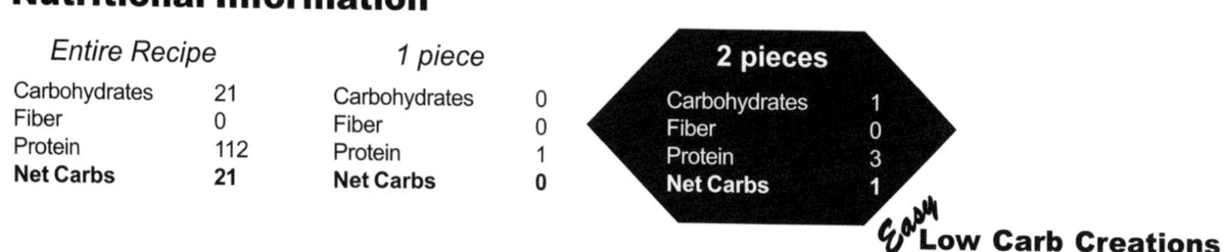

Entire Recipe	
Carbohydrates	21
Fiber	0
Protein	112
Net Carbs	**21**

1 piece	
Carbohydrates	0
Fiber	0
Protein	1
Net Carbs	**0**

2 pieces	
Carbohydrates	1
Fiber	0
Protein	3
Net Carbs	**1**

Nichole's Stuffed Mushrooms

Makes approximately 24 mushrooms / 12 servings

1 16-ounce package fresh mushrooms, stems removed
1 stick butter
1 tablespoon minced garlic

1 8-ounce package cream cheese with chives and onions
1 cup shredded cheddar cheese

Directions

1. Preheat oven to 350 degrees.
2. In medium skillet over medium-low heat, cook mushroom caps in butter and garlic 10 minutes. Cool.
3. In prepared 8 x 8-inch baking dish, place mushrooms.
4. Fill mushroom caps with cream cheese.
5. Top mushrooms with cheddar cheese.
6. Bake 15 minutes or until cheese melts.

Nutritional Information

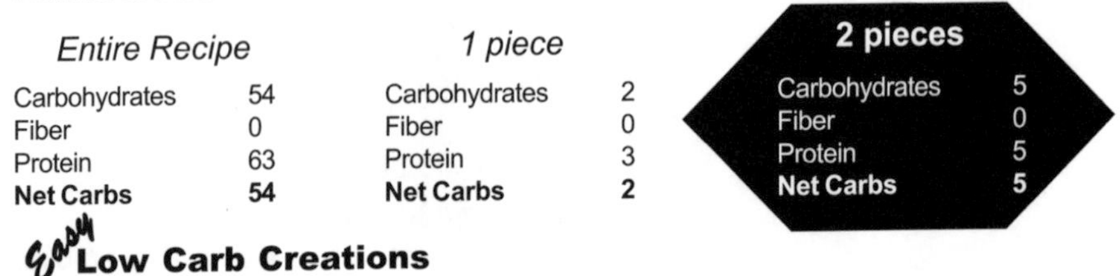

Entire Recipe	
Carbohydrates	54
Fiber	0
Protein	63
Net Carbs	**54**

1 piece	
Carbohydrates	2
Fiber	0
Protein	3
Net Carbs	**2**

2 pieces	
Carbohydrates	5
Fiber	0
Protein	5
Net Carbs	**5**

Party Beef Balls

Makes approximately 40 meatballs / 20 servings

2 pounds lean ground beef
2 eggs, beaten
2 teaspoons salt
1/2 teaspoon pepper
1 large onion, finely chopped
1 tablespoon Worcestershire sauce
1 tablespoon oregano
1 tablespoon soy sauce

1 1/2 cups BBQ Sauce (see recipe page 161)

Directions

1. Preheat oven to 350 degrees.
2. In large bowl, combine first 8 ingredients.
3. Shape meat mixture into 40 small, 1-inch balls. On prepared sheet cake pan, place meatballs.
4. Bake 45 minutes or until centers of meatballs are no longer pink.
5. Into slow cooker, place meatballs; cover with barbecue sauce.
6. Cook on low 1 hour or until hot; serve with toothpicks.

Nutritional Information

Entire Recipe	
Carbohydrates	43
Fiber	3
Protein	155
Net Carbs	**40**

1 piece	
Carbohydrates	1
Fiber	0
Protein	4
Net Carbs	**1**

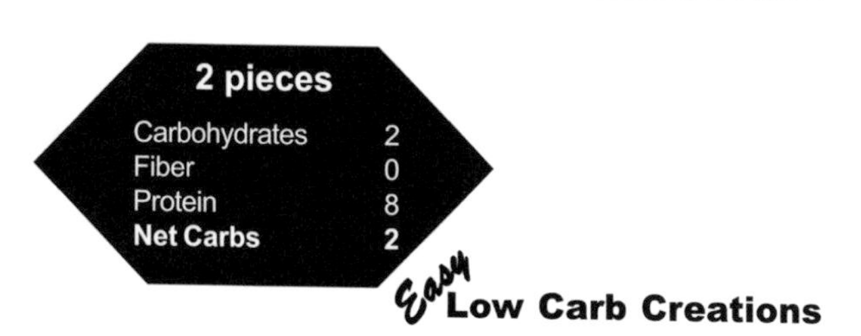

2 pieces	
Carbohydrates	2
Fiber	0
Protein	8
Net Carbs	**2**

Peanut Pineapple Bites

Makes 36 pieces / 18 servings

1 8-ounce package cream cheese, softened

1/4 cup peanut butter
1 tablespoon sugar substitute*
1 8-ounce can crushed pineapple, well drained
1/4 teaspoon hot pepper sauce (optional)

12 ribs celery, cut into thirds

1/2 cup peanuts, chopped

Directions

1. In medium bowl, beat cream cheese.
2. To same bowl, beat in next 3 (or 4) ingredients.
3. Fill celery pieces with cream cheese mixture.
4. Sprinkle with chopped nuts.

Nutritional Information

Entire Recipe		*1 piece*	
Carbohydrates	31	Carbohydrates	1
Fiber	8	Fiber	0
Protein	25	Protein	1
Net Carbs	**23**	**Net Carbs**	**1**

2 pieces	
Carbohydrates	2
Fiber	0
Protein	1
Net Carbs	**2**

Pepperoni-Cheese-Spinach Mini-Cups

Makes 48 pieces / 24 servings

1 10-ounce package sliced pepperoni

1 10-ounce package frozen chopped spinach, thawed, drained
2 cups ricotta cheese
1 1/2 cups freshly grated Parmesan cheese
1 8-ounce package fresh mushrooms, finely chopped
1/4 cup onion, finely chopped
1 teaspoon oregano
1/2 teaspoon salt
2 eggs, slightly beaten

1/4 cup sour cream

Directions

1. Preheat oven to 350 degrees.
2. In bottom of each prepared miniature muffin cup, place a pepperoni slice; set aside.
3. Cut remaining pepperoni slices into 48 wedges.
4. In large bowl, combine spinach and next 7 ingredients; spoon mixture into muffin cups.
5. Bake 20 to 25 minutes or until lightly browned.
6. Cool 10 minutes; on serving plate, place Mini-Cups.
7. On top of each Mini-Cup, place dollop sour cream and pepperoni wedge.

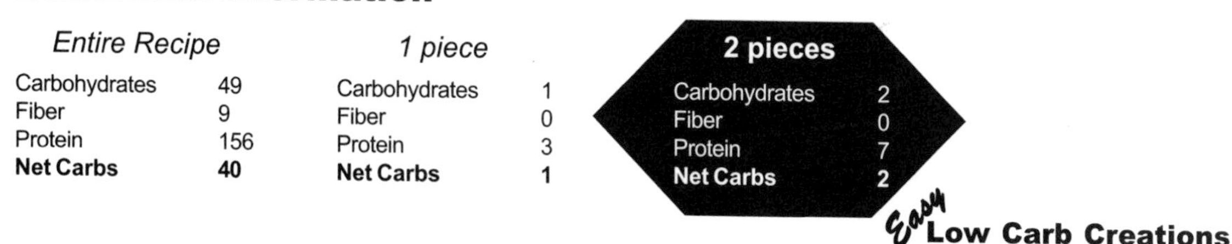

Nutritional Information

	Entire Recipe	*1 piece*	**2 pieces**
Carbohydrates	49	1	2
Fiber	9	0	0
Protein	156	3	7
Net Carbs	**40**	**1**	**2**

Pickle Pick-Ups

Makes approximately 80 pieces / 40 servings

1 16-ounce jar baby dill pickles, drained
2 2.5-ounce packages smoked ham
1 8-ounce package whipped cream cheese

Directions

1. On paper towel, place pickles to dry.
2. While pickles are "drying," spread cream cheese on one side of ham slice, being careful to cover entire slice with thin layer.
3. Overlap second piece of ham on the first piece and spread cream cheese on it in the same way.
4. On end of each ham slice, place pickle and roll like a jelly roll.
5. Cover and chill 1 hour.
6. To serve, slice into 1/2 inch rounds.

Nutritional Information

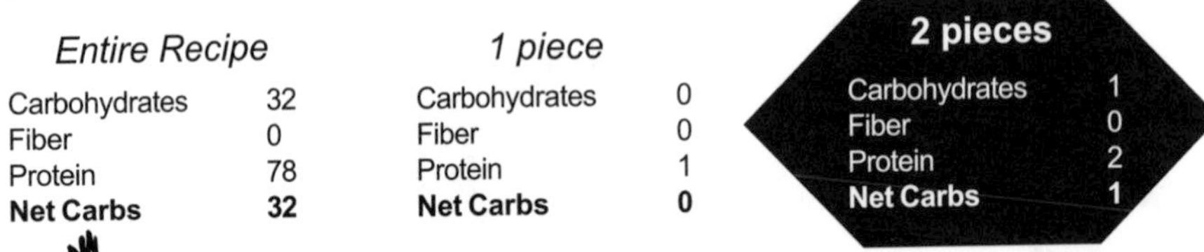

	Entire Recipe	*1 piece*	**2 pieces**
Carbohydrates	32	0	1
Fiber	0	0	0
Protein	78	1	2
Net Carbs	**32**	**0**	**1**

Pineapple Cheese Ball

Makes approximately 78 tablespoons / 39 servings

2 8-ounce packages cream cheese, softened
1 8-ounce can crushed pineapple, drained
1 teaspoon seasoned salt
1/4 cup green pepper, finely chopped
2 tablespoons onion, finely chopped

1 1/2 cups chopped pecans

Directions

1. In medium bowl, mix first 5 ingredients.
2. Shape ingredients into 3 balls and chill 1 hour.
3. Roll balls in chopped pecans.
4. Cover and chill 2 hours.
5. Serve with fresh vegetables, cooked vegetables, or meat.

Nutritional Information

Entire Recipe

Carbohydrates	122
Fiber	19
Protein	50
Net Carbs	**103**

1 tablespoon

Carbohydrates	1
Fiber	0
Protein	1
Net Carbs	**1**

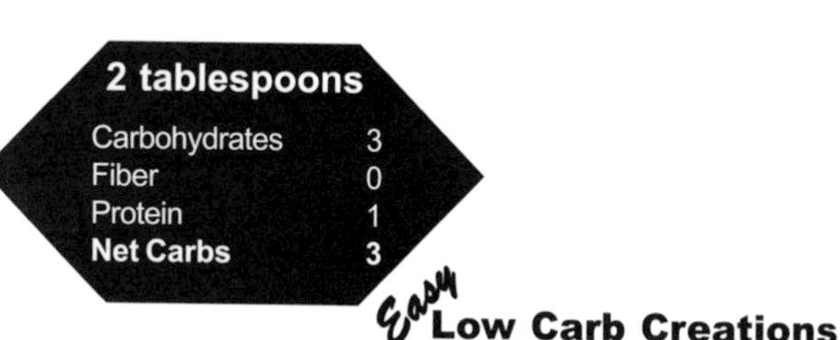

2 tablespoons

Carbohydrates	3
Fiber	0
Protein	1
Net Carbs	**3**

Spiced Pecans

Makes approximately 4 cups / 8 servings

1 egg white
1 tablespoon water

1 teaspoon vanilla
1 teaspoon salt
1 tablespoon cinnamon
1/2 teaspoon nutmeg
1 cup sugar substitute*

1 pound pecans

Directions

1. Preheat oven to 300 degrees.
2. In large bowl, beat egg white and water until foamy.
3. To beaten egg whites, add next 5 ingredients; beat.
4. To same bowl, add pecans; stir until well coated.
5. Onto prepared sheet cake pan, pour pecan mixture.
6. Bake 45 minutes, stirring every 15 minutes.

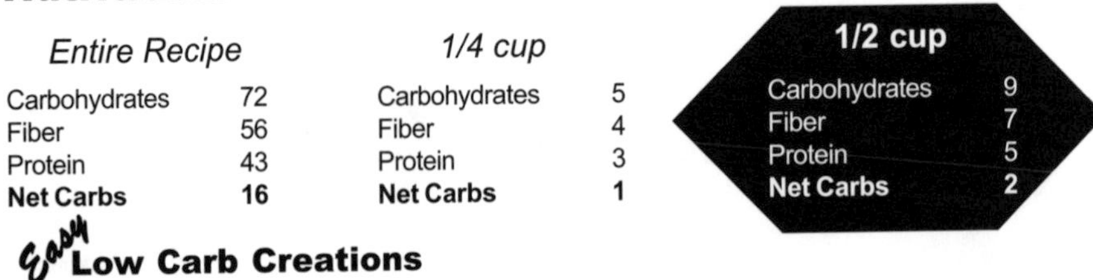

Nutritional Information

	Entire Recipe	1/4 cup	1/2 cup
Carbohydrates	72	5	9
Fiber	56	4	7
Protein	43	3	5
Net Carbs	**16**	**1**	**2**

Stuffed Cherry Tomatoes

Makes approximately 48 pieces / 24 servings

1 pound bacon, cut into 1/2-inch pieces

1/2 cup green onions

1/2 cup mayonnaise or salad dressing

24 cherry tomatoes

Directions

1. In skillet over medium-high heat, cook bacon until crisp; drain.
2. In food chopper, finely chop bacon and green onions.
3. In small bowl, combine bacon, green onions and mayonnaise; mix well.
4. Cut each tomato in half; scoop out pulp with small spoon.
5. Fill tomatoes with bacon mixture; place in large dish.
6. Cover and chill 1 hour.

Nutritional Information

Entire Recipe		*1 piece*	
Carbohydrates	16	Carbohydrates	0
Fiber	2	Fiber	0
Protein	42	Protein	1
Net Carbs	**14**	**Net Carbs**	**0**

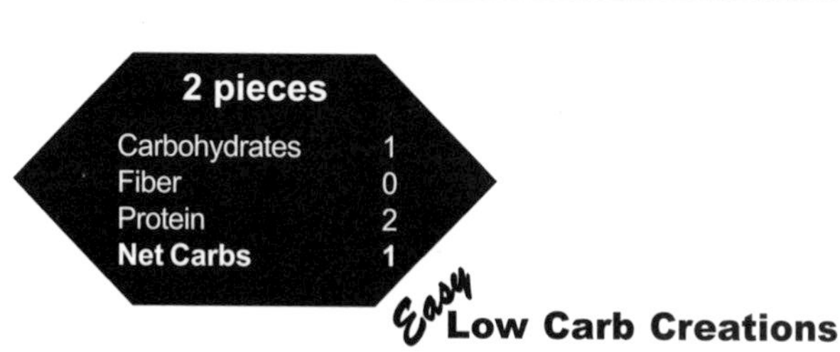

Stuffed Mushrooms with Bacon

Makes approximately 24 pieces / 12 servings

1 pound bacon, cut into 1/2-inch pieces

1 small onion, quartered

1 16-ounce package fresh mushrooms, stems removed

3/4 cup mayonnaise
1/2 cup shredded cheddar cheese

Directions

1. Preheat oven to 350 degrees.
2. In skillet over medium-high heat, cook bacon until crisp; drain.
3. In food chopper, finely chop cooked bacon and onion.
4. In prepared 9 x 13-inch baking dish, place mushroom caps.
5. In medium bowl, combine remaining ingredients, including chopped bacon and onion.
6. Fill mushroom caps with bacon/cheese mixture.
7. Bake 30 minutes or until mushrooms are tender.

Nutritional Information

Entire Recipe		*1 piece*		**2 pieces**	
Carbohydrates	23	Carbohydrates	1	Carbohydrates	2
Fiber	2	Fiber	0	Fiber	0
Protein	71	Protein	3	Protein	6
Net Carbs	**21**	**Net Carbs**	**1**	**Net Carbs**	**2**

Stuffed Mushrooms with Parmesan Cheese

Net Carbs 1

Makes approximately 24 pieces / 12 servings

1 medium onion, quartered
1 16-ounce package fresh mushrooms, stems removed and reserved

1/4 cup butter
1 teaspoon garlic salt

1/2 cup grated Parmesan cheese

Directions

1. Preheat oven to 350 degrees.
2. In food chopper, finely chop onion and mushroom stems.
3. In skillet over medium-high heat, melt butter; add garlic salt.
4. To same skillet, add mushroom caps and cook 2 to 3 minutes or until tender.
5. Remove mushroom caps from skillet; reserve liquid.
6. In prepared 8 x 8-inch baking dish, place mushroom caps.
7. In same skillet with reserved liquid, cook chopped mushroom stems and onions 2 to 3 minutes or until tender.
8. Fill mushroom caps with cooked stems and onions.
9. Sprinkle filled mushrooms with Parmesan cheese; bake 15 minutes or until cheese melts.

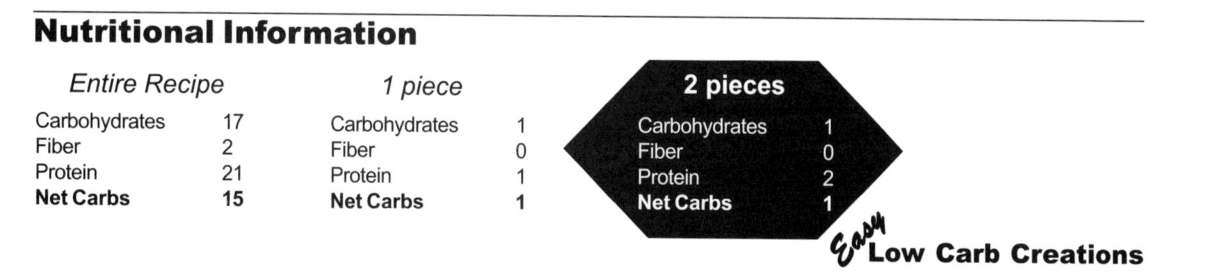

Nutritional Information

Entire Recipe	
Carbohydrates	17
Fiber	2
Protein	21
Net Carbs	**15**

1 piece	
Carbohydrates	1
Fiber	0
Protein	1
Net Carbs	**1**

2 pieces	
Carbohydrates	1
Fiber	0
Protein	2
Net Carbs	**1**

Beef

Net Carbs	Recipe	Page
2	Bacon Burgers	41
5	Baked Steak	42
2	Beef Kabobs	43
1	Chuck Roast with Sauce	44
6	Cubed Steak Parmesan	45
3	Grilled Teriyaki Burgers	46
6	Italian Meatballs (Meatloaf)	47
1	Marinated Chuck Roast	48

Bacon Burgers

Makes 6 servings

Net Carbs 2

Beef

1 pound lean ground beef
2 eggs, beaten
1/3 cup grated Parmesan cheese
1 4-ounce can mushrooms, drained, finely chopped
2 tablespoons stuffed green olives, finely chopped
2 tablespoons onion, finely chopped
2 tablespoons green pepper, finely chopped

6 slices bacon

1 large tomato, cut into 6 slices
6 stuffed green olives

Directions

1. In large bowl, combine first 7 ingredients; shape into 6 patties.
2. Around each patty, wrap bacon slice.
3. Coat outdoor grill grates with non-stick spray.
4. Over medium-hot coals, cook burgers 5 minutes on each side or until desired doneness. For gas grill, follow instructions for grilling hamburgers.
5. Serve burgers with tomato slice and olive on top.

Nutritional Information

Entire Recipe

Carbohydrates	13
Fiber	2
Protein	112
Net Carbs	**11**

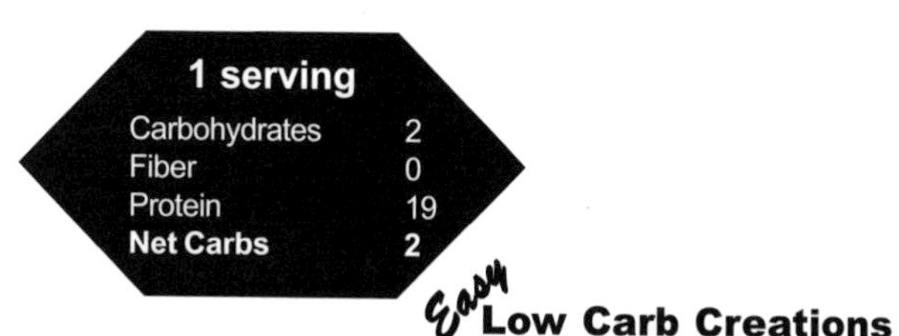

1 serving

Carbohydrates	2
Fiber	0
Protein	19
Net Carbs	**2**

Baked Steak

Makes 12 servings

Net Carbs 5

Beef

3 pounds boneless top sirloin steak, 1 1/2-inch thick
2 teaspoons olive oil

1/4 teaspoon salt
1/8 teaspoon pepper
2 teaspoons garlic powder

1 small green pepper, cut into 1/8-inch rings
1 small onion, cut into 1/8-inch rings
1 14-ounce can Italian-style stewed tomatoes, drained
1/2 cup ketchup

Directions

1. Preheat oven to 350 degrees.
2. Cut steak into 12 equal pieces.
3. Dry steak with paper towels; spread oil on both sides of steak.
4. In large skillet over medium-high heat, cook meat 4 to 5 minutes on each side.
5. Into prepared 9 x 13-inch baking dish, place steak; season with next 3 ingredients.
6. On top of steak, pile green pepper and onion rings; add stewed tomatoes and top with ketchup.
7. Bake 1 1/2 to 2 hours or until desired tenderness.

Nutritional Information

Entire Recipe

Carbohydrates	72
Fiber	11
Protein	396
Net Carbs	**61**

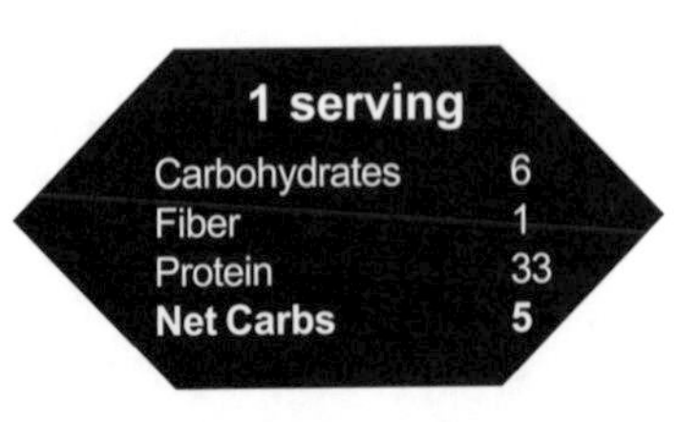

1 serving	
Carbohydrates	6
Fiber	1
Protein	33
Net Carbs	**5**

Beef Kabobs

Makes 8 skewers

1/2 cup vegetable oil
1/4 cup vinegar
1/4 cup onion, chopped
1 teaspoon salt
2 teaspoons Worcestershire sauce

3 pounds boneless sirloin steak, cut into 1 1/2-inch cubes

1/4 cup butter

1 teaspoon garlic salt
2 large onions, cut into eighths

1 8-ounce package fresh mushrooms

2 green peppers, cut into eighths

Directions

1. In large bowl, combine first 5 ingredients to make marinade.
2. To marinade, add meat; stir to coat. Cover and chill 4 hours.
3. In skillet over medium heat, melt butter; stir in garlic and onions. Cook 3 to 4 minutes or until onions are tender; remove onions from skillet.
4. In same skillet, add mushrooms. Cook 3 to 4 minutes; remove mushrooms from skillet.
5. In same skillet, add peppers. Cook 2 to 3 minutes; remove peppers from skillet.
6. Alternating meat with vegetables, thread pieces onto 8 skewers.
7. Coat outdoor grill grates with non-stick spray.
8. Over hot coals, cook kabobs 10 to 15 minutes on each side until desired doneness. For gas grill, follow instructions for grilling sirloin steak.

Nutritional Information

Entire Recipe

Carbohydrates	20
Fiber	4
Protein	395
Net Carbs	**16**

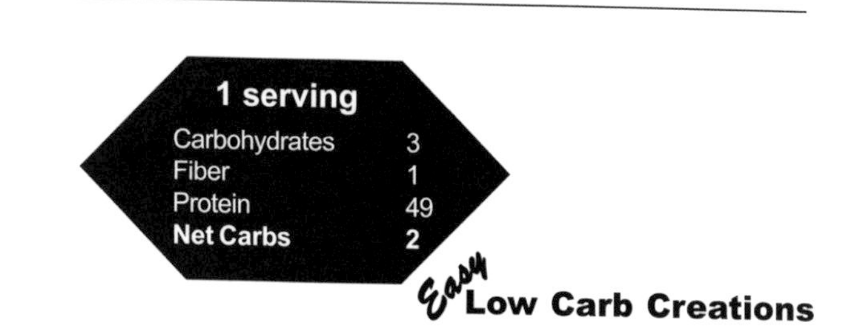

Chuck Roast with Sauce

Makes 12 servings

Beef

1 8-ounce can tomato sauce
1/2 cup beef broth
1 medium onion, chopped

1 3-4 pound boneless chuck roast

2 tablespoons vegetable oil
1/2 cup cider vinegar
1/4 cup ketchup
2 teaspoons Worcestershire sauce
1 teaspoon mustard
1 teaspoon paprika
1/8 teaspoon garlic powder

Directions

1. In shallow dish or large freezer bag, combine first 3 ingredients; add roast. Cover and chill 8 hours.
2. Preheat oven to 350 degrees.
3. Remove roast from marinade; in prepared roasting pan, place roast.
4. In small bowl, combine marinade and remaining ingredients; pour over roast.
5. Cover roast and bake 2 1/2 to 3 hours or until tender.
6. Skim fat from sauce and serve sauce with roast.

Nutritional Information

Entire Recipe

Carbohydrates	8
Fiber	2
Protein	529
Net Carbs	**6**

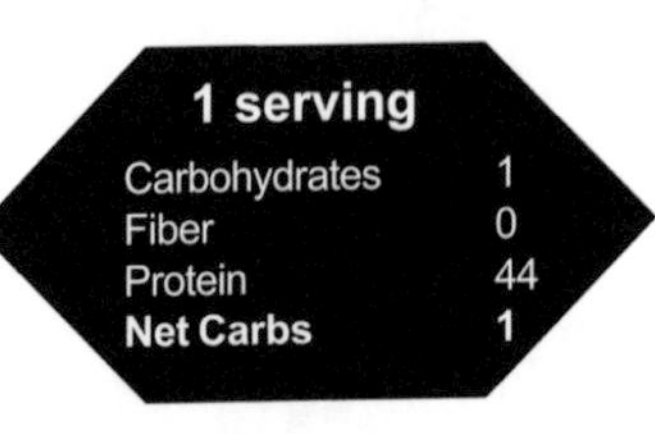

Cubed Steak Parmesan

Makes 6 servings

2 eggs
2 tablespoons water
1/8 teaspoon pepper

2 tablespoons flour
1/2 cup grated Parmesan cheese, divided

3 tablespoons vegetable oil
2 pounds beef cubed steaks, cut into 6 pieces

1 15-ounce can pizza sauce

Directions

1. Preheat oven to 325 degrees.
2. In medium bowl, beat first 3 ingredients.
3. In small bowl, combine flour and 2 tablespoons Parmesan cheese.
4. Dip steaks in egg mixture.
5. Then dip steaks in flour mixture.
6. In large skillet over medium-high heat, heat oil; cook steaks 4 to 5 minutes on both sides.
7. In prepared 9 x 13-inch baking dish, place steaks.
8. Cover steaks with pizza sauce and sprinkle with remaining Parmesan cheese. Bake 1 hour.

Nutritional Information

Entire Recipe

Carbohydrates	39
Fiber	7
Protein	269
Net Carbs	**32**

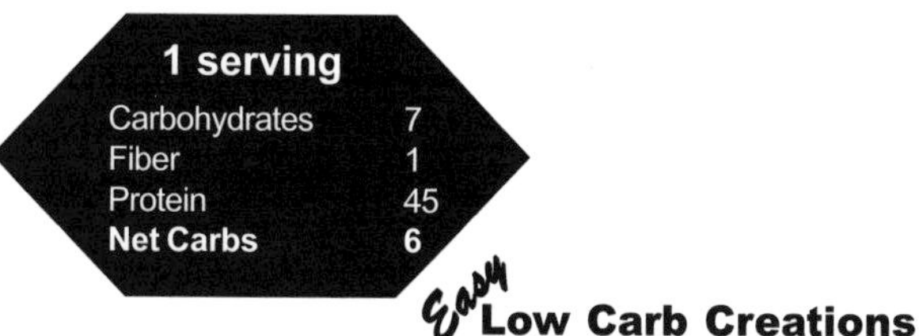

1 serving	
Carbohydrates	7
Fiber	1
Protein	45
Net Carbs	**6**

Grilled Teriyaki Burgers

Makes 6 servings

Net Carbs 3

Beef

1 pound lean ground beef
2 eggs
5 saltine crackers, crushed
1/3 cup water chestnuts, finely chopped
1/4 cup green pepper, finely chopped
2 green onions, finely chopped
1 tablespoon brown sugar substitute, equivalent measure
2 tablespoons water
1 tablespoon lemon juice
1 tablespoon soy sauce
1/2 teaspoon ground ginger

Directions

1. In large bowl, combine all ingredients; shape into 6 patties.
2. Cover grill grates with foil.
3. Over medium-hot coals, cook burgers 5 minutes on each side or until desired doneness. For gas grill, follow instructions for grilling hamburgers.

Nutritional Information

Entire Recipe

Carbohydrates	19
Fiber	2
Protein	83
Net Carbs	**17**

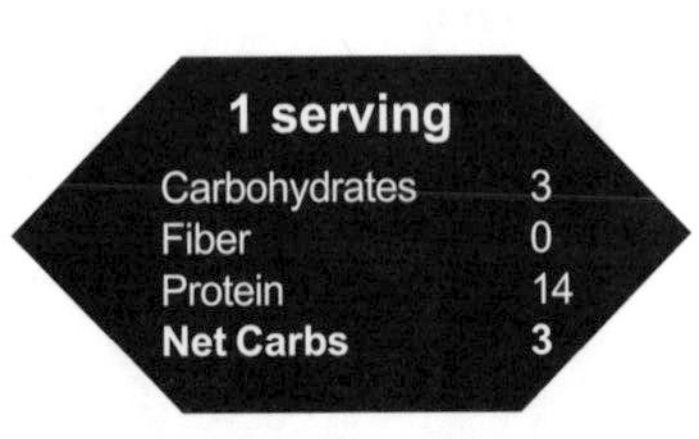

1 serving	
Carbohydrates	3
Fiber	0
Protein	14
Net Carbs	3

Italian Meatballs (Meatloaf)

Makes 36 meatballs or large meatloaf makes 12 servings

2 pounds lean ground beef
1 pound Italian sausage
15 saltine crackers, crushed
3 eggs
2 teaspoons basil
1 tablespoon parsley flakes
1 1/2 teaspoons oregano
1 teaspoon minced garlic
1/2 teaspoon salt
1/8 teaspoon pepper
1/3 cup grated Parmesan cheese
1/3 cup grated Romano cheese
1/2 medium onion, finely chopped
1/3 cup half-and-half

1 15-ounce can pizza sauce, divided

Directions

1. Preheat oven to 350 degrees.
2. In large bowl, combine first 14 ingredients and 1/3 cup pizza sauce with hands.

For Meatballs:

3. Shape into 2-inch balls; place on prepared sheet cake pan.
4. Bake meatballs 45 minutes.
5. Heat remaining pizza sauce and pour over meatballs to serve. (Can be kept hot in slow-cooker)

For Meatloaf:

3. Shape into large loaf and place in 9 x 13-inch prepared pan.
4. Bake meatloaf 1 hour 15 minutes.
5. On top of meatloaf, pour remaining pizza sauce. Bake additional 15 minutes.

Nutritional Information

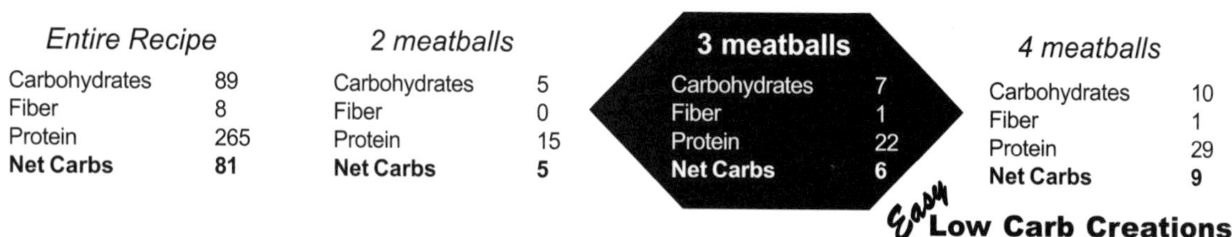

	Entire Recipe	*2 meatballs*	**3 meatballs**	*4 meatballs*
Carbohydrates	89	5	7	10
Fiber	8	0	1	1
Protein	265	15	22	29
Net Carbs	**81**	**5**	**6**	**9**

Marinated Chuck Roast

Makes 16 servings

4 pounds boneless chuck roast

1/2 teaspoon meat tenderizer
1/4 teaspoon garlic powder
1/4 teaspoon ginger
1/2 cup soy sauce
1/2 cup lemon juice
2 tablespoons brown sugar substitute, equivalent measure
1 tablespoon Worcestershire sauce
3/4 cup onions, chopped

Directions

1. In shallow dish or large freezer bag, place roast.
2. In small bowl, combine remaining ingredients; pour over meat; cover and chill 8 hours.
3. When ready to roast, preheat oven to 350 degrees.
4. In prepared roasting pan, place meat .
5. Roast 3 1/2 hours or until desired tenderness.

Nutritional Information

Entire Recipe

Carbohydrates	8
Fiber	2
Protein	529
Net Carbs	**6**

1 serving

Carbohydrates	1
Fiber	0
Protein	33
Net Carbs	**1**

Breakfast Main Dishes

Net Carbs	Recipe	Page
4	Bacon and Egg Casserole	50
4	Baked Bacon and Eggs	51
2	Baked Ham and Cheese Omelet	52
2	Baked Ham and Eggs	53
2	Baked Sausage and Eggs	54
2	Reuben Omelet	55
10	Sausage Gravy	56

Bacon and Egg Casserole

Makes 9 servings

1 1/2 pounds bacon, cut into 1/2-inch pieces

1/2 cup onion, chopped
1 1/2 teaspoons flour

1 1/4 cups half-and-half
1 1/2 cups shredded cheddar cheese

6 eggs, hard-cooked, sliced
3/4 cup sliced almonds, toasted

Net Carbs 4

Directions

1. Preheat oven to 350 degrees.
2. In large skillet over medium-high heat, cook bacon until crisp. Remove bacon; reserve 2 tablespoons drippings.
3. In same skillet, cook onion in bacon drippings until tender; blend in flour.
4. To onion mixture, add half-and-half; cook and stir until mixture thickens. Add cheese; stir until melted.
5. In bottom of prepared 8 x 8-inch baking dish, arrange half the egg slices.
6. Cover eggs with half the cheese sauce, half the almonds and half the crumbled bacon.
7. Repeat layers.
8. Bake 30 minutes or until hot and bubbly.

Nutritional Information

Entire Recipe

Carbohydrates	43
Fiber	13
Protein	148
Net Carbs	**30**

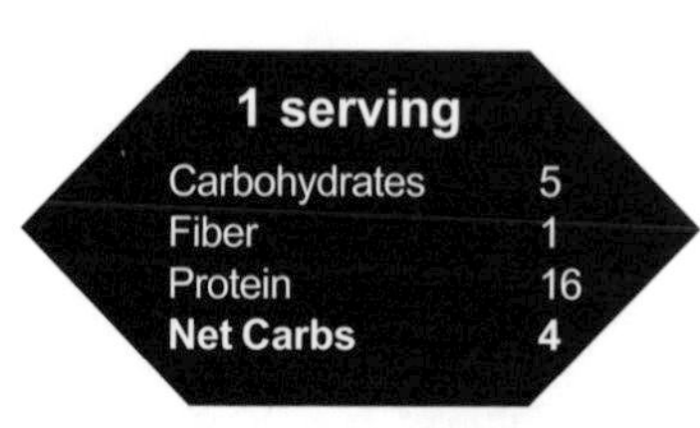

1 serving

Carbohydrates	5
Fiber	1
Protein	16
Net Carbs	**4**

Baked Bacon and Eggs

Makes 9 servings

8 eggs

1 cup milk
1/2 teaspoon seasoned salt
2 cups shredded Colby/Monterey Jack cheese

1 pound bacon, cut into 1/2-inch pieces

3 green onions, chopped
2 4-ounce cans sliced mushrooms, drained

1 cup shredded cheddar cheese

Net Carbs 4

Breakfast

Directions

1. Preheat oven to 350 degrees.
2. In large bowl, beat eggs.
3. To beaten eggs, add next 3 ingredients; stir well.
4. In large skillet over medium-high heat, cook bacon until crisp. Remove bacon; reserve 2 tablespoons drippings.
5. In same skillet, cook onions in bacon drippings until tender; add mushrooms and cook additional 2 minutes.
6. To egg mixture, add cooked bacon and onion mixture; stir well.
7. Into prepared 2-quart baking dish, pour mixture.
8. Bake 50 to 55 minutes.
9. Remove casserole from oven; sprinkle with cheddar cheese.

Nutritional Information

Entire Recipe

Carbohydrates	36
Fiber	0
Protein	173
Net Carbs	**36**

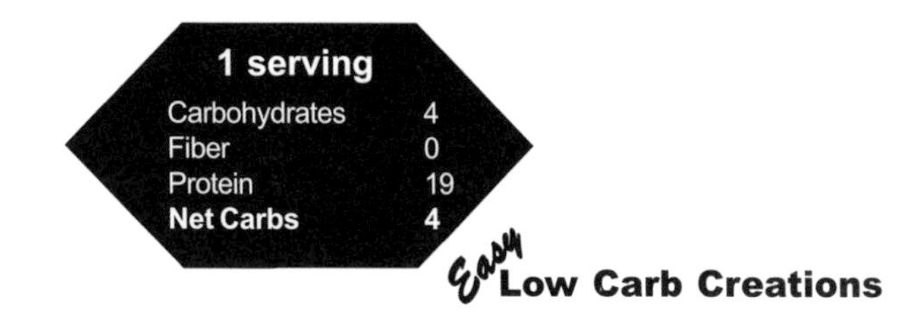

1 serving	
Carbohydrates	4
Fiber	0
Protein	19
Net Carbs	**4**

Baked Ham and Cheese Omelet

Makes 12 servings

1 1/2 cups cooked ham, chopped
12 eggs, slightly beaten
2 cups shredded cheddar cheese
2 teaspoons mustard
1 cup milk
1/4 teaspoon salt
1/8 teaspoon pepper
2 tablespoons butter, melted

Directions

1. Preheat oven to 325 degrees.
2. In large bowl, combine all ingredients.
3. Into prepared 9 x 13-inch pan, pour mixture.
4. Bake 1 hour.

This recipe can be prepared the night before, refrigerated and baked in the morning.

Nutritional Information

Entire Recipe

Carbohydrates	25
Fiber	0
Protein	172
Net Carbs	**25**

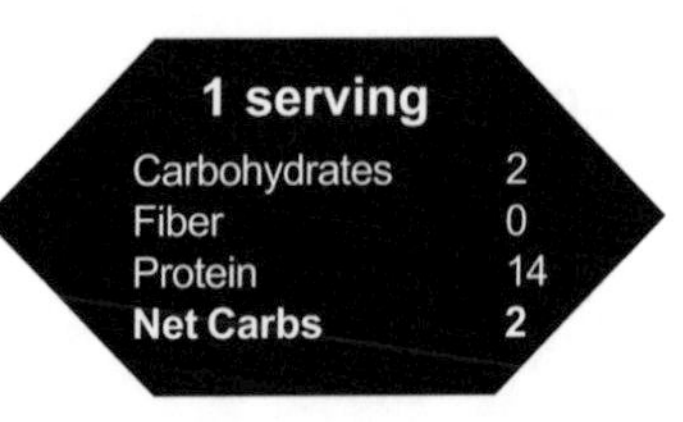

1 serving	
Carbohydrates	2
Fiber	0
Protein	14
Net Carbs	**2**

Baked Ham and Eggs

Makes 12 servings

12 eggs, slightly beaten
1 cup cooked ham, chopped
1 small onion, chopped
1 large tomato, chopped
2 cups shredded cheddar cheese
1/4 teaspoon salt
1/8 teaspoon pepper

Directions

1. Preheat oven to 325 degrees.
2. In large bowl, combine all ingredients.
3. Into prepared 9 x 13-inch baking dish, pour mixture.
4. Bake 1 hour.

This recipe can be prepared the night before, refrigerated and baked in the morning.

Nutritional Information

Entire Recipe

Carbohydrates	20
Fiber	0
Protein	175
Net Carbs	**20**

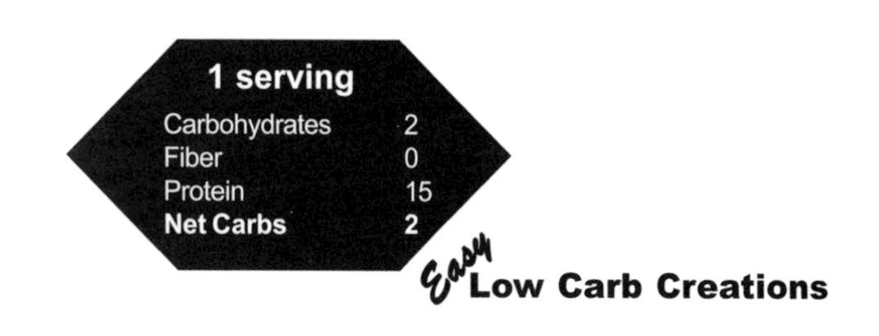

1 serving	
Carbohydrates	2
Fiber	0
Protein	15
Net Carbs	**2**

Baked Sausage and Eggs

Makes 12 servings

1 pound ground sausage

12 eggs, slightly beaten
1 cup half-and-half
1/2 teaspoon salt
1/4 teaspoon pepper
1 teaspoon mustard
2 cups shredded cheddar cheese

Net Carbs 2

Breakfast

Directions

1. Preheat oven to 325 degrees.
2. In skillet over medium-high heat, cook sausage, stirring until meat is brown and crumbly; drain.
3. In large bowl, combine cooked sausage with remaining ingredients.
4. In prepared 9 x 13-inch baking dish, pour mixture.
5. Bake 1 hour.

This recipe can be prepared the night before, refrigerated and baked in the morning.

Nutritional Information

Entire Recipe

Carbohydrates	20
Fiber	0
Protein	176
Net Carbs	**20**

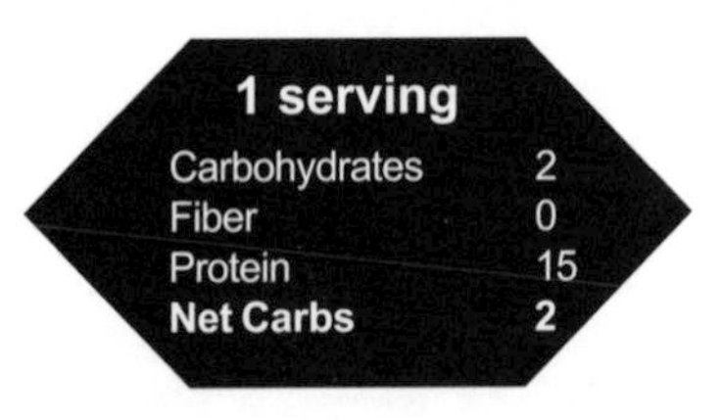

Reuben Omelet

Makes 1 serving

3 ounces thin-sliced corned beef
1/4 cup sauerkraut, drained

2 teaspoons vegetable oil
2 eggs, beaten
Dash salt
Dash pepper

2 ounces shredded Swiss cheese

Net Carbs 2

Directions

1. In medium skillet over medium heat, heat corned beef and sauerkraut. Do not mix.
2. In large skillet over medium heat, heat oil. Add eggs, spreading them to form a rectangle; sprinkle with salt and pepper.
3. Down center of omelet, sprinkle cheese.
4. When eggs are firm, place corned beef and sauerkraut on top of them.
5. Fold sides over filling.
6. Flip omelet to cook other side.

Nutritional Information

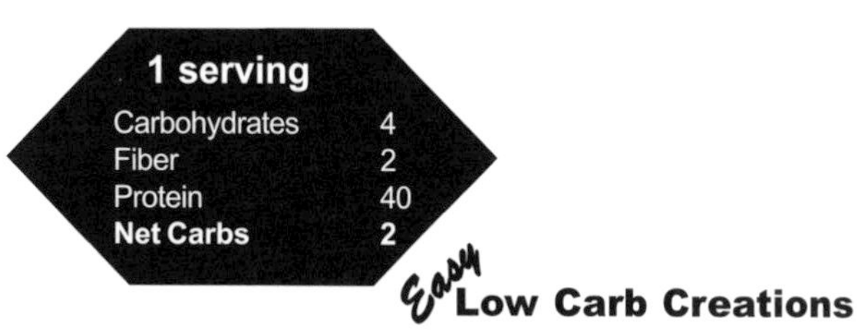

1 serving	
Carbohydrates	4
Fiber	2
Protein	40
Net Carbs	**2**

Sausage Gravy

Makes 6 servings

Net Carbs 10

Breakfast

1 pound ground sausage

1/4 cup flour

1 1/2 cups half-and-half
2 cups milk

1/4 teaspoon salt
1/4 teaspoon pepper

Directions

1. In large skillet over medium-high heat, cook sausage, stirring until meat is brown and crumbly. Drain and reserve drippings.
2. To skillet with sausage and 3 tablespoons or less drippings, stir in flour; cook and stir until golden brown.
3. To same skillet, slowly add next 2 ingredients; bring gravy to boil.
4. Reduce heat to medium-low; simmer until thickened, stirring constantly.
5. Season with salt and pepper.

Serving option

Serve prepared gravy over fried or scrambled eggs. Recipe makes enough gravy to cover 12 eggs.

Nutritional Information

Entire Recipe	
Carbohydrates	59
Fiber	0
Protein	91
Net Carbs	**59**

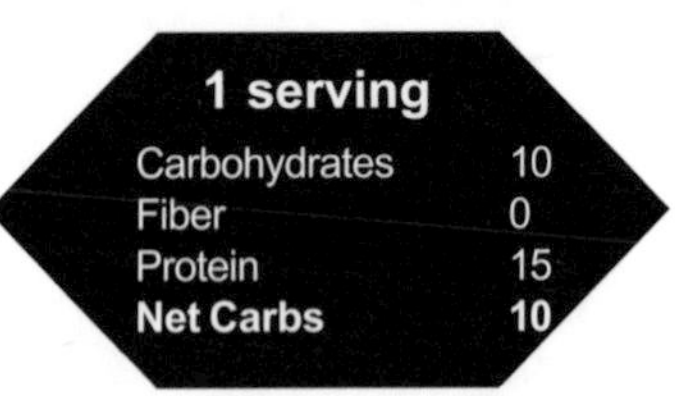

1 serving	
Carbohydrates	10
Fiber	0
Protein	15
Net Carbs	**10**

Net Carbs	Recipe	Page

Net Carbs	Recipe	Page
2	Baked Ham Salad	58
5	Cabbage Un-Rolls	59
2	Cheese-Stuffed Beef Rolls	60
4	Chicken Bacon Casserole	61
3	Chicken Broccoli Casserole	62
8	Creamy Chicken Broccoli Casserole	63
6	Crunchy Chicken Casserole	64
3	Green Bean Hamburger Casserole	65
4	Hot Chicken Salad	66
11	Lasagna	67
3	Nichole's Cabbage Casserole	68
3	Pizza Casserole	69
8	Sausage-Stuffed Eggplant	70
6	Stuffed Green Peppers	71
10	Taco-Filled Peppers	72

Baked Ham Salad

Makes 9 servings

3 cups cooked ham, chopped
1 cup celery, chopped
2 tablespoons stuffed green olives, chopped
2 eggs, hard-cooked, chopped
1/4 cup onion, finely chopped
1 tablespoon lemon juice
1 teaspoon mustard
3/4 cup mayonnaise
1 cup shredded cheddar cheese

1 cup sliced almonds

Directions

Net Carbs 2

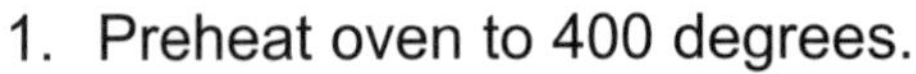

1. Preheat oven to 400 degrees.
2. In large bowl, combine first 9 ingredients.
3. Into prepared 8 x 8-inch baking dish, pour mixture.
4. Sprinkle casserole with almonds.
5. Bake 20 minutes or until hot and bubbly.

Nutritional Information

Entire Recipe

Carbohydrates	35
Fiber	19
Protein	214
Net Carbs	**16**

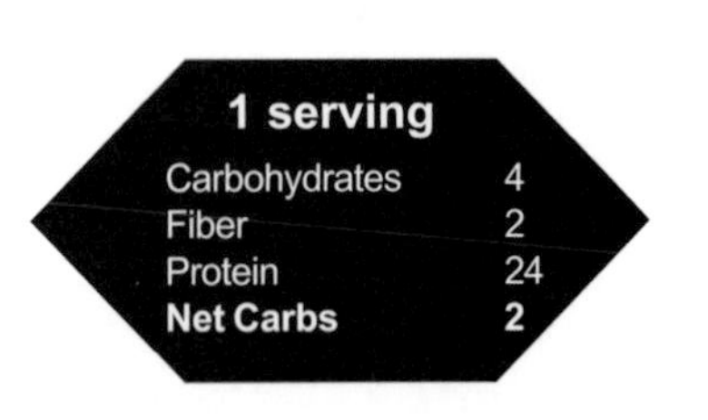

1 serving	
Carbohydrates	4
Fiber	2
Protein	24
Net Carbs	**2**

Cabbage Un-rolls

Makes 12 servings

1 1/2 pounds lean ground beef
1 medium onion, chopped

1 medium cabbage head

1 25-ounce jar spaghetti sauce
2 teaspoons garlic salt, divided

2 cups shredded mozzarella cheese

Directions

1. Preheat oven to 350 degrees.
2. In skillet over medium heat, cook ground beef and onion with 1 teaspoon garlic salt, stirring until meat is brown and crumbly; drain.
3. Into prepared 9 x 13-inch baking dish, place cooked meat.
4. Cut cabbage into wedges and place on top of meat.
5. To spaghetti sauce, add remaining garlic salt; over meat and cabbage, pour sauce.
6. Cover with foil and bake 45 minutes.
7. Uncover casserole; sprinkle with cheese. Bake additional 15 minutes.

Nutritional Information

Entire Recipe

Carbohydrates	96
Fiber	34
Protein	245
Net Carbs	**62**

1 serving

Carbohydrates	8
Fiber	3
Protein	20
Net Carbs	**5**

Cheese-Stuffed Beef Rolls

Makes 6 servings

1 15.5-ounce jar spaghetti sauce

1 egg, beaten
1/4 teaspoon oregano
1/4 teaspoon garlic powder
1 15-ounce container ricotta or cottage cheese
1/4 cup grated Parmesan cheese
2 cups shredded mozzarella cheese, divided

6 thin slices deli roast beef (1/2 pound)

2 medium zucchinis, sliced into 1/8-inch rounds

Net Carbs 2

Casseroles

Directions

1. Preheat oven to 375 degrees.
2. In bottom of prepared 9 x 13-inch baking dish, spread 1/2 cup spaghetti sauce.
3. In large bowl, combine next five ingredients and 1 cup mozzarella cheese.
4. On end of each beef slice, spoon equal amounts of cheese mixture.
5. Roll each filled beef slice like jelly roll; arrange seam-side down in baking dish.
6. Around sides of baking dish, place zucchini slices.
7. Over beef rolls and zucchini slices, pour remaining spaghetti sauce.
8. Bake 40 minutes or until hot and bubbly.
9. Top beef rolls with remaining cheese; bake additional 5 minutes.

Nutritional Information

Entire Recipe	
Carbohydrates	13
Fiber	2
Protein	88
Net Carbs	**11**

1 serving	
Carbohydrates	2
Fiber	0
Protein	15
Net Carbs	**2**

Chicken Bacon Casserole

Makes 6 servings

1/4 cup butter
6 boneless, skinless chicken breasts

1 10.75-ounce can condensed cream of mushroom soup
1 8-ounce container sour cream

1/2 cup sliced almonds

1/2 pound bacon, cut into 1/2-inch pieces

Directions

1. Preheat oven to 350 degrees.
2. Into prepared 9 x 13-inch baking dish, place butter and melt in preheated oven; remove from oven.
3. In baking dish with melted butter, add chicken.
4. In small bowl, combine next 2 ingredients; pour over chicken.
5. Sprinkle chicken with almonds; bake 1 hour or until chicken is tender and no longer pink.
6. In small skillet over medium heat, cook bacon until crisp; drain.
7. Sprinkle cooked bacon on top of casserole before serving.

Nutritional Information

Entire Recipe

Carbohydrates	35
Fiber	9
Protein	198
Net Carbs	**26**

1 serving

Carbohydrates	6
Fiber	2
Protein	33
Net Carbs	**4**

Chicken Broccoli Casserole

Makes 12 servings

2 10-ounce packages frozen, chopped broccoli

2 pounds cooked chicken breast, thinly sliced

1 10.75-ounce can condensed cream of mushroom soup
1/2 cup milk

2 cups shredded cheddar cheese

Directions

1. Preheat oven to 375 degrees.
2. Cook broccoli according to package directions.
3. In prepared 9 x 13-inch baking dish, spoon drained broccoli.
4. Place cooked chicken over broccoli.
5. In small bowl, combine next 2 ingredients; pour over chicken.
6. Top casserole with cheese; bake 30 minutes or until hot and bubbly.
7. Let stand 5 minutes before serving.

Nutritional Information

Entire Recipe

Carbohydrates	50
Fiber	14
Protein	251
Net Carbs	**36**

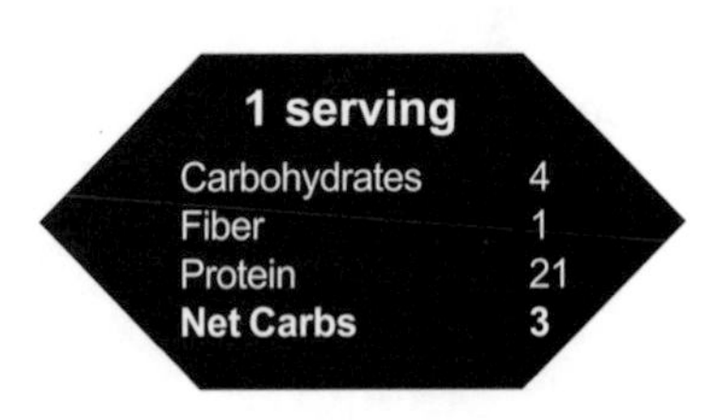

1 serving	
Carbohydrates	4
Fiber	1
Protein	21
Net Carbs	**3**

Creamy Chicken Broccoli Casserole

Makes 6 servings

2 10-ounce packages frozen chopped broccoli, thawed
6 boneless, skinless chicken breasts, cut into pieces

1 10.75-ounce can condensed cream of chicken soup
1/4 cup sour cream
1/4 cup mayonnaise or salad dressing

Directions

1. Preheat oven to 350 degrees.
2. In prepared 9 x 13-inch baking dish, place thawed broccoli; arrange chicken over broccoli.
3. In small bowl, combine next 3 ingredients; pour soup mixture over chicken.
4. Bake 1 hour.

Net Carbs 8

Nutritional Information

Entire Recipe

Carbohydrates	63
Fiber	15
Protein	178
Net Carbs	**48**

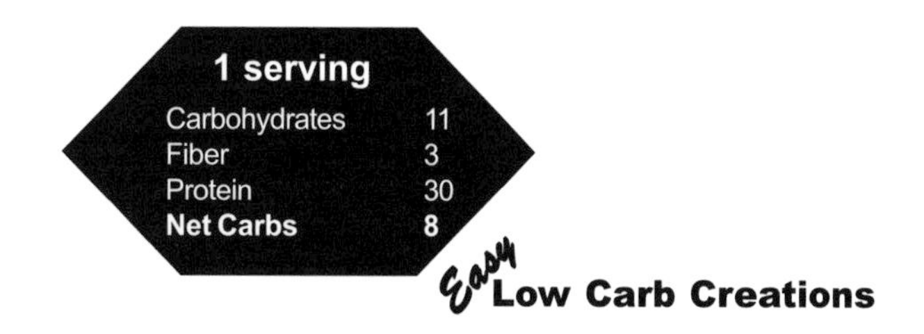

1 serving

Carbohydrates	11
Fiber	3
Protein	30
Net Carbs	**8**

Crunchy Chicken Casserole

Makes 9 servings

1 10-ounce package baby carrots
2 tablespoons water

3 4-ounce cans mushrooms, drained
1/2 cup celery, thinly sliced
1/2 cup sliced almonds, toasted, divided
4 boneless, skinless chicken breasts, cut into cubes

1/2 cup white wine (or chicken broth)
3/4 cup chicken broth
1/2 teaspoon garlic salt
1/2 teaspoon pepper

Paprika

Net Carbs 6

Directions

1. Preheat oven to 375 degrees.
2. In microwave-safe dish, combine carrots and 2 tablespoons water. Cover and microwave on high 5 minutes; drain.
3. In prepared 9 x 13-inch baking dish, layer vegetables, 1/4 cup almonds and chicken.
4. In small bowl, combine next 4 ingredients.
5. Over chicken and vegetables, pour broth mixture; sprinkle with paprika.
6. Cover and bake 35 minutes or until chicken is tender and no longer pink.
7. Baste chicken with sauce and top with remaining toasted almonds.

Nutritional Information

Entire Recipe

Carbohydrates	65
Fiber	12
Protein	136
Net Carbs	**53**

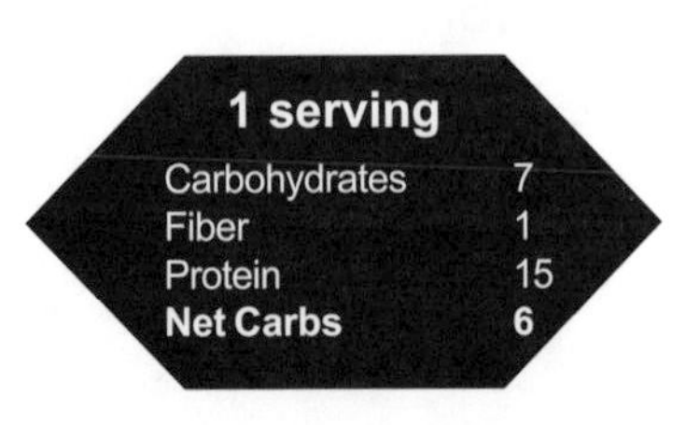

1 serving	
Carbohydrates	7
Fiber	1
Protein	15
Net Carbs	**6**

Green Bean Hamburger Casserole

Makes 12 servings

2 pounds lean ground beef
1 medium onion, chopped

2 14.5-ounce cans green beans, drained
1 1/2 packages dry sloppy Joe sauce mix
1 12-ounce can tomato sauce
1 4-ounce can mushroom stems and pieces, drained

2 cups shredded cheddar cheese

Directions

Net Carbs 3

1. Preheat oven to 350 degrees.
2. In large skillet over medium-high heat, cook ground beef and onion, stirring until meat is brown and crumbly; drain.
3. Into prepared 2-quart casserole dish, place meat mixture.
4. In medium bowl, combine next four ingredients; pour over meat.
5. Top casserole with grated cheddar cheese; bake 30 minutes.

Nutritional Information

Entire Recipe

Carbohydrates	64
Fiber	24
Protein	230
Net Carbs	**40**

1 serving

Carbohydrates	5
Fiber	2
Protein	19
Net Carbs	**3**

Hot Chicken Salad

Makes 12 servings

2 pounds cooked chicken breast, chopped
1 cup sliced almonds, toasted
2 cups celery, sliced
1 tablespoon lemon juice
1 cup mayonnaise or salad dressing
2 cups shredded cheddar cheese
3 eggs, hard-cooked, chopped
2 teaspoons onion, finely chopped
1/2 teaspoon salt
1/8 teaspoon pepper

Directions

1. Preheat oven to 400 degrees.
2. In large bowl, combine all ingredients.
3. Into prepared 9 x 13-inch baking dish, pour mixture.
4. Bake 20 minutes or until hot and bubbly.
5. Let stand 5 minutes before serving.

Nutritional Information

Entire Recipe

Carbohydrates	73
Fiber	20
Protein	291
Net Carbs	**53**

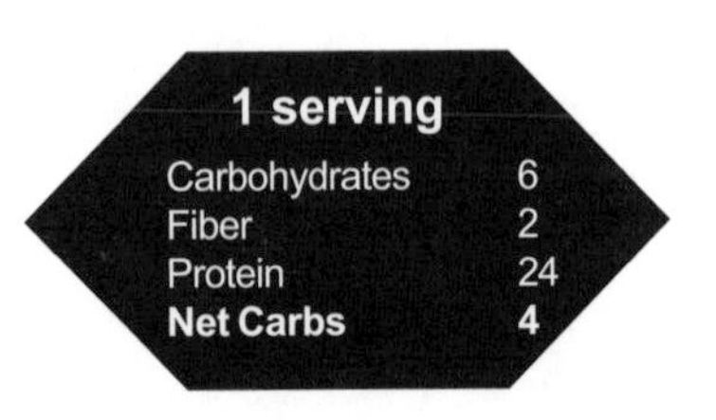

Lasagna

Makes 12 servings

1 1/2 pounds lean ground beef
1 large onion, chopped

1 32-ounce jar spaghetti sauce

1 cup Parmesan cheese, divided
1 24-ounce carton small curd cottage cheese
1 tablespoon parsley
1 1/2 teaspoons salt
1 teaspoon oregano

3 medium zucchinis, sliced into 1/8-inch rounds

4 cups shredded mozzarella cheese

Directions

1. Preheat oven to 350 degrees.
2. In large skillet over medium-high heat, cook ground beef and onions, stirring until meat is brown and crumbly; drain.
3. To beef in skillet, stir in spaghetti sauce.
4. In medium bowl, combine 1/2 cup Parmesan cheese and next 4 ingredients.
5. Into prepared 9 x 13-inch baking dish, place layer of zucchini slices.
6. Cover zucchini slices with all cottage cheese mixture.
7. Over cottage cheese mixture, spread 1/2 the spaghetti sauce.
8. Over spaghetti sauce, layer 2 cups mozzarella cheese and remaining zucchini slices.
9. Over zucchini slices, spread remaining spaghetti sauce.
10. Top casserole with remaining cheeses. Bake, covered, 20 minutes. Remove foil and bake additional 30 minutes.
11. Remove casserole from oven; let stand 15 minutes.

Nutritional Information

Entire Recipe

Carbohydrates	155
Fiber	27
Protein	446
Net Carbs	**128**

1 serving

Carbohydrates	13
Fiber	2
Protein	37
Net Carbs	**11**

Nichole's Cabbage Casserole

Makes 12 servings

1 pound lean ground beef
1 onion, chopped
1/4 teaspoon garlic powder
1/2 teaspoon salt
1/4 teaspoon pepper

1 16-ounce can tomato sauce

3 cups cabbage, chopped

2 cups shredded cheddar cheese

Directions

1. Preheat oven to 350 degrees.
2. In large skillet over medium-high heat, cook ground beef and next 4 ingredients until meat is brown and crumbly; drain.
3. To beef in skillet, stir in tomato sauce; simmer 1 to 2 minutes. Remove from heat.
4. To hot mixture, stir in cabbage.
5. Into prepared 9 x 13-inch baking dish, pour mixture. Bake 45 minutes.
6. Top casserole with cheese; bake additional 15 minutes.

Nutritional Information

Entire Recipe

Carbohydrates	58
Fiber	25
Protein	144
Net Carbs	**33**

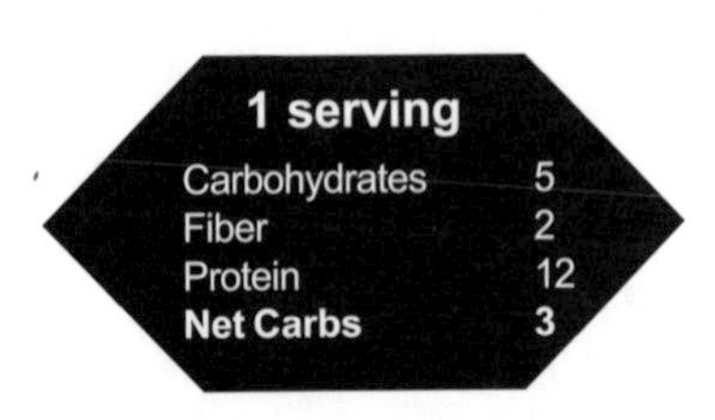

1 serving	
Carbohydrates	5
Fiber	2
Protein	12
Net Carbs	**3**

Pizza Casserole

Makes 12 servings

1 pound ground sausage

2 eggs, slightly beaten
1 cup grated Parmesan cheese, divided

1 green pepper, chopped
1 small onion, cut in small slices
1 4-ounce can mushrooms, drained
1 cup shredded mozzarella cheese
1/2 cup Gouda cheese, cut into small pieces
1/2 cup Muenster cheese, cut into small pieces
1/2 cup shredded cheddar cheese
1 3.5-ounce package sliced pepperoni
1 15-ounce can pizza sauce

Net Carbs 3

Directions

1. Preheat oven to 350 degrees.
2. In skillet over medium-high heat, cook sausage, stirring until meat is brown and crumbly; drain.
3. In medium bowl, combine eggs, 1/4 cup Parmesan cheese and cooked sausage.
4. Into prepared 9 x 13-inch baking dish, press meat mixture.
5. Over meat mixture, layer next 9 ingredients.
6. Sprinkle casserole with remaining Parmesan cheese.
7. Bake 30 minutes or until hot and bubbly.

Nutritional Information

Entire Recipe

Carbohydrates	48
Fiber	9
Protein	259
Net Carbs	**39**

1 serving

Carbohydrates	4
Fiber	1
Protein	22
Net Carbs	**3**

Sausage-Stuffed Eggplant

Makes 8 servings

2 medium eggplants (about 1 1/4 pounds each)

1 pound Italian sausage

1 tablespoon olive oil
3/4 cup carrots, chopped

1 4-ounce can sliced mushrooms, drained
1 1/2 cups shredded mozzarella cheese

Directions

Net Carbs 8

Casseroles

1. Preheat oven to 375 degrees.
2. Cut eggplants in half lengthwise; remove pulp, leaving a 1/4-inch shell.
3. Chop pulp and set aside.
4. In skillet over medium-high heat, cook sausage, stirring until meat is brown and crumbly; drain and set aside.
5. Wipe skillet clean with paper towel.
6. In skillet over medium heat, heat olive oil; add eggplant pulp and carrots; cook 10 minutes or until tender.
7. To same skillet, stir in cooked sausage, mushrooms and cheese.
8. Into prepared 12 x 15-inch baking dish, place eggplant shells.
9. Fill shells with sausage mixture; bake 20 to 25 minutes.

Nutritional Information

Entire Recipe

Carbohydrates	74
Fiber	10
Protein	87
Net Carbs	**64**

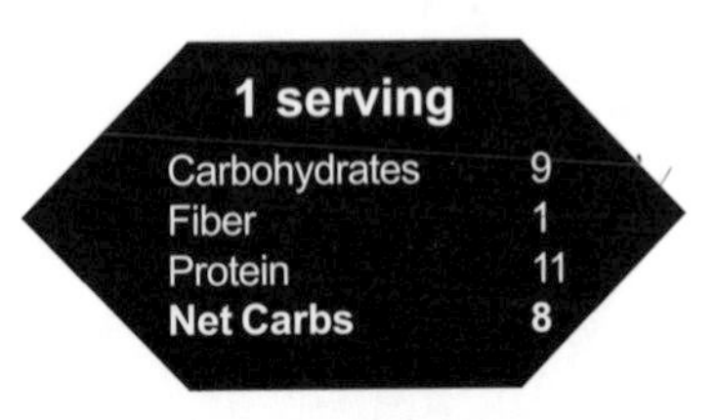

1 serving

Carbohydrates	9
Fiber	1
Protein	11
Net Carbs	**8**

Stuffed Green Peppers

Makes 12 servings

6 green peppers, cut in half lengthwise, seeds removed

1/2 pound bacon, cut into 1/2-inch pieces
1 large onion, finely chopped
2 ribs celery, finely chopped

1 teaspoon parsley
3 1/8-inch thick cooked ham slices, finely chopped
1 1/2 pounds cooked deli roast beef, finely chopped

2 slices bread

1 egg, slightly beaten
1/4 teaspoon salt
1/8 teaspoon pepper

1 cup shredded cheddar cheese
1 cup shredded mozzarella cheese

Directions

1. Preheat oven to 350 degrees.
2. In microwave-safe baking dish, place half of peppers in single layer with 3 tablespoons water; cover and microwave on high 4 to 5 minutes until peppers are fork tender; drain; set aside. Repeat with remaining peppers.
3. In large skillet over medium-high heat, cook bacon until almost done. Add onions and celery; cook until tender.
4. In same skillet, add next 3 ingredients; stir well. Reduce heat to low; cover and cook 20 minutes, stirring often.
5. Moisten bread with water; crumble into meat mixture; cook 2 minutes. Remove from heat; stir in next 3 ingredients.
6. In prepared 9 x 13-inch baking dish, place peppers and fill them with meat mixture.
7. Bake 10 minutes; sprinkle peppers with cheeses. Bake additional 10 minutes.

Nutritional Information

Entire Recipe

Carbohydrates	79
Fiber	9
Protein	378
Net Carbs	**70**

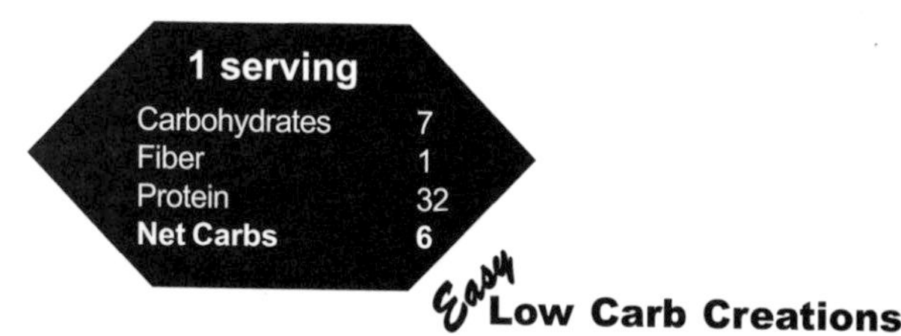

1 serving

Carbohydrates	7
Fiber	1
Protein	32
Net Carbs	**6**

Taco-Filled Peppers

Makes 8 servings

1 pound lean ground beef

1 1.25-ounce package taco seasoning mix
1 8-ounce can chili beans, drained
1 cup salsa
1/2 cup water

4 medium green peppers

1 medium tomato, chopped
1 cup shredded cheddar cheese
1/2 cup sour cream

Directions

1. Preheat oven to 350 degrees.
2. In large skillet over medium-high heat, cook ground beef, stirring until meat is brown and crumbly; drain.
3. To beef in skillet, stir in next 4 ingredients; bring to boil. Reduce heat to low and simmer 5 minutes.
4. Cut peppers in half lengthwise; remove and discard seeds and stems.
5. In microwave-safe dish, place peppers with 2 tablespoons water; cover. Microwave on high 4 to 5 minutes; drain.
6. In prepared 9 x 13-inch baking dish, place peppers.
7. Into each pepper, spoon 1/2 cup meat mixture.
8. Cover with foil and bake 15 to 20 minutes or until hot and peppers are crisp-tender.
9. Top each stuffed pepper with cheese, tomato and dollop of sour cream.

Nutritional Information

Entire Recipe

Carbohydrates	104
Fiber	21
Protein	119
Net Carbs	**83**

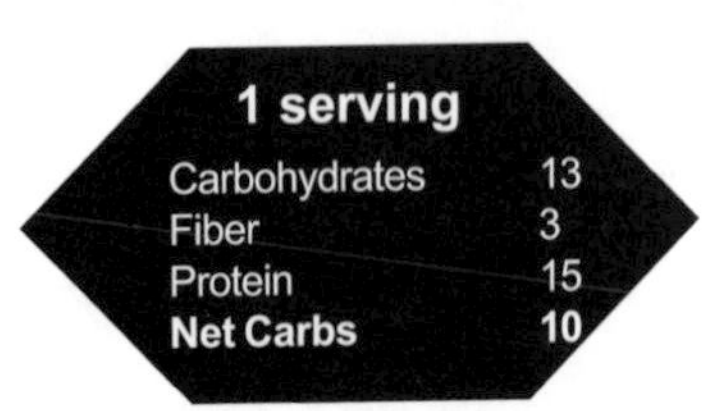

Chicken and Turkey Main Dishes

Net Carbs	Recipe	Page
4	Apple-Rosemary Chicken	74
6	Bourbon Chicken and Gravy	75
4	Chicken Divan	76
6	Chicken Rosé	77
7	Chicken with Artichokes	78
2	Grilled Chicken Patties	79
1	Lemon-Dilled Chicken	80
0	Marinated Grilled Chicken	81
0	Parmesan Chicken	82
3	Pineapple Chicken	83
5	Quick Chicken Cacciatore	84
8	Teriyaki Chicken Kabobs	85

Apple-Rosemary Chicken

Makes 6 servings

1/2 cup apple juice
1/4 cup white wine vinegar
1/4 cup vegetable oil
1 teaspoon rosemary
1/4 teaspoon salt
1/4 teaspoon pepper

6 boneless, skinless chicken breasts
2 apples, cored, sliced into 1/2-inch thick rings

Directions

1. In shallow baking dish, combine first 6 ingredients to make marinade.
2. To marinade, add chicken and apples; cover and chill 30 minutes. Discard marinade.
3. Spray outdoor grill grates with non-stick cooking spray.
4. Over medium-hot coals, cook chicken 10 to 12 minutes on each side.
5. On grill with chicken, place apples; cook 3 minutes on each side or until apples are crisp-tender.
6. Remove chicken from grill when tender and no longer pink. For gas grill, follow instructions for grilling chicken.

Net Carbs 4

Nutritional Information

Entire Recipe

Carbohydrates	35
Fiber	9
Protein	133
Net Carbs	**26**

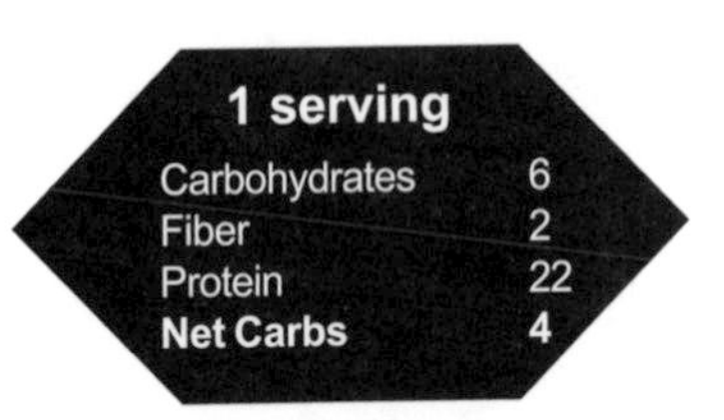

1 serving	
Carbohydrates	6
Fiber	2
Protein	22
Net Carbs	**4**

Bourbon Chicken and Gravy

Makes 6 servings

4 boneless, skinless chicken breasts, cut into 12 pieces
1/4 cup butter
3/4 cup bourbon, divided

1 medium onion, finely chopped
2 tablespoons parsley
1 teaspoon thyme
1/2 teaspoon salt
1/8 teaspoon pepper

1/4 cup sour cream

Directions

1. In large skillet over medium-high heat, melt butter; add chicken and cook 3 to 4 minutes on each side.
2. To chicken in skillet, add 1/4 cup bourbon.
3. Ignite bourbon with long match and let burn until flames die.
4. To same skillet, add next 5 ingredients and remaining 1/2 cup bourbon, stirring until blended.
5. Bring chicken mixture to boil. Cover; reduce heat and simmer 30 minutes or until chicken is tender and no longer pink.
6. Remove chicken to serving bowl.
7. To drippings in skillet over high heat, add sour cream; bring to boil while stirring constantly.
8. Reduce to medium heat; cook gravy until thickened; serve over chicken.

Nutritional Information

Entire Recipe

Carbohydrates	35
Fiber	2
Protein	92
Net Carbs	**33**

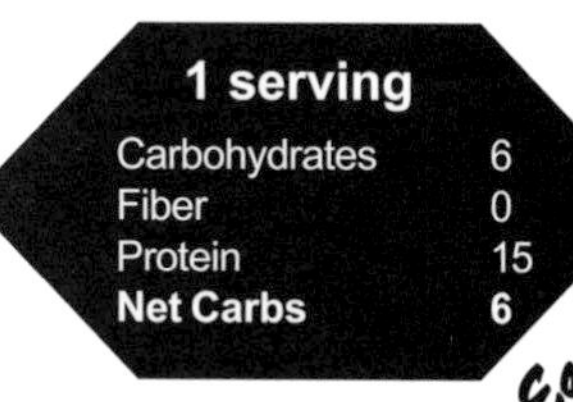

1 serving

Carbohydrates	6
Fiber	0
Protein	15
Net Carbs	**6**

Chicken Divan

Makes 9 servings

1 16-ounce package frozen broccoli spears

1 1/2 pounds sliced, cooked chicken, cut into pieces

3 tablespoons butter
1 tablespoon flour

1 1/2 cups half-and-half
4 egg yolks

2 tablespoons sherry cooking wine
1/2 cup grated Parmesan cheese
1/4 teaspoon salt
1/8 teaspoon pepper

Directions

1. Preheat oven to 350 degrees.
2. In microwave-safe bowl, add broccoli and 2 tablespoons water. Cover and microwave on high 6 minutes; drain.
3. In prepared 2-quart shallow baking dish, layer chicken and broccoli spears.
4. Meanwhile, in saucepan over medium heat, melt butter; blend in flour; cook and stir until smooth and bubbly.
5. To same saucepan, gradually stir in half-and-half; bring to boil, stirring constantly. Remove saucepan from heat.
6. Into small bowl, beat egg yolks. Gradually stir half of hot mixture into beaten yolks; immediately blend back into remaining hot mixture.
7. To same saucepan, stir in next 4 ingredients. Over broccoli, pour sauce. Bake 40 minutes or until hot and bubbly.

Nutritional Information

Entire Recipe

Carbohydrates	42
Fiber	10
Protein	191
Net Carbs	**32**

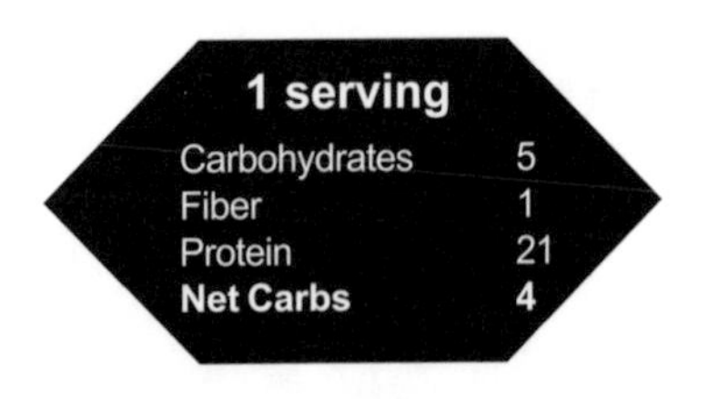

1 serving	
Carbohydrates	5
Fiber	1
Protein	21
Net Carbs	**4**

Chicken Rosé

Makes 6 servings

1 16-ounce package fresh sliced mushrooms
4 boneless, skinless chicken breasts, cut into 12 pieces

1 tablespoon cornstarch
1 tablespoon water

2 tablespoons olive oil
3/4 cup rosé wine
1/4 cup soy sauce
1/2 teaspoon minced garlic
2 tablespoons brown sugar, equivalent measure
1/4 teaspoon oregano

Directions

1. Preheat oven to 350 degrees.
2. Into prepared 9 x 13-inch baking dish, layer sliced mushrooms and chicken.
3. In small bowl, combine cornstarch and water, stirring until smooth.
4. Into cornstarch mixture, stir next 6 ingredients and pour over chicken.
5. Bake 50 to 60 minutes or until chicken is tender and no longer pink.

Nutritional Information

Entire Recipe

Carbohydrates	35
Fiber	0
Protein	115
Net Carbs	**35**

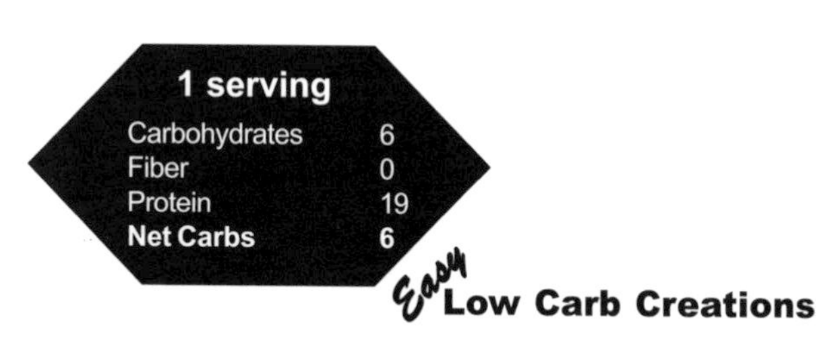

Chicken with Artichokes

Makes 6 servings

4 boneless, skinless chicken breasts, cut into 12 pieces
1/2 teaspoon celery salt

2 tablespoons olive oil

3 small fresh onions, quartered
1 14-ounce can artichoke hearts, drained, halved
1 teaspoon parsley
2 tablespoons water
1 teaspoon Italian seasoning
1/8 teaspoon garlic powder

6 tomatoes, cored and coarsely chopped
1/4 cup white grape juice

1/4 cup grated Parmesan cheese

Directions

Net Carbs 7

1. Preheat oven to 350 degrees.
2. In prepared 2-quart casserole dish, place chicken; sprinkle with celery salt and set aside.
3. In large skillet over medium-high heat, heat oil. Add next 6 ingredients; cook and stir 5 minutes or until onion is tender.
4. To same skillet, stir in tomato and grape juice; pour mixture over chicken.
5. Cover and bake 50 minutes or until chicken is tender and no longer pink.
6. Sprinkle chicken with cheese and bake, uncovered, additional 5 minutes or until cheese melts.

Nutritional Information

Entire Recipe

Carbohydrates	51
Fiber	10
Protein	107
Net Carbs	**41**

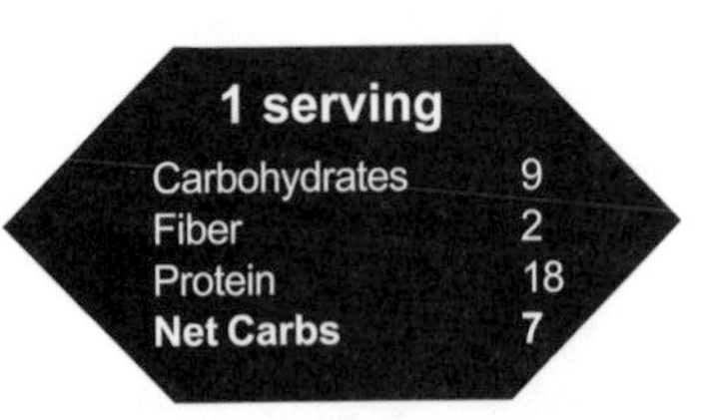

1 serving	
Carbohydrates	9
Fiber	2
Protein	18
Net Carbs	**7**

Grilled Chicken Patties

Makes 8 servings

1 1/2 pounds ground chicken or turkey
1/2 cup green pepper, finely chopped
1/3 cup fresh mushrooms, finely chopped
2 tablespoons stuffed green olives, finely chopped
2 cups shredded sharp cheddar cheese
1/2 teaspoon salt
1/4 teaspoon pepper

1 tablespoon butter
2 medium onions, sliced into rings

Directions

1. In medium bowl, combine first 7 ingredients; shape mixture into 8 patties; cover and chill.
2. In large skillet over medium-low heat, melt butter. Add onion rings; cook until tender and brown; keep warm.
3. Coat outdoor grill grates with non-stick spray.
4. Over medium-hot coals, cook chicken patties 15 minutes on each side or until tender and no longer pink. For gas grill, follow instructions for grilling chicken.
5. Serve patties with hot onions on top.

Nutritional Information

Entire Recipe

Carbohydrates	22
Fiber	5
Protein	254
Net Carbs	**17**

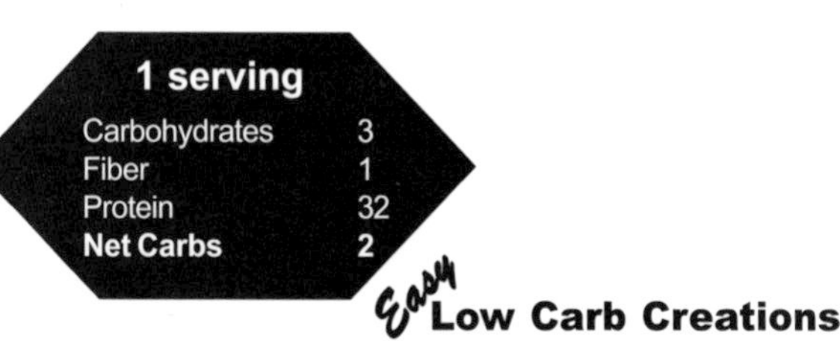

1 serving

Carbohydrates	3
Fiber	1
Protein	32
Net Carbs	**2**

Lemon-Dilled Chicken

Makes 4 servings

4 boneless, skinless chicken breasts

2 tablespoons olive oil
2 tablespoons lemon juice
1 teaspoon minced garlic
1/2 teaspoon dill weed
1/2 teaspoon salt

Directions

1. Position oven rack for broiling, about 4-inches from heat.
2. Set oven temperature to broil/high.
3. On prepared broiler pan, place chicken.
4. In small bowl, mix together remaining ingredients; brush chicken with mixture.
5. Broil chicken 6 to 8 minutes; brush with remaining mixture; broil other side of breasts additional 6 to 8 minutes or until chicken is tender and no longer pink.

Nutritional Information

Entire Recipe

Carbohydrates	2
Fiber	0
Protein	93
Net Carbs	**2**

1 serving	
Carbohydrates	1
Fiber	0
Protein	23
Net Carbs	**1**

Marinated Grilled Chicken

Makes 6 servings

6 boneless, skinless chicken breasts
1 16-ounce bottle Italian salad dressing

Directions

1. In large bowl, place chicken breasts; over chicken, pour salad dressing; cover and chill 3 hours. Discard marinade.
2. Coat outdoor grill grates with non-stick spray.
3. Over medium-hot coals, cook breasts 20 minutes on each side or until chicken is tender and no longer pink. For gas grill, follow instructions for grilling chicken.

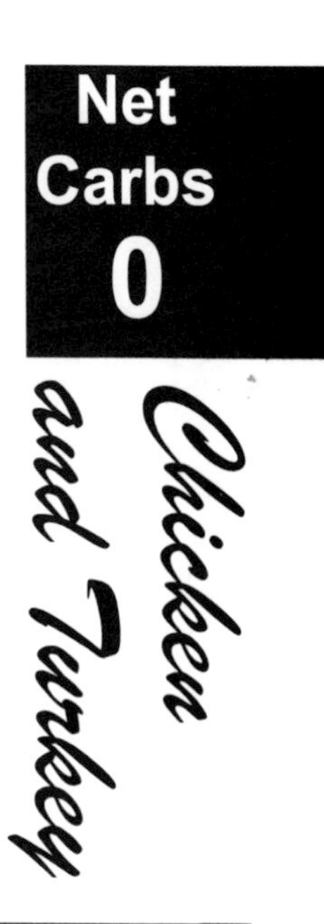

Nutritional Information

Entire Recipe

Carbohydrates	0
Fiber	0
Protein	156
Net Carbs	**0**

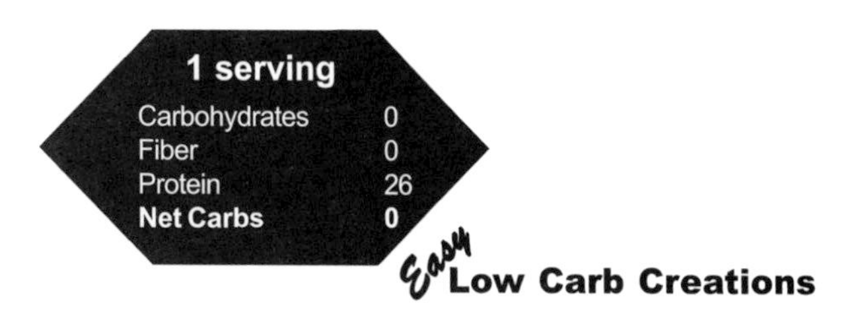

1 serving

Carbohydrates	0
Fiber	0
Protein	26
Net Carbs	**0**

Parmesan Chicken

Makes 6 servings

2 eggs

1 cup grated Parmesan cheese

6 boneless, skinless chicken breasts

Directions

1. Preheat oven to 350 degrees.
2. In medium bowl, beat eggs slightly.
3. In separate bowl, place Parmesan cheese.
4. Dip each chicken breast in egg, then in Parmesan cheese.
5. In prepared 9 x 13-inch baking dish, place chicken.
6. Bake 50 to 60 minutes or until chicken is tender and no longer pink.

Nutritional Information

Entire Recipe

Carbohydrates	1
Fiber	0
Protein	180
Net Carbs	**1**

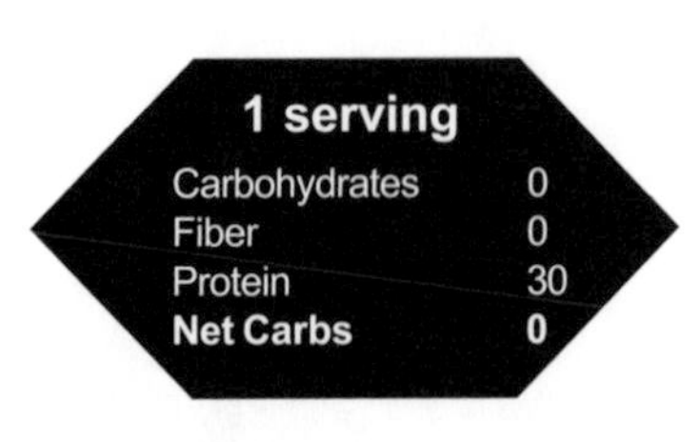

1 serving	
Carbohydrates	0
Fiber	0
Protein	30
Net Carbs	**0**

Pineapple Chicken

Makes 6 servings

2 tablespoons vegetable oil
4 boneless, skinless chicken breasts, cut into 1/8-inch strips
1 teaspoon salt
1/4 teaspoon pepper

1 20-ounce can pineapple chunks, drained, reserving juice

2 tablespoons soy sauce
2 teaspoons cornstarch
1 teaspoon vinegar

Directions

1. In large skillet over high heat, heat oil. Add chicken strips; sprinkle with salt and pepper. Cook and stir 7 to 8 minutes; drain.
2. To chicken, add pineapple; cook additional 2 to 3 minutes.
3. In small bowl, combine the reserved pineapple juice and remaining ingredients.
4. To chicken over medium heat, slowly add pineapple juice mixture; cook and stir until thickened.

Net Carbs 3

Nutritional Information

Entire Recipe

Carbohydrates	17
Fiber	1
Protein	93
Net Carbs	**16**

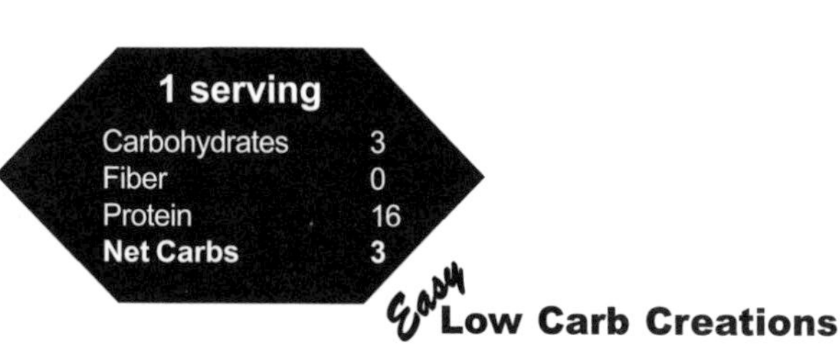

1 serving

Carbohydrates	3
Fiber	0
Protein	16
Net Carbs	**3**

Quick Chicken Cacciatore

Makes 8 servings

1 tablespoon olive oil
4 boneless, skinless chicken breasts, cut into halves

1 medium green pepper, cut into strips
1 onion, sliced into rings
1 8-ounce package fresh sliced mushrooms

1 15-ounce can tomato sauce
1 4-ounce can chopped green chilies, drained
1/2 teaspoon basil
1/2 teaspoon oregano
1/4 teaspoon garlic powder
1/8 teaspoon cayenne pepper

Directions

1. In large skillet over high heat, heat oil; add chicken. Cook 4 to 5 minutes on each side; reduce heat to medium-low.
2. Over chicken, place vegetables.
3. In medium bowl, combine remaining ingredients. Over vegetables and chicken, pour tomato sauce mixture.
4. Cover chicken and simmer 20 minutes or until chicken is tender and no longer pink.

Net Carbs 5

Nutritional Information

Entire Recipe

Carbohydrates	49
Fiber	9
Protein	225
Net Carbs	**40**

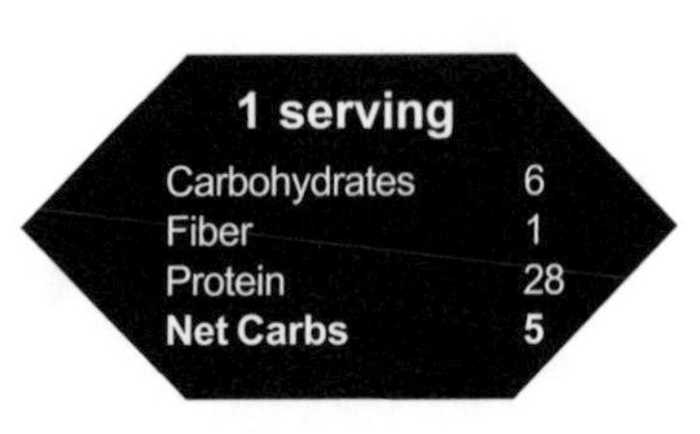

1 serving	
Carbohydrates	6
Fiber	1
Protein	28
Net Carbs	**5**

Teriyaki Chicken Kabobs

Makes 8 servings

6 boneless, skinless chicken breasts, cut into 1 1/2-inch cubes
1 10-ounce bottle teriyaki marinade

1/4 cup butter
1 teaspoon garlic salt
2 large onions, cut into eighths

1 8-ounce package fresh mushrooms

2 green peppers, cut into eighths

1 20-ounce can pineapple chunks, drained

Directions

1. In large bowl, combine chicken and marinade; cover and chill 3 hours.
2. In skillet over medium heat, melt butter; stir in garlic salt and onions. Cook 3 to 4 minutes or until onions are tender; remove onions from skillet.
3. In same skillet, add mushrooms. Cook 3 to 4 minutes; remove mushrooms from skillet.
4. In same skillet, add peppers. Cook 2 to 3 minutes; remove peppers from skillet.
5. Alternating meat with vegetables and pineapple, thread pieces onto 8 skewers.
6. Coat outdoor grill grates with non-stick spray.
7. Over hot coals, cook kabobs 10 to 15 minutes on each side or until chicken is tender and no longer pink. For gas grill, follow instructions for grilling chicken.

Nutritional Information

Entire Recipe

Carbohydrates	72
Fiber	5
Protein	186
Net Carbs	**67**

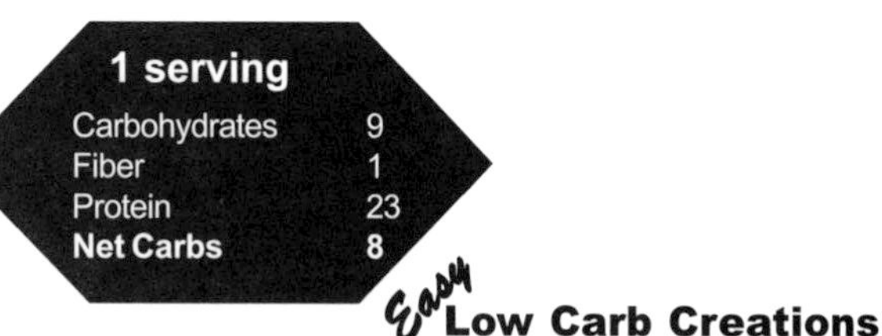

1 serving

Carbohydrates	9
Fiber	1
Protein	23
Net Carbs	**8**

Desserts

Net Carbs	Recipe	Page
13	Baked Apples (Microwave)	87
16	Bing Cherry Supreme	88
7	Butterscotch Peanut Butter Mousse	89
7	Cheesecake Pie	90
7	Cheesecake Supreme	91
3	Cherry-Diet Cola Dessert	92
9	Chilled Cheesecake	93
2	Chocolate Cheesecake Singles	94
2	Chocolate Peanut Pops	95
6	Chocolate Pie	96
7	Chocolate Silk Pie	97
8	Cream Cheese Puffs	98
9	Four Layer Dessert	99
13	Frozen Peanut Butter Dessert	100
0	Frozen Pops	101
12	Fruit Fluff	102
9	Fruity Cheese Fluff	103
4	Layered Gelatin Dessert	104
5	Lemon Cream Nutty Delight	105
7	Lime Dessert	106
10	Margueritaville Pecan Pie	107
4	Peanut Butter Cookies	108
13	Peanut Butter Pie	109
6	Pumpkin Chiffon Dessert	110
7	Pumpkin Cream Pie	111
12	Pumpkin Fluff	112
7	Strawberry Pecan Dessert	113
5	Strawberry White Chocolate Mousse	114
7	Vanilla Silk Pie	115

Baked Apples (Microwave)

Makes 4 servings

4 apples

1/4 cup sugar substitute*
2 tablespoons butter
1/2 teaspoon cinnamon

Directions

1. Core apples and slice thin circle of peel from top of each apple.
2. In prepared 8 x 8-inch microwave-safe baking dish, place apples.
3. Into cavity of each apple, spoon sugar substitute*, cinnamon, and butter.
4. Cover and microwave on high 4 to 5 minutes or until apples are tender.
5. Let apples stand 2 minutes before testing tenderness.

Nutritional Information

Entire Recipe

Carbohydrates	72
Fiber	20
Protein	0
Net Carbs	**52**

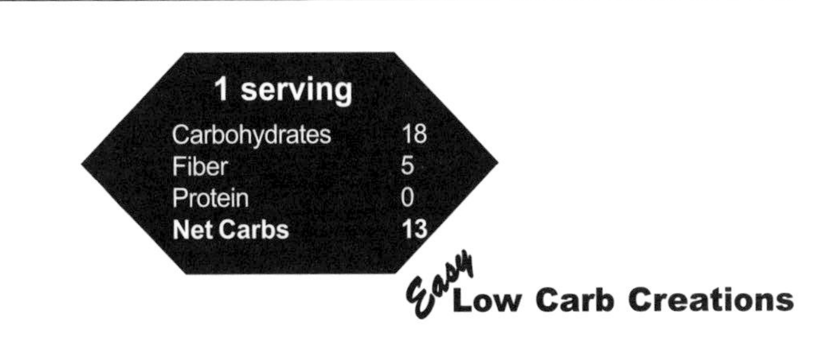

1 serving

Carbohydrates	18
Fiber	5
Protein	0
Net Carbs	**13**

Bing Cherry Supreme

Makes 12 servings

1 8-ounce package cream cheese, softened
1/4 cup sugar substitute*

1 8-ounce carton whipped topping

1 15-ounce can dark pitted cherries, drained
1 20-ounce can crushed pineapple, drained
1/2 cup pecan pieces

Directions

1. In large bowl, beat first 2 ingredients.
2. To cream cheese mixture, fold in whipped topping.
3. To same bowl, stir in remaining ingredients.
4. Cover and chill 3 hours.

Nutritional Information

Entire Recipe

Carbohydrates	206
Fiber	14
Protein	24
Net Carbs	**192**

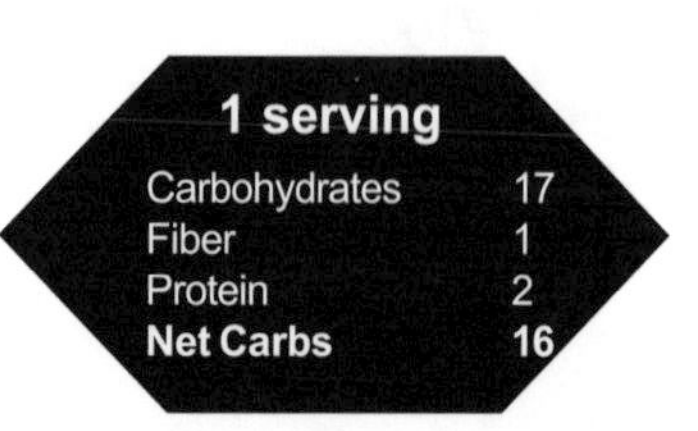

1 serving	
Carbohydrates	17
Fiber	1
Protein	2
Net Carbs	**16**

Butterscotch Peanut Butter Mousse

Makes 6 servings

2 ounces cream cheese, softened
3 tablespoons peanut butter
1 tablespoon sugar substitute*

1 cup whipping cream
1 cup water

1 1-ounce package sugar-free butterscotch instant pudding mix

Directions

1. In medium bowl, add first 3 ingredients; beat 1 minute.
2. To peanut butter mixture, gradually add whipping cream while beating; beat until thickened. Continue to beat while adding water.
3. To same bowl, add pudding mix; mix 1 minute.
4. Into 6 dessert dishes, pour pudding mixture; cover and chill 1 hour.

May substitute sugar-free chocolate instant pudding mix, but add 3 carbs per serving.

Nutritional Information

Entire Recipe

Carbohydrates	42
Fiber	3
Protein	14
Net Carbs	**39**

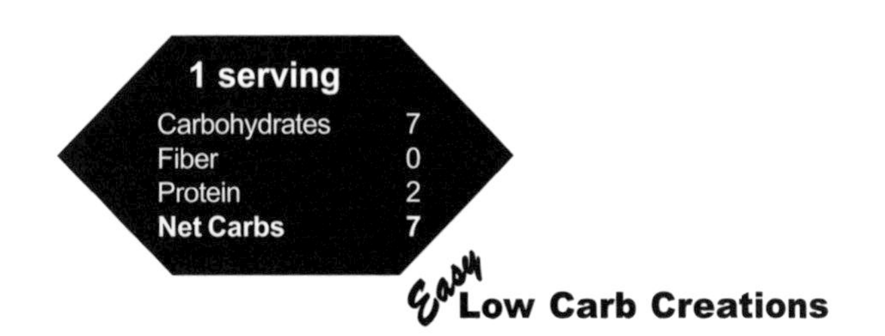

1 serving	
Carbohydrates	7
Fiber	0
Protein	2
Net Carbs	**7**

Cheesecake Pie

Makes 12 servings

1 unbaked 9-inch walnut crust (see recipe page 10)

2 8-ounce packages cream cheese, softened
2/3 cup plus 3 tablespoons sugar substitute*, divided
1/4 teaspoon almond extract

3 eggs

1 cup sour cream
1 teaspoon vanilla extract

1 tablespoon chocolate sprinkles

Directions

1. Preheat oven to 350 degrees.
2. In large bowl, beat cream cheese, 2/3 cup sugar substitute* and almond extract until light and fluffy.
3. To cream cheese mixture, add eggs, 1 at a time, beating after each addition.
4. Into pie crust, pour cream cheese mixture.
5. Bake 35 minutes or until knife comes out clean.
6. In medium bowl, blend together sour cream, 3 tablespoons sugar substitute* and vanilla.
7. Over hot pie, spread sour cream mixture; let stand until cool.
8. Cover and chill 3 hours.
9. Add sprinkles to pie before serving.

Nutritional Information

Entire Recipe

Carbohydrates	110
Fiber	21
Protein	73
Net Carbs	**89**

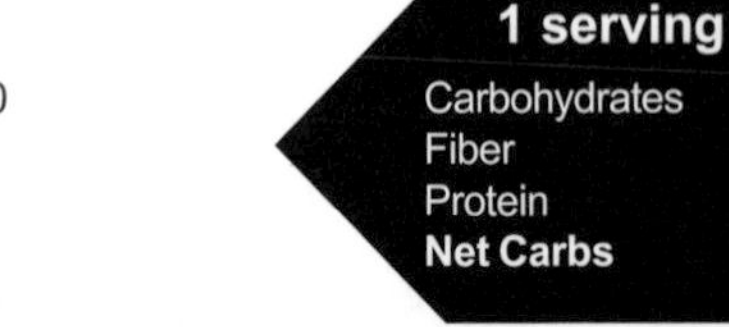

1 serving

Carbohydrates	9
Fiber	2
Protein	6
Net Carbs	**7**

Cheesecake Supreme

Makes 12 servings

1 8-inch pecan crust ingredients pressed into 9-inch spring form pan (see recipe page 9)

2 8-ounce packages plus 1 3-ounce package cream cheese, softened
1 cup sugar substitute*

2 teaspoons grated lemon peel
1/4 teaspoon vanilla
3 eggs

Directions

1. Preheat oven to 350 degrees.
2. In large bowl, beat cream cheese.
3. To cream cheese, gradually add 1 cup sugar substitute*; beat until fluffy.
4. To same bowl, add lemon peel and vanilla; add eggs, one at a time, beating after each addition.
5. Over pecan crust, pour cream cheese mixture.
6. Bake 1 hour or until knife comes out clean.
7. Cool to room temperature.

Use of all-fruit topping or fresh strawberries or blueberries is optional, but adds carbohydrates.

Nutritional Information

Entire Recipe

Carbohydrates	99
Fiber	16
Protein	76
Net Carbs	**83**

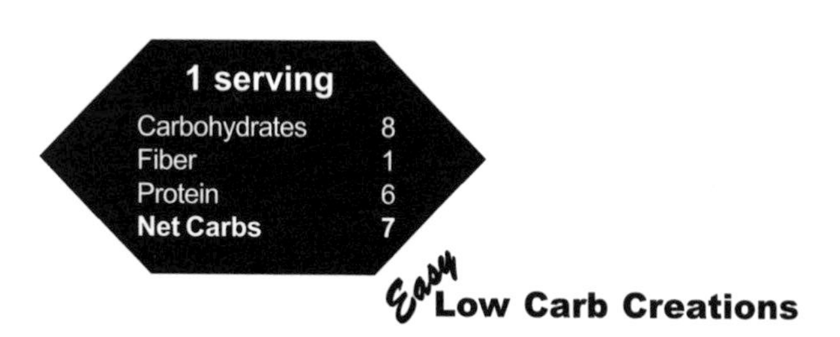

1 serving	
Carbohydrates	8
Fiber	1
Protein	6
Net Carbs	**7**

Cherry-Diet Cola Dessert

Makes 15 servings

1 20-ounce can crushed pineapple, drained, reserving juice
2 .3-ounce packages sugar-free cherry gelatin

1 8-ounce package cream cheese, softened

1 12-ounce can diet cola
1 cup pecan pieces

Directions

1. To reserved pineapple juice, add water to make 2 cups liquid. Heat to boiling.
2. In electric blender, combine gelatin and boiling liquid; blend until dissolved.
3. To blender, add cream cheese and blend until smooth.
4. Into 9 x 13-inch glass dish, pour mixture.
5. To same dish, stir in pineapple, diet cola and pecans.
6. Cover and chill 3 hours or until firm.

Nutritional Information

Entire Recipe

Carbohydrates	57
Fiber	11
Protein	43
Net Carbs	**46**

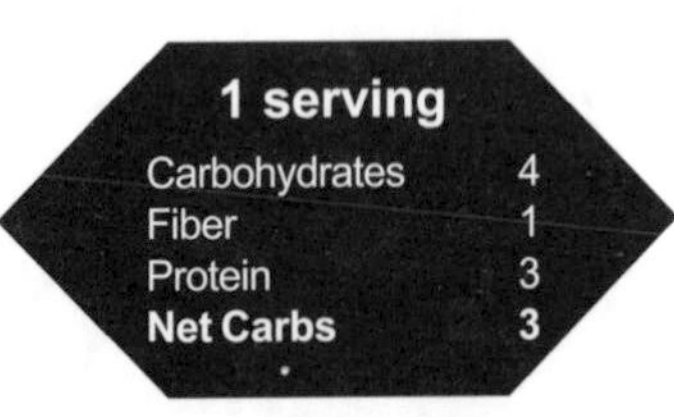

1 serving	
Carbohydrates	4
Fiber	1
Protein	3
Net Carbs	3

Chilled Cheesecake

Makes 12 servings

1 baked 9-inch pecan crust (see recipe page 10)

1 .3-ounce package sugar-free lemon gelatin
1 cup boiling water

1/2 cup sugar substitute*
1 8-ounce package cream cheese, softened
2 teaspoons vanilla

1 12-ounce carton whipped topping

Directions

1. In electric blender, combine gelatin and boiling water; blend until dissolved.
2. To blender, add next 3 ingredients; blend until smooth. Pour into large bowl.
3. Chill until slightly thickened.
4. Into gelatin mixture, fold whipped topping.
5. Into pie crust, pour mixture; cover and chill 3 hours or until firm.

Use of all-fruit topping or fresh strawberries or blueberries is optional, but adds carbohydrates.

Nutritional Information

Entire Recipe	
Carbohydrates	136
Fiber	21
Protein	41
Net Carbs	**115**

1 serving	
Carbohydrates	11
Fiber	2
Protein	3
Net Carbs	**9**

Chocolate Cheesecake Singles

Makes 16 servings

16 muffin cup liners

1/2 cup pecans, chopped, divided

3/4 cup sugar substitute*
3 tablespoons unsweetened cocoa
1/2 teaspoon ground cinnamon
1 cup ricotta cheese
1/4 cup half-and-half
2 eggs
2 teaspoons vanilla extract

3 egg whites
1/2 teaspoon salt

Directions

1. Preheat oven to 225 degrees.
2. Coat 16 paper muffin cup liners with non-stick cooking spray.
3. In bottom of muffin cup liners, evenly sprinkle 3 tablespoons chopped nuts.
4. In electric blender, combine next 7 ingredients; blend on high until smooth; pour into large bowl and set aside.
5. In medium bowl, combine egg whites and salt; beat at medium speed with electric mixer until stiff peaks form.
6. Into chocolate mixture, fold beaten egg whites.
7. Into muffin liners, spoon batter, filling each 3/4 full.
8. Bake 30 minutes; turn off oven. Leave Cheesecake Singles in oven additional 30 minutes.
9. Remove Cheesecake Singles to wire racks to cool. Sprinkle with remaining chopped nuts; cover and chill.

Nutritional Information

Entire Recipe

Carbohydrates	29
Fiber	6
Protein	52
Net Carbs	**23**

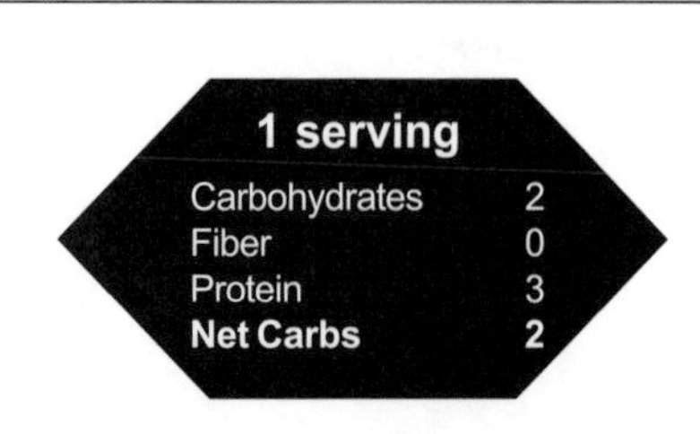

Chocolate Peanut Pops

Makes 8 servings

1 1-ounce package sugar-free chocolate instant pudding mix
4 cups half-and-half, divided

1/2 cup Spanish peanuts, chopped

1 1-ounce package sugar-free vanilla instant pudding mix
1/2 cup peanut butter

8 5-ounce paper cups
8 popsicle sticks
8 4-inch squares of aluminum foil

Directions

1. Prepare chocolate pudding according to package directions using 2 cups half-and-half.
2. Into paper cups, spoon equal amount chocolate pudding mixture.
3. On top of pudding layer, sprinkle peanuts.
4. Prepare vanilla pudding according to package directions using remaining 2 cups half-and-half and peanut butter.
5. Into cups over peanuts, spoon equal amount vanilla pudding mixture.
6. In middle of each foil piece, cut slit and cover cups.
7. In each cup, place popsicle stick.
8. Freeze 4 hours or until firm.
9. To serve pops, remove cups.

Nutritional Information

Entire Recipe

Carbohydrates	18
Fiber	2
Protein	7
Net Carbs	**16**

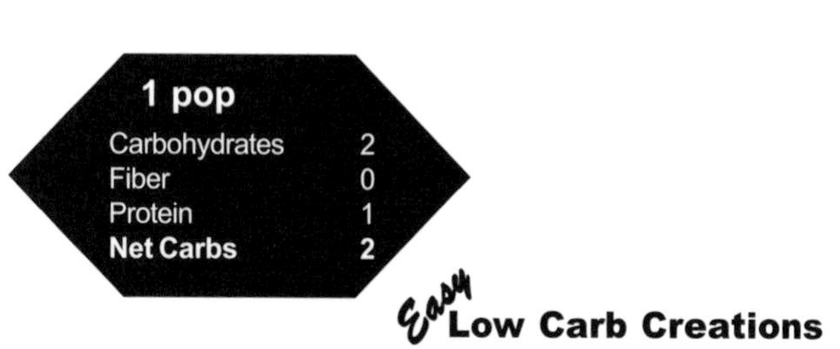

1 pop

Carbohydrates	2
Fiber	0
Protein	1
Net Carbs	**2**

Chocolate Pie

Makes 12 servings

1 baked 9-inch pecan crust (see recipe page 10)

2 tablespoons butter
2 squares (2 ounces) unsweetened chocolate

1 cup sugar substitute*
2 tablespoons cornstarch
1/2 teaspoon salt

3 cups half-and-half
4 egg yolks, slightly beaten

2 teaspoons vanilla

Canned pasteurized sweetened whipped cream

Directions

1. In microwave-safe bowl, place chocolate and butter. Microwave on high 1 minute or until butter and chocolate melt. Stir and set aside.
2. In medium saucepan, combine next 3 ingredients.
3. To same saucepan, gradually stir in half-and-half and egg yolks.
4. In same saucepan over medium heat, cook and stir constantly. Bring to boil. Boil and stir 1 minute; remove from heat.
5. To same saucepan, stir in vanilla and chocolate mixture until well-blended.
6. Into pie crust, pour pie filling. Cover and chill 3 hours or until firm.
7. Top each serving with whipped cream.

Nutritional Information

Entire Recipe

Carbohydrates	94
Fiber	26
Protein	43
Net Carbs	**68**

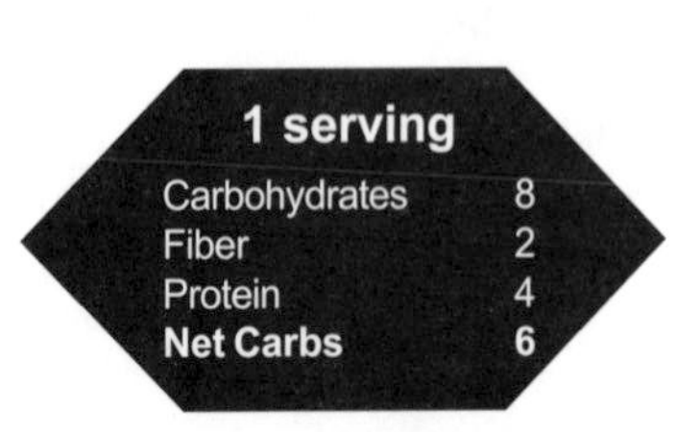

1 serving	
Carbohydrates	8
Fiber	2
Protein	4
Net Carbs	**6**

Chocolate Silk Pie

Makes 8 servings

1 baked 8-inch pecan crust (see recipe page 9)

1 cup sour cream
1 cup half-and-half

1 1-ounce package sugar-free chocolate instant pudding mix

Canned pasteurized sweetened whipped cream

Directions

1. In large bowl, beat sour cream and half-and-half until smooth.
2. In same bowl, blend in pudding mix until smooth and slightly thickened.
3. Into crust, pour pie filling; chill 3 hours or until firm.
4. Top each serving with whipped cream.

Nutritional Information

Entire Recipe

Carbohydrates	69
Fiber	16
Protein	24
Net Carbs	**53**

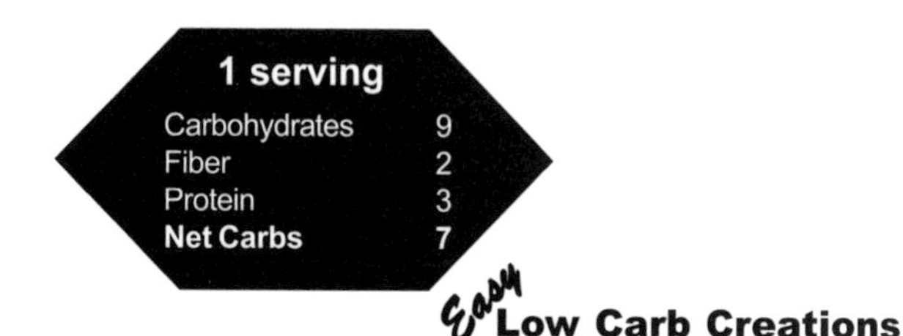

1 serving	
Carbohydrates	9
Fiber	2
Protein	3
Net Carbs	**7**

Cream Cheese Puffs

Makes 10 servings

1 8-ounce package cream cheese, softened
1/2 cup sugar substitute*
1/2 teaspoon vanilla

1 cup whipping cream

Canned pasteurized sweetened whipped cream
1 pint strawberries, sliced

Directions

1. In medium bowl, beat together first 3 ingredients until fluffy.
2. To same bowl, slowly add cream; beat until thickened, scraping sides of bowl often.
3. On sheet cake pan covered with waxed paper, drop 10 even mounds of mixture; use spoon to make well in each mound.
4. Cover Cream Cheese Puffs and freeze 2 hours.
5. Before serving, fill shells with whipped cream and strawberries.

May use black raspberries, blueberries or other fruit for filling.

Nutritional Information

Entire Recipe

Carbohydrates	88
Fiber	11
Protein	20
Net Carbs	**77**

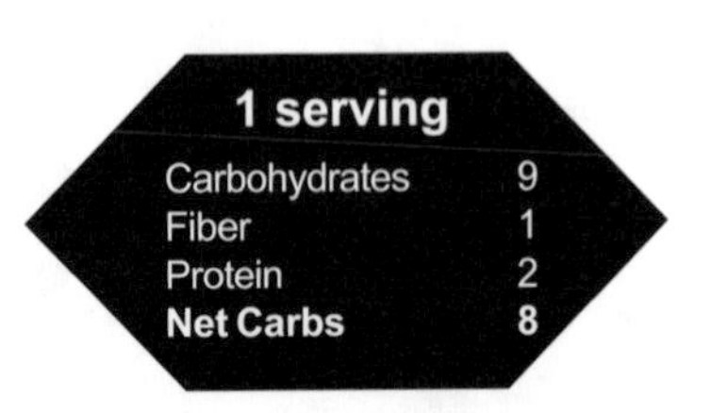

1 serving	
Carbohydrates	9
Fiber	1
Protein	2
Net Carbs	**8**

Four Layer Dessert

Makes 18 servings

1 baked 9 x 13-inch pecan crust (see recipe page 11)

1 8-ounce package cream cheese, softened
1/2 cup sugar substitute*

1 12-ounce carton whipped topping, divided

2 1-ounce packages sugar-free butterscotch instant pudding mix
3 cups half-and-half

Directions

1. In large bowl, beat first 2 ingredients*.
2. To same bowl, fold in half of whipped topping.
3. On crust, spread cream cheese mixture.
4. In large bowl, prepare both pudding mixes according to package directions, using 3 cups half-and-half.
5. Onto cream cheese layer, spread pudding mixture.
6. Top pudding layer with remaining whipped topping.
7. Cover and chill 3 hours or until firm.

Variations

Use sugar-free lemon pudding.
Use sugar-free white chocolate and sugar-free chocolate pudding swirled together.
Use sugar-free pistachio pudding and top with chopped pistachio nuts (substitute pistachios for the pecans in the crust).

Nutritional Information

Entire Recipe

Carbohydrates	217
Fiber	45
Protein	50
Net Carbs	**172**

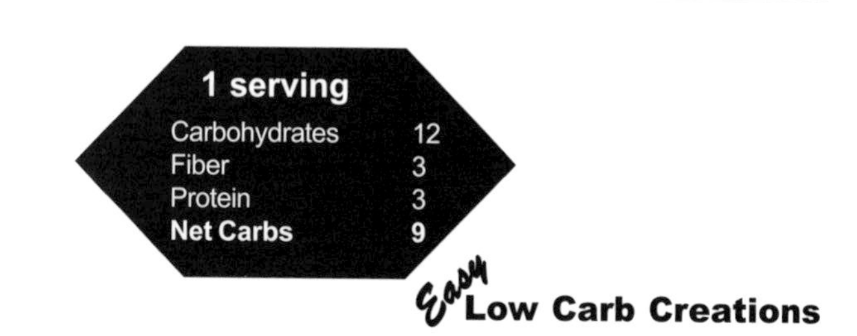

1 serving

Carbohydrates	12
Fiber	3
Protein	3
Net Carbs	**9**

Net Carbs 13

Frozen Peanut Butter Dessert

Makes 18 servings

1 baked 9 x 13-inch baked peanut crust (see recipe page 11)

1 8-ounce package cream cheese, softened

2 cups peanut butter
1 cup sugar substitute*

1 cup half-and-half

1 8-ounce carton whipped topping

Directions

1. In large bowl, beat cream cheese.
2. Into cream cheese, blend next 2 ingredients.
3. To same bowl, beat in half-and-half.
4. To peanut butter mixture, fold in whipped topping.
5. Onto 9 x 13-inch crust, pour filling.
6. Cover and freeze 4 hours or until firm.

May be prepared without peanut crust; to do so, subtract 3 net carbs per serving.

Nutritional Information

Entire Recipe

Carbohydrates	274
Fiber	44
Protein	224
Net Carbs	**230**

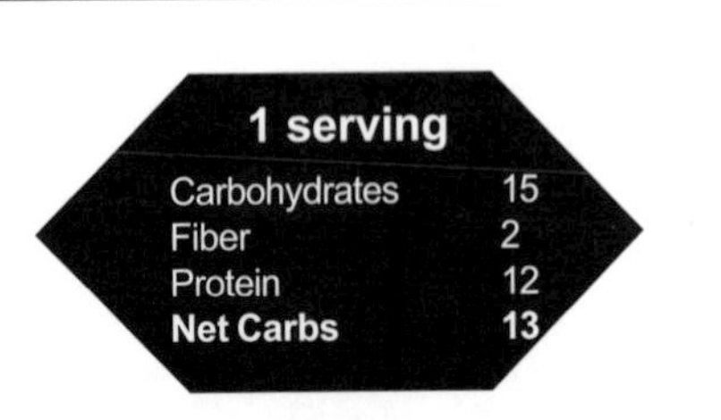

Frozen Pops

Makes 8 servings

1 .3-ounce package sugar-free gelatin (any flavor)
1 small package sugar-free drink mix (any flavor)
2 cups boiling water

2 cups cold water

8 5-ounce paper cups
8 popsicle sticks
8 4-inch squares aluminum foil

Directions

1. In large bowl, stir first three ingredients until dissolved.
2. To same bowl, stir in 2 cups cold water.
3. Into popsicle holders or paper cups, pour liquid to 3/4 full.
4. In middle of each foil piece, cut slit and cover cups.
5. In each cup, place popsicle stick.
6. Freeze 4 hours or until firm.
7. To serve frozen pops, remove cups.

Nutritional Information

Entire Recipe

Carbohydrates	0
Fiber	0
Protein	0
Net Carbs	**0**

1 pop

Carbohydrates	0
Fiber	0
Protein	0
Net Carbs	**0**

Net Carbs 12

Fruit Fluff

Makes 14 servings

2 .3-ounce packages sugar-free orange gelatin
1 24-ounce container small curd cottage cheese
2 11-ounce cans mandarin oranges, drained

1 8-ounce carton whipped topping

Directions

1. In large bowl, combine first 3 ingredients.
2. To same bowl, fold in whipped topping.
3. Cover and chill 1 hour.

Variations

Substitute lime gelatin and crushed pineapple.

Substitute strawberry gelatin and chopped strawberries.

Substitute raspberry gelatin and frozen red raspberries.

Nutritional Information

Entire Recipe

Carbohydrates	165
Fiber	0
Protein	146
Net Carbs	**165**

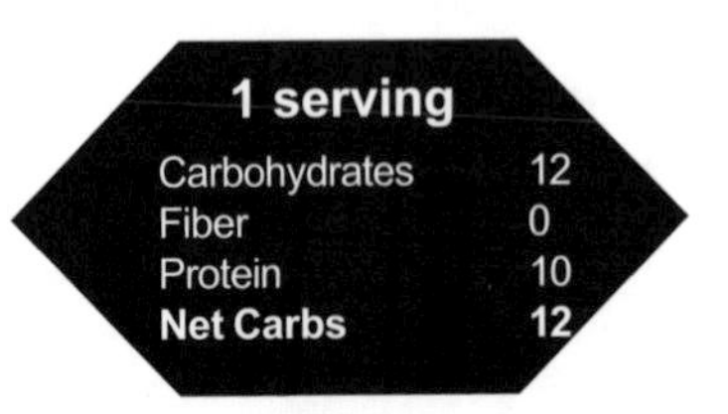

1 serving	
Carbohydrates	12
Fiber	0
Protein	10
Net Carbs	**12**

Fruity Cheese Fluff

Makes 18 servings

1 .3-ounce package sugar-free lemon gelatin
1 cup boiling water

1/2 cup reserved pineapple juice
1/2 cup cold water

1 11-ounce can mandarin oranges, drained
1 15.25-ounce can crushed pineapple, drained, reserving juice
2 cups shredded cheddar cheese
1/2 cup coconut

1 8-ounce carton whipped topping

Directions

1. In medium bowl, combine gelatin and boiling water; stir until dissolved.
2. To gelatin, stir in pineapple juice and cold water.
3. To same bowl, stir in next 4 ingredients. Chill until partially set.
4. To gelatin mixture, stir in whipped topping.
5. Cover and chill 3 hours or until firm.

Nutritional Information

Entire Recipe

Carbohydrates	160
Fiber	1
Protein	32
Net Carbs	**159**

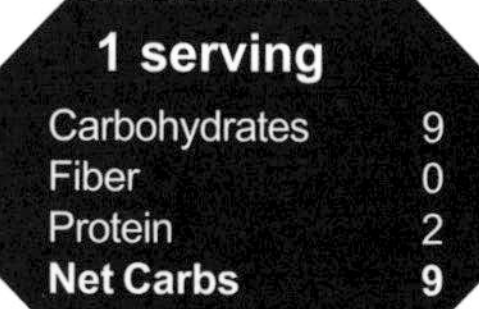

1 serving

Carbohydrates	9
Fiber	0
Protein	2
Net Carbs	**9**

Layered Gelatin Dessert

Makes 18 servings

2 .3-ounce packages sugar-free lime gelatin
2 cups boiling water
2 cups cold water

1 .3-ounce package sugar-free lemon gelatin
1 cup boiling water
1 3-ounce package cream cheese

1 8-ounce can crushed pineapple, drained
1 8-ounce carton whipped topping

2 .3-ounce packages sugar-free cherry gelatin
2 cups boiling water
2 cups cold water

Directions

1. First layer: In 9 x 13-inch glass dish, combine lime gelatin and 2 cups boiling water; stir until dissolved. Stir in 2 cups cold water. Chill until set.
2. Second layer: In electric blender, combine lemon gelatin and 1 cup boiling water; blend until gelatin dissolves. Add cream cheese; blend on low until smooth.
3. Into large bowl, pour lemon gelatin/cream cheese mixture; stir in pineapple; chill until slightly thickened.
4. Into same bowl, stir whipped topping; chill until thickened. Spread over first layer. Chill until firm.
5. Third layer: In medium bowl, combine cherry gelatin and 2 cups boiling water; stir until dissolved. Stir in 2 cups cold water. Chill until slightly thickened.
6. Over second layer, pour slightly thickened cherry gelatin. Cover and chill 3 hours or until firm.

Nutritional Information

Entire Recipe

Carbohydrates	66
Fiber	0
Protein	6
Net Carbs	**66**

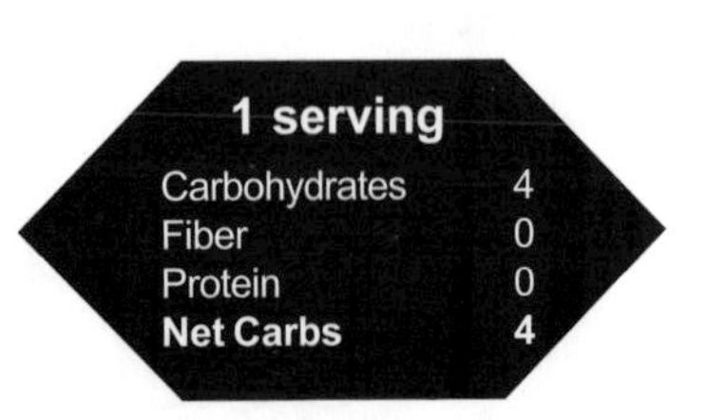

1 serving	
Carbohydrates	4
Fiber	0
Protein	0
Net Carbs	**4**

Net Carbs 5

Lemon Cream Nutty Delight

Makes 18 servings

1 8-ounce package cream cheese, softened
1 12-ounce can diet lemon-lime soda
2 teaspoons vanilla

2 .3-ounce packages sugar-free lemon gelatin
2 1/2 cups boiling water

1 15.25-ounce can crushed pineapple, drained
1 cup pecan pieces

Directions

1. In electric blender, combine first 3 ingredients; blend on low until smooth.
2. In 9 x 13-inch dish, combine gelatin and boiling water, stirring until dissolved.
3. To same dish, add cream cheese mixture, pineapple and pecans; stir well.
4. Cover and chill 3 hours or until firm.

Nutritional Information

Entire Recipe

Carbohydrates	114
Fiber	16
Protein	75
Net Carbs	**98**

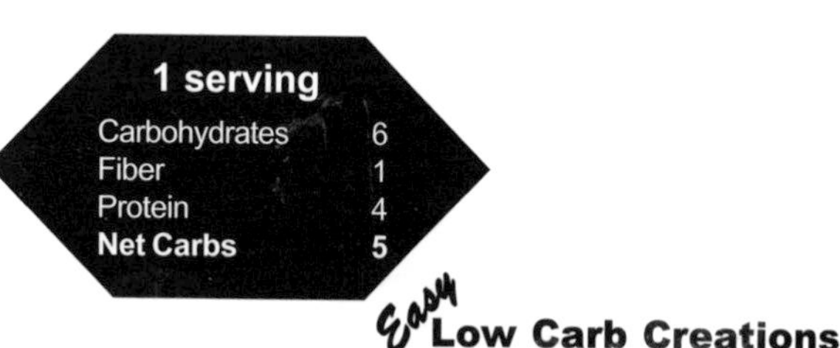

Lime Dessert

Makes 12 servings

1 .3-ounce package sugar-free lime gelatin
1 cup boiling water

1/2 cup cold water
1 8-ounce package cream cheese, softened

1 12-ounce can crushed pineapple, drained

1 8-ounce carton whipped topping
1 cup walnut pieces

Directions

1. In electric blender, combine gelatin and boiling water; blend until dissolved.
2. To blender, add next 2 ingredients; blend until smooth.
3. To medium bowl, pour cream cheese mixture; stir in pineapple; chill until slightly thickened.
4. Into gelatin mixture, fold whipped topping and walnuts.
5. Cover and chill 3 hours or until firm.

Nutritional Information

Entire Recipe

Carbohydrates	101
Fiber	12
Protein	20
Net Carbs	**89**

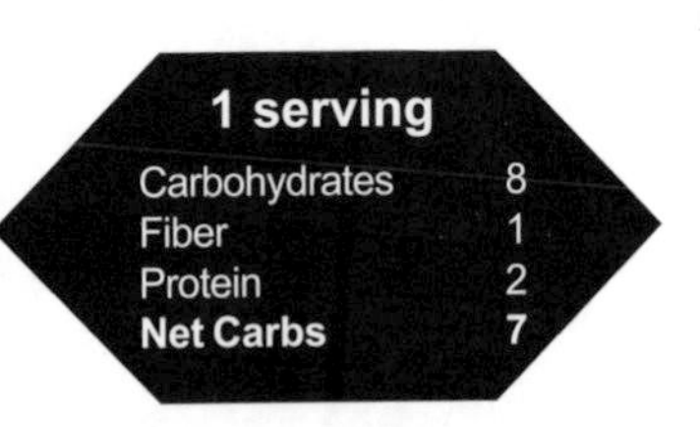

Pecan Pie

vings

Net Carbs 10

(see recipe page 10)

ened

1. In large bowl, beat cream cheese.
2. To cream cheese, add next 2 ingredients; beat until mixture is light and fluffy.
3. To same bowl, slowly add remaining ingredients while beating.
4. Into pie crust, pour filling; cover and chill 3 hours or until firm.

Desserts

Nutritional Information

Entire Recipe

Carbohydrates	141
Fiber	21
Protein	77
Net Carbs	**120**

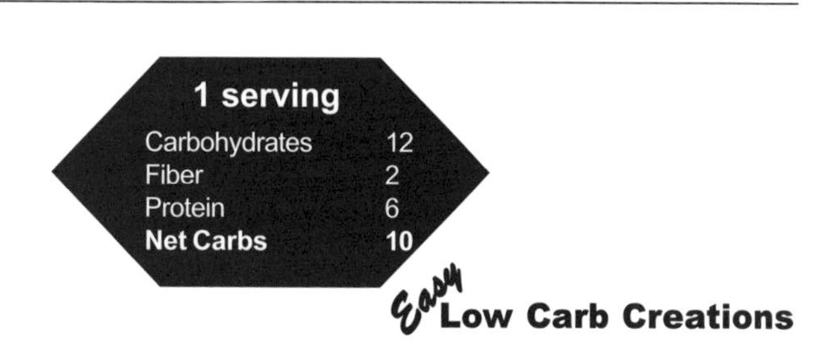

Peanut Butter Cookies

Makes 2 dozen / 12 servings

1 egg

1 cup peanut butter
3/4 cup plus 2 tablespoons sugar substitute*
1 teaspoon vanilla

Directions

1. Preheat oven to 350 degrees.
2. In medium bowl, beat egg slightly.
3. To same bowl, combine remaining ingredients.
4. Shape cookie dough into teaspoon-sized balls; place 2 inches apart on baking sheet; flatten with fork.
5. Bake 16 to18 minutes or until set.
6. Cool cookies 5 minutes; remove to cooling racks.

Nutritional Information

Entire Recipe	
Carbohydrates	56
Fiber	16
Protein	60
Net Carbs	**40**

1 cookie	
Carbohydrates	2
Fiber	1
Protein	3
Net Carbs	**1**

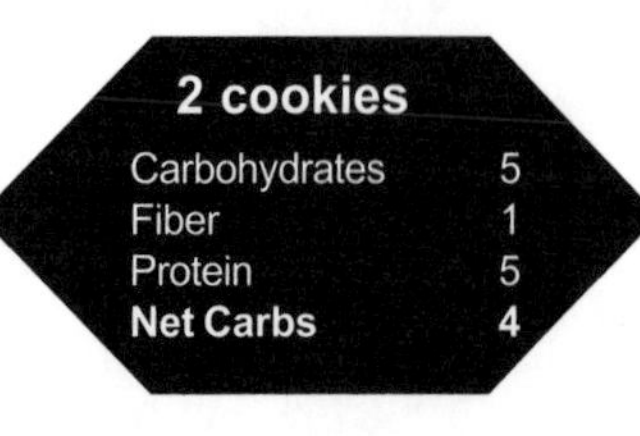

2 cookies	
Carbohydrates	5
Fiber	1
Protein	5
Net Carbs	**4**

Peanut Butter Pie

Makes 12 servings

1 baked 9-inch peanut pie crust (see recipe page 10)

2 1-ounce packages sugar-free vanilla cook-type pudding mix
4 cups half-and-half

1/2 cup peanut butter
1/2 cup sugar substitute*

Canned pasteurized sweetened whipped cream

Directions

1. In large saucepan, prepare both vanilla pudding mixes according to box directions, using 4 cups half-and-half.
2. To cooked pudding in pan, add next 2 ingredients; stir until dissolved.
3. Into peanut pie crust, pour pie filling; cover and chill 3 hours or until firm.
4. Top each serving with whipped cream.

Nutritional Information

Entire Recipe

Carbohydrates	182
Fiber	24
Protein	92
Net Carbs	**158**

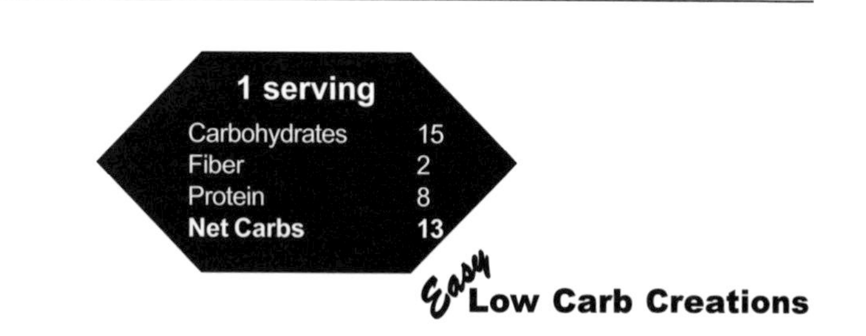

Pumpkin Chiffon Dessert

Makes 12 servings

1 baked 9-inch walnut crust, 1 teaspoon cinnamon added to recipe
(see recipe page 10)

1 tablespoon unflavored gelatin
1/4 cup cold water

3 egg yolks

1/2 cup sugar substitute*
1 1/4 cups canned pumpkin
1/2 cup milk
1/4 teaspoon salt
1/2 teaspoon cinnamon
1/2 teaspoon nutmeg

1 8-ounce carton whipped topping

Directions

1. In 1/4 cup cold water, soak gelatin; set aside.
2. In medium saucepan, beat egg yolks slightly.
3. To same saucepan, add next 6 ingredients. Over medium heat, cook and stir constantly, until thickened.
4. Remove saucepan from heat; stir in soaked gelatin until dissolved.
5. Chill pumpkin mixture 1 hour.
6. Into pumpkin mixture, fold whipped topping.
7. Into pie crust, pour pie filling; cover and chill 3 hours or until firm.

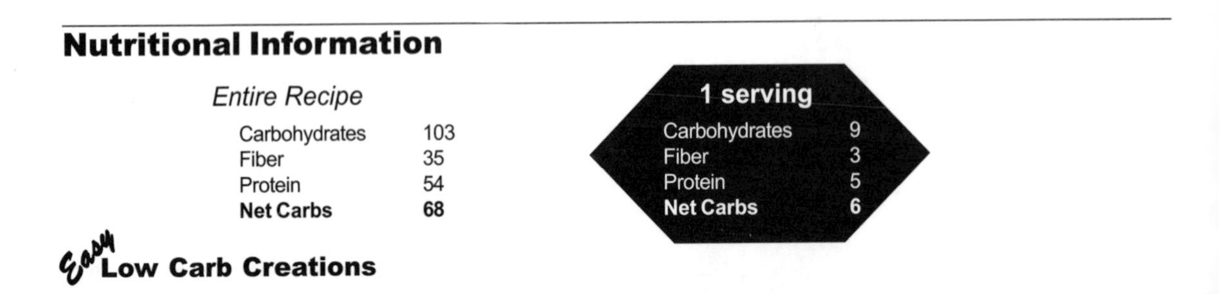

Nutritional Information

Entire Recipe

Carbohydrates	103
Fiber	35
Protein	54
Net Carbs	**68**

1 serving

Carbohydrates	9
Fiber	3
Protein	5
Net Carbs	**6**

Pumpkin Cream Pie

Makes 12 servings

1 baked 9-inch walnut crust (see recipe page 10)

2 1-ounce packages sugar-free vanilla cook-type pudding mix
3 tablespoons sugar substitute*
1 1/2 teaspoons pumpkin pie spice
1 1/2 cups half-and-half
1 egg, slightly beaten
1 15-ounce can pumpkin

Canned pasteurized sweetened whipped cream

Directions

1. In medium saucepan over medium heat, combine pudding mixes and next 5 ingredients; cook and stir until mixture boils.
2. Remove saucepan from heat. Cool 5 minutes, stirring pie filling twice.
3. Into pie crust, pour pie filling. Cover and chill 3 hours or until firm.
4. Top each serving with whipped cream.

Nutritional Information

Entire Recipe

Carbohydrates	116
Fiber	41
Protein	42
Net Carbs	**75**

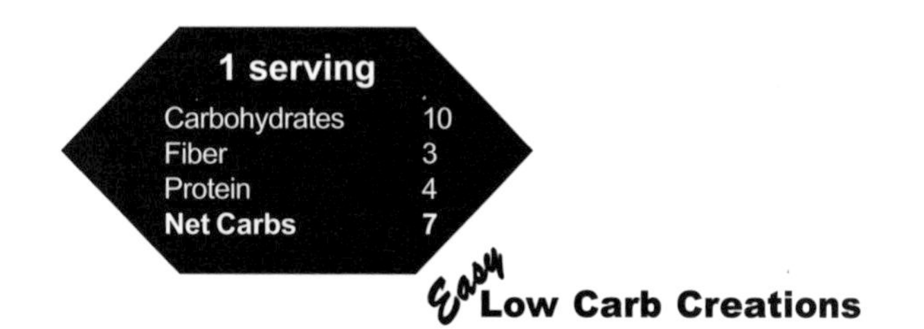

Pumpkin Fluff

Makes 8 servings

1 1-ounce package sugar-free butterscotch instant pudding mix
1 1/2 cups half-and-half

1 cup canned pumpkin
1 teaspoon pumpkin pie spice

1 8-ounce carton whipped topping

Directions

1. In large bowl, combine first 2 ingredients. Beat 2 minutes.
2. To pudding, blend in pumpkin and spice.
3. To pumpkin mixture, fold in whipped topping.
4. Into dessert dishes, spoon Pumpkin Fluff; cover and chill 3 hours or until firm.

Nutritional Information

Entire Recipe

Carbohydrates	104
Fiber	10
Protein	24
Net Carbs	**94**

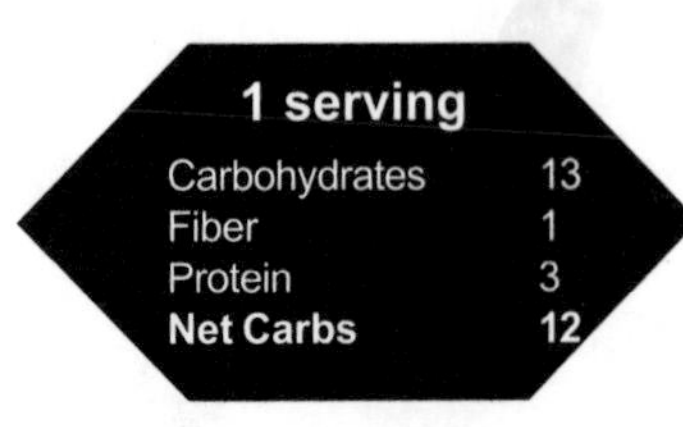

1 serving

Carbohydrates	13
Fiber	1
Protein	3
Net Carbs	**12**

Strawberry Pecan Dessert

Makes 18 servings

1 baked 9 x 13-inch pecan crust (see recipe page 11)

1 8-ounce package cream cheese, softened
1 cup sugar substitute*

1 8-ounce carton whipped topping

2 .3-ounce packages sugar-free strawberry gelatin
2 cups boiling water

2 10-ounce packages unsweetened frozen strawberries, partially thawed.

Directions

1. In large bowl, beat cream cheese and sugar substitute* until fluffy.
2. To same bowl, fold in whipped topping.
3. Over pecan crust, spread cream cheese mixture.
4. In medium bowl, combine gelatin and boiling water; stir until dissolved.
5. Into same bowl, stir strawberries; chill until slightly thickened.
6. Over cream cheese layer, pour strawberry mixture; cover and chill 3 hours or until firm.

Nutritional Information

Entire Recipe

Carbohydrates	176
Fiber	48
Protein	126
Net Carbs	**128**

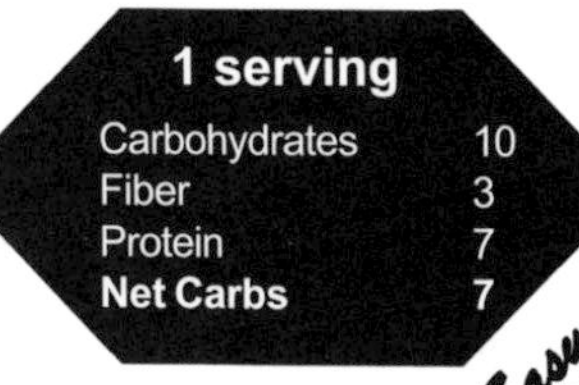

1 serving	
Carbohydrates	10
Fiber	3
Protein	7
Net Carbs	7

Strawberry White Chocolate Mousse

Makes 6 servings

2 ounces cream cheese, softened
5 strawberries
1 tablespoon sugar substitute*

1 cup whipping cream
3/4 cup water

1 package sugar-free white chocolate instant pudding mix

Directions

1. In medium bowl, add first 3 ingredients; beat 1 minute.
2. To cream cheese mixture, gradually add whipping cream while beating; beat until thickened. Continue to beat while adding water.
3. To same bowl, add pudding mix; mix 1 minute.
4. Into 6 dessert dishes, pour pudding mixture; cover and chill 1 hour.

Nutritional Information

Entire Recipe

Carbohydrates	35
Fiber	3
Protein	5
Net Carbs	**32**

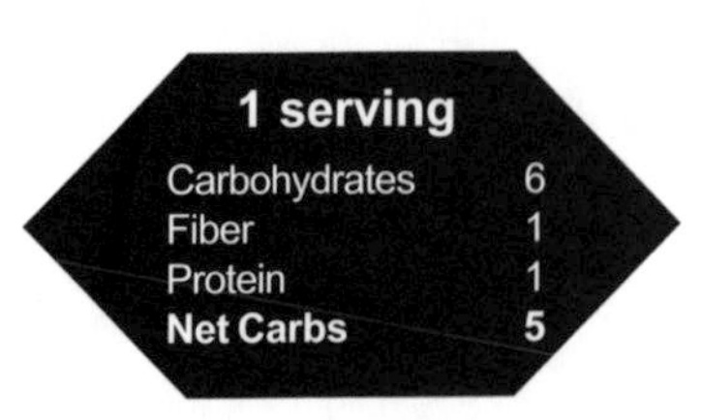

Vanilla Silk Pie

Makes 8 servings

1 baked 8-inch pecan crust (see recipe page 9)

1 cup sour cream
1 cup half-and-half

1 1-ounce package sugar-free vanilla instant pudding mix

Directions

1. In large bowl, beat sour cream and half-and-half until smooth.
2. In same bowl, blend in pudding mix until smooth and slightly thickened.
3. Into crust, pour pie filling; chill 3 hours or until firm.

Nutritional Information

Entire Recipe

Carbohydrates	75
Fiber	16
Protein	32
Net Carbs	**59**

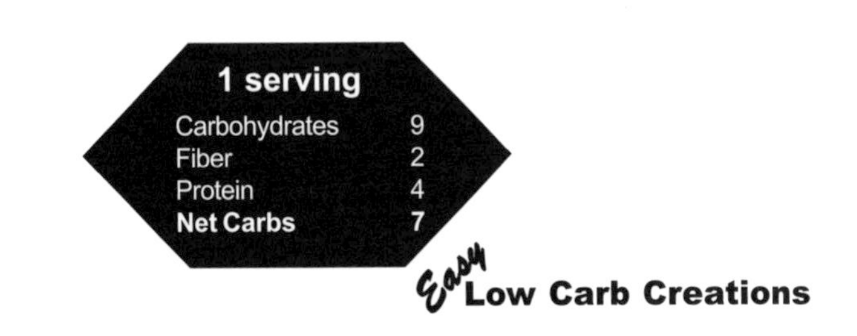

1 serving

Carbohydrates	9
Fiber	2
Protein	4
Net Carbs	**7**

Main Dish Salads

Net Carbs	Recipe	Page
7	Almond Chicken Salad	117
3	Avocado Chicken Salad	118
2	Bacon and Egg Salad	119
6	Beef Faijta Salad	120
9	Chili Salad	121
3	Crabmeat Salad	122
3	Grilled Chicken Caesar Salad	123
12	Ham Salad	124
12	Joni's Chicken Salad	125
9	Layered Tex-Mex Salad	126
1	Oriental Crunch Salad	127
11	Taco Salad	128
2	Tuna Salad	129

Almond Chicken Salad

Makes 8 servings

Net Carbs 7

Main Dish Salads

2 pounds cooked chicken breast, cubed
1 cup celery, chopped
1 cup seedless red grapes, halved
1/2 cup sliced almonds, toasted
1/2 teaspoon salt
1/4 teaspoon pepper
3/4 cup mayonnaise or salad dressing
1/4 cup sour cream

Directions

1. In large bowl, combine all ingredients; mix thoroughly.
2. Cover and chill 1 hour.

Nutritional Information

Entire Recipe

Carbohydrates	69
Fiber	14
Protein	199
Net Carbs	**55**

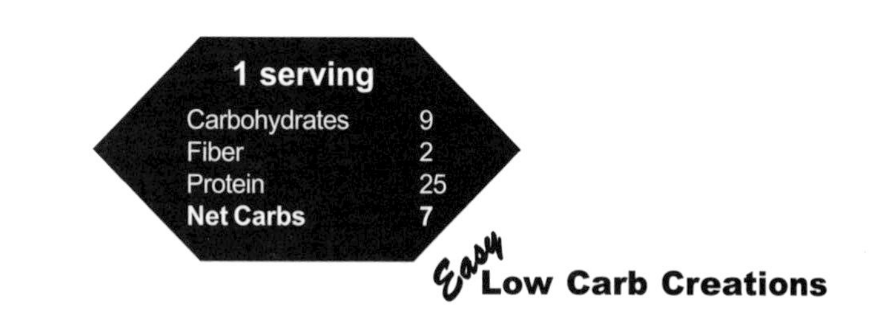

1 serving

Carbohydrates	9
Fiber	2
Protein	25
Net Carbs	**7**

Avocado Chicken Salad

Makes 10 servings

Net Carbs 3

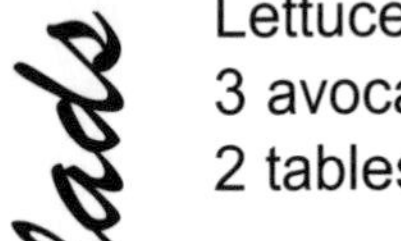

Main Dish Salads

2 pounds chicken breast, cooked, chopped
1 1/2 cups celery, chopped
4 eggs, hard-cooked, chopped
1/2 cup slivered almonds, toasted
1/2 cup pineapple tidbits, drained, reserving juice
1/2 cup mayonnaise or salad dressing

Lettuce leaves
3 avocados, peeled, seeded, sliced
2 tablespoons lemon or lime juice

Directions

1. In large bowl, combine first 6 ingredients and 1 tablespoon reserved pineapple juice.
2. On individual serving plates, place lettuce leaves.
3. On lettuce leaves, arrange sliced avocados.
4. To keep avocado green, brush surface with lemon or lime juice.
5. Onto avocado slices, heap chicken salad mixture.

Nutritional Information

Entire Recipe

Carbohydrates	73
Fiber	36
Protein	244
Net Carbs	**37**

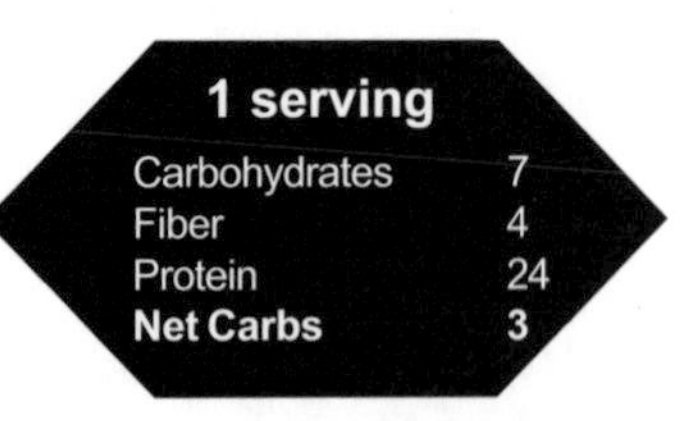

1 serving	
Carbohydrates	7
Fiber	4
Protein	24
Net Carbs	**3**

Bacon and Egg Salad

Makes 6 servings

Net Carbs 2

1/2 pound bacon, cut into 1/2-inch pieces

8 eggs, hard-cooked, chopped
1 cup celery, chopped
1/4 cup green onion, sliced

1/2 cup mayonnaise or salad dressing
1 teaspoon caraway seeds
1/4 teaspoon salt
1/4 teaspoon pepper

1 teaspoon parsley

Directions

1. In skillet over medium-high heat, cook bacon until crisp; drain.
2. In large bowl, combine cooked bacon and next 3 ingredients. Set aside.
3. In small bowl, combine next 4 ingredients.
4. Fold dressing into egg mixture; cover and chill.
5. Sprinkle with parsley before serving.

Nutritional Information

Entire Recipe

Carbohydrates	9
Fiber	2
Protein	53
Net Carbs	**7**

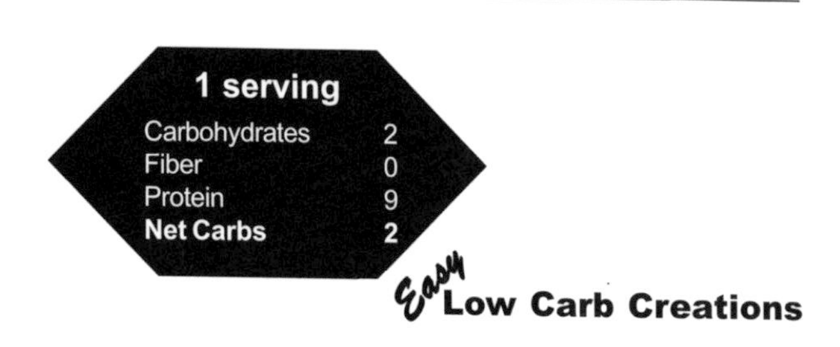

1 serving	
Carbohydrates	2
Fiber	0
Protein	9
Net Carbs	**2**

Beef Fajita Salad

Makes 8 servings

1 1/2 pounds sirloin steak
1/3 cup lime juice
1 1/2 teaspoons minced garlic
1/2 teaspoon ground cumin
1/2 teaspoon pepper

4 cups romaine lettuce, torn into bite-sized pieces
4 cups leaf lettuce, torn into bite-sized pieces
2 medium tomatoes, cut into wedges
1/2 cup red onion, sliced thinly, separated into rings
2 cups shredded cheddar cheese

1 cup picante sauce
1/2 cup sour cream
1 cup Guacamole Dip (see recipe page 27)

Directions

1. Trim fat from steak and discard fat. In sealable plastic bag or large glass bowl, place steak.
2. To steak, add lime juice and next 3 ingredients; seal or cover; chill 6 to 8 hours.
3. Spray outdoor grill grates with non-stick cooking spray.
4. Over medium-hot coals, cook steak 10 minutes on each side until desired doneness. For gas grill, follow instructions for grilling steaks.
5. Cut steak diagonally across grain into 1/4-inch slices.
6. On individual serving plates, arrange equal amounts of salad greens, steak, tomato, onion and cheese.
7. Serve each salad with 2 tablespoons each picante sauce, guacamole, and 1 tablespoon sour cream.

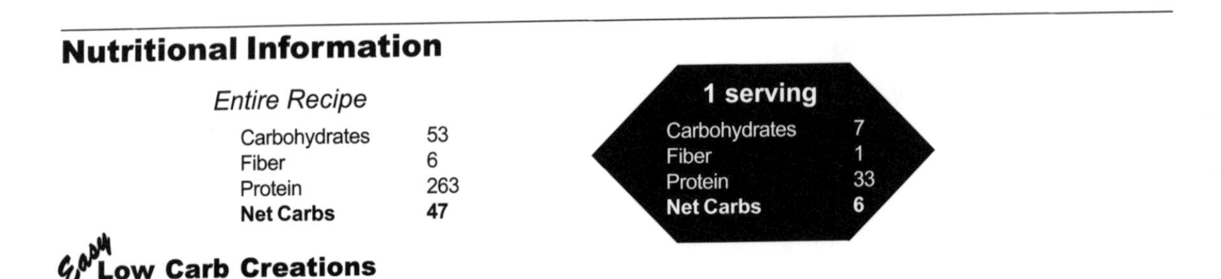

Nutritional Information

Entire Recipe

Carbohydrates	53
Fiber	6
Protein	263
Net Carbs	**47**

1 serving

Carbohydrates	7
Fiber	1
Protein	33
Net Carbs	**6**

Chili Salad

Makes 8 servings

1 1/2 pounds lean ground beef

1 package dry chili mix
1/2 cup water
1 15-ounce can chili beans, undrained
1 14.5-ounce can diced tomatoes, undrained

1/2 cup sour cream
3 tablespoons mayonnaise
1 fresh tomato, chopped
1/4 cup fresh cilantro
1/8 teaspoon pepper

8 cups leaf lettuce, torn into bite-sized pieces

1 red bell pepper, thinly sliced
3 green onions, sliced
2 cups shredded cheddar cheese
1/4 cup sliced, ripe black olives

Directions

1. In large skillet over medium-high heat, cook ground beef, stirring until meat is brown and crumbly; drain.
2. To beef in skillet, stir in next 4 ingredients; blend well. Bring to boil; reduce heat and simmer 10 minutes.
3. Meanwhile, in small bowl, combine next 5 ingredients; chill.
4. On individual serving plates, layer lettuce, chili meat and next 4 ingredients; drizzle chilled dressing over top.

Nutritional Information

Entire Recipe

Carbohydrates	113
Fiber	37
Protein	196
Net Carbs	**76**

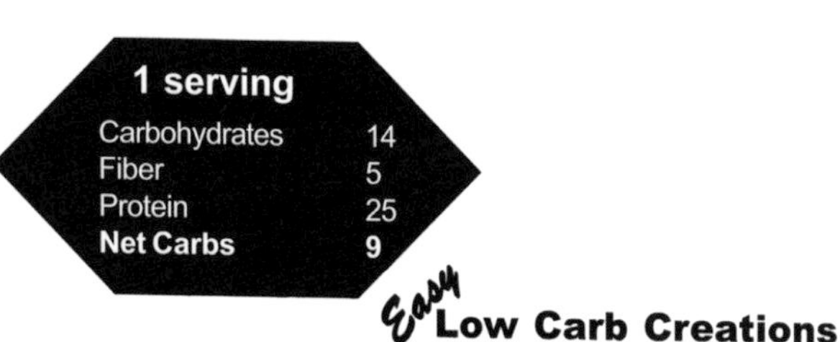

1 serving	
Carbohydrates	14
Fiber	5
Protein	25
Net Carbs	**9**

Crabmeat Salad

Makes 6 servings

1 pound flaked crabmeat (imitation works fine)
2 cups broccoli, cut into florets

3/4 cup mayonnaise or salad dressing
2 tablespoons brown sugar substitute, equivalent measure
1 teaspoon cider vinegar

Directions

1. In medium bowl, place crabmeat and broccoli.
2. In small bowl, combine remaining ingredients to make dressing.
3. Over crabmeat mixture, pour dressing; stir well to coat.
4. Cover and chill 1 hour.

Nutritional Information

Entire Recipe

Carbohydrates	31
Fiber	9
Protein	84
Net Carbs	**22**

1 serving	
Carbohydrates	5
Fiber	2
Protein	14
Net Carbs	**3**

Grilled Chicken Caesar Salad

Makes 8 servings

Net Carbs 3

6 boneless, skinless chicken breasts
1/4 cup olive oil

1/4 teaspoon basil
1/4 teaspoon oregano
1/2 teaspoon garlic salt
1/2 teaspoon pepper

8 cups romaine lettuce, torn into bite-sized pieces
2 tomatoes, thinly sliced

1 8-ounce bottle Caesar salad dressing
1 cup fresh grated Parmesan cheese

Directions

1. Brush chicken with oil.
2. In small bowl, combine next 4 ingredients; sprinkle over chicken.
3. Spray outdoor grill grates with non-stick cooking spray.
4. Over medium-hot coals, cook chicken 15 minutes on each side or until tender and no longer pink. For gas grill, follow instructions for grilling chicken.
5. On individual serving plates, arrange lettuce and tomato.
6. Cut chicken into 1/4-inch strips; place on top of salad.
7. Drizzle salad with Caesar salad dressing; top with Parmesan cheese.

Nutritional Information

Entire Recipe

Carbohydrates	27
Fiber	2
Protein	231
Net Carbs	**25**

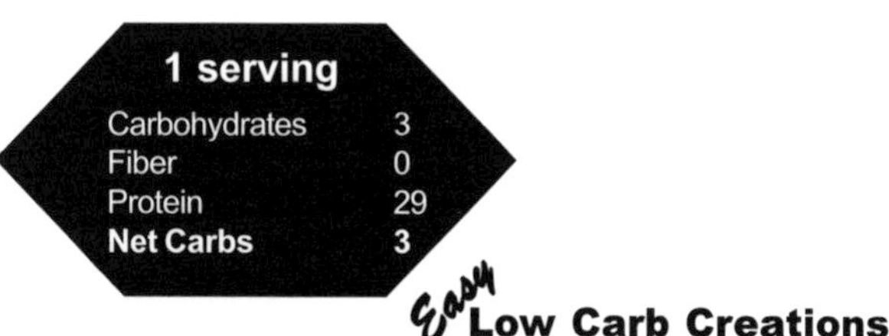

1 serving	
Carbohydrates	3
Fiber	0
Protein	29
Net Carbs	**3**

Ham Salad

Makes 8 servings

4 eggs, hard-cooked
1/2 pound beef bologna
1/2 pound minced ham
1/2 pound sweet dill pickles

1 cup salad dressing or mayonnaise

Directions

1. Into large bowl, grind together first 4 ingredients using food grinder, processor or chopper.
2. To same bowl, add salad dressing; mix well.
3. Cover and chill 1 hour.
4. Serve alone or with celery, tomatoes or lettuce.

Nutritional Information

Entire Recipe

Carbohydrates	99
Fiber	0
Protein	155
Net Carbs	**99**

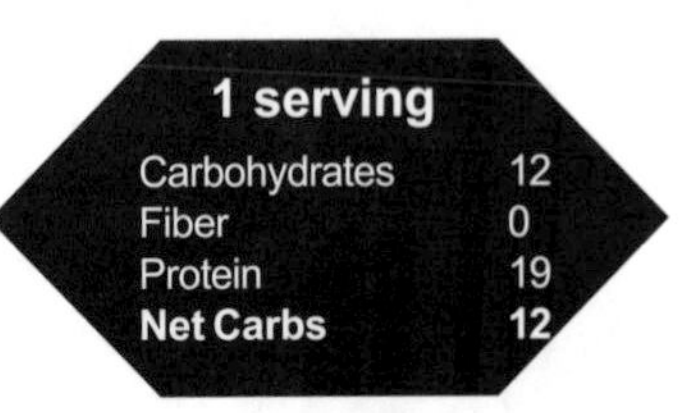

1 serving

Carbohydrates	12
Fiber	0
Protein	19
Net Carbs	**12**

Joni's Chicken Salad

Makes 12 servings

6 boneless, skinless chicken breasts

1 20-ounce can crushed pineapple with juice
4 ounces smoked almonds, finely chopped
1 1/2 cups salad dressing or mayonnaise

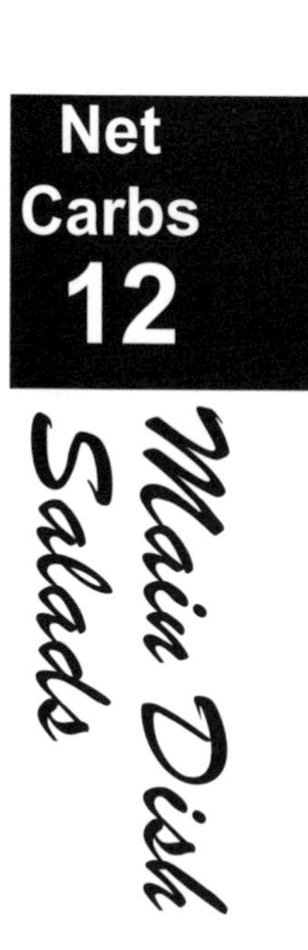

Directions

1. In large pan, place chicken; cover chicken with water. Over medium-high heat, bring to boil; reduce heat and simmer 45 minutes or until chicken is tender and no longer pink.
2. In large bowl, shred chicken breasts into small pieces using two forks.
3. To same bowl, add remaining ingredients; mix well.
4. Cover and chill 1 hour.
5. Serve alone or with tomatoes, lettuce or celery.

Nutritional Information

Entire Recipe

Carbohydrates	171
Fiber	18
Protein	205
Net Carbs	**153**

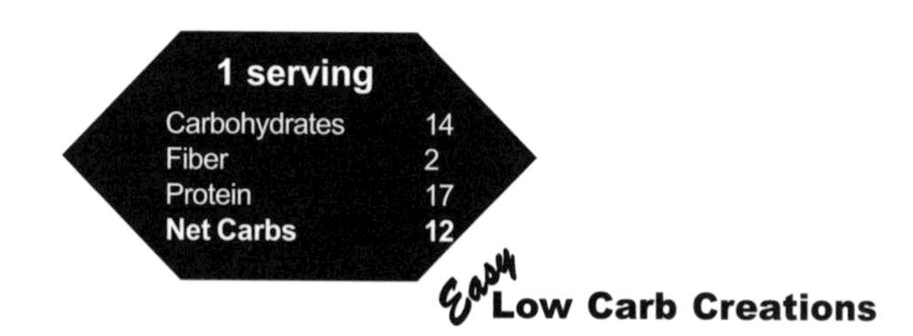

1 serving

Carbohydrates	14
Fiber	2
Protein	17
Net Carbs	**12**

Layered Tex-Mex Salad

Makes 12 servings

Net Carbs 9

Main Dish Salads

3 ripe avocados, chopped
1/2 cup onion, chopped, divided
3 large tomatoes, chopped, divided

1 pound lean ground beef
1 package taco seasoning mix

1 16-ounce can refried beans

1/2 head lettuce, shredded

2 ounces tortilla chips, broken
1 cup sour cream
2 cups shredded cheddar cheese
1 7-ounce can sliced, ripe black olives, drained

Directions

1. In medium bowl, combine avocados, 1/4 cup onion and 1/2 cup tomatoes; chill.
2. In skillet over medium-high heat, cook ground beef with remaining 1/4 cup onion, stirring until meat is brown and crumbly; drain.
3. To beef in skillet, add taco seasoning packet; cook per package directions.
4. To meat mixture, add refried beans; continue cooking 1 to 2 minutes or until beans are hot.
5. In medium bowl, toss lettuce with remaining chopped tomato.
6. In 9 x 13-inch dish, layer ingredients in the following order: tortilla chips, avocado mixture, sour cream, ground beef mixture, lettuce mixture, cheese, olives.

Nutritional Information

Entire Recipe

Carbohydrates	131
Fiber	21
Protein	156
Net Carbs	**110**

1 serving

Carbohydrates	11
Fiber	2
Protein	13
Net Carbs	**9**

Oriental Crunch Salad

Makes 8 servings

Net Carbs 1

1/4 cup sugar substitute*
1 teaspoon pepper
1/2 cup vegetable oil
1/4 cup plus 2 tablespoons vinegar
1/2 teaspoon minced garlic

8 cups leaf lettuce, torn into bite-sized pieces
1/4 cup green onion, sliced
1/2 cup celery, sliced
1 1/2 pounds cooked chicken breast, cut into 1/8-inch strips
1/4 cup almonds, toasted
2 tablespoons sesame seeds, toasted

Directions

1. In small sealable container, combine first 5 ingredients. Seal lid and shake. Chill.
2. On individual serving plates, layer remaining ingredients in order given.
3. Serve each salad with chilled dressing.

Nutritional Information

Entire Recipe

Carbohydrates	18
Fiber	5
Protein	135
Net Carbs	**13**

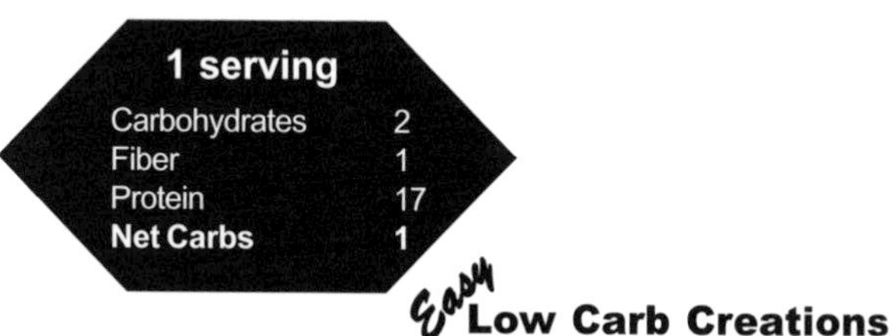

Taco Salad

Makes 8 servings

1 1/2 pounds lean ground beef
1 package taco seasoning mix

8 cups head lettuce, shredded
1/4 cup green onions, sliced
1 15-ounce can chili beans, rinsed, drained
2 tomatoes, chopped
1 8-ounce bottle creamy Italian dressing
2 cups shredded Mexican-blend cheese

Directions

1. In skillet over medium-high heat, cook ground beef, stirring until meat is brown and crumbly; drain.
2. To beef in skillet, add taco seasoning packet; cook per package directions.
3. In large bowl, layer lettuce and next 5 ingredients; toss.
4. On individual serving plates, place lettuce mixture.
5. Top each salad with cooked ground beef.

Can be served with salsa, sour cream and/or Guacamole Dip (see recipe page 27) for additional carbs.

Nutritional Information

Entire Recipe

Carbohydrates	115
Fiber	27
Protein	190
Net Carbs	**88**

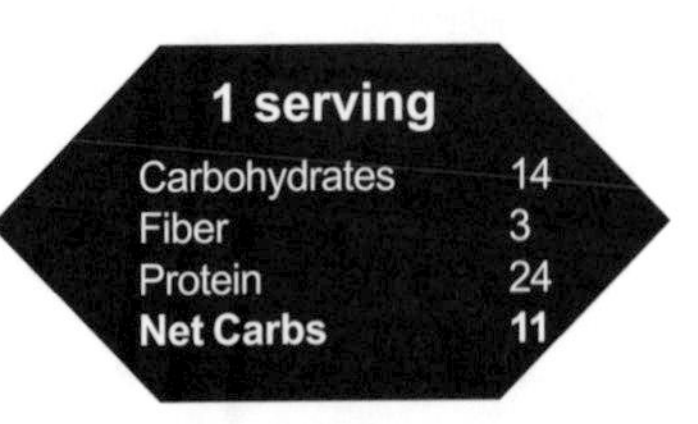

Tuna Salad

Makes 5 servings

1 12-ounce can tuna packed in water, drained
Dash salt
Dash pepper
2 teaspoons sugar substitute*
1/4 teaspoon cider vinegar
4 eggs, hard-cooked, chopped
2/3 cup celery, chopped
2 tablespoons sweet pickle relish
1/2 cup salad dressing or mayonnaise

Directions

1. In medium bowl, combine all ingredients.
2. Cover and chill 1 hour.
3. Serve alone or with celery, tomatoes or lettuce.

Nutritional Information

Entire Recipe

Carbohydrates	12
Fiber	1
Protein	95
Net Carbs	**11**

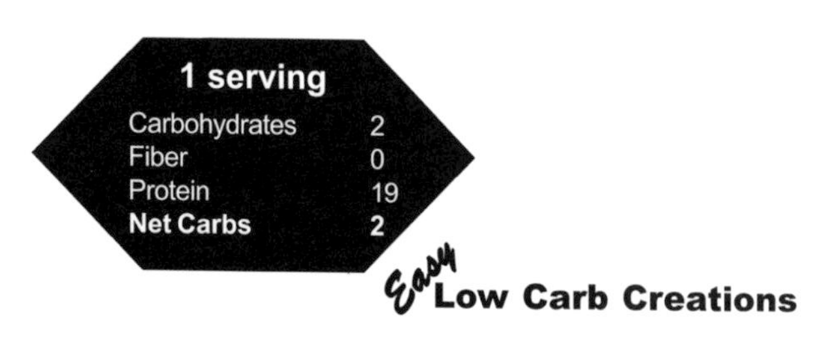

Pork Main Dishes

Net Carbs	Recipe	Page
9	Foodles (Pork Barbeque)	131
3	Grilled Beer Brats	132
5	Ham and Cheese Rolls	133
7	Ham Roll-Ups	134
3	Oriental Grilled Chops	136
8	Oven Bar-B-Cue Ribs	137
3	Pork Kabobs	138

Foodles (Pork Barbeque)

Makes 12 servings

4 pounds pork shoulder steak, cut into large pieces
1 28-ounce can diced tomatoes
1 cup Worcestershire sauce
1 cup ketchup
2 onions, chopped
2 tablespoons sugar substitute*
1 teaspoon minced garlic
1/2 teaspoon salt
1/4 teaspoon pepper

Directions

1. In large pot, combine all ingredients.
2. Over medium heat, cook, stirring occasionally, 3 hours or until meat falls apart.

Nutritional Information

Entire Recipe

Carbohydrates	118
Fiber	10
Protein	479
Net Carbs	**108**

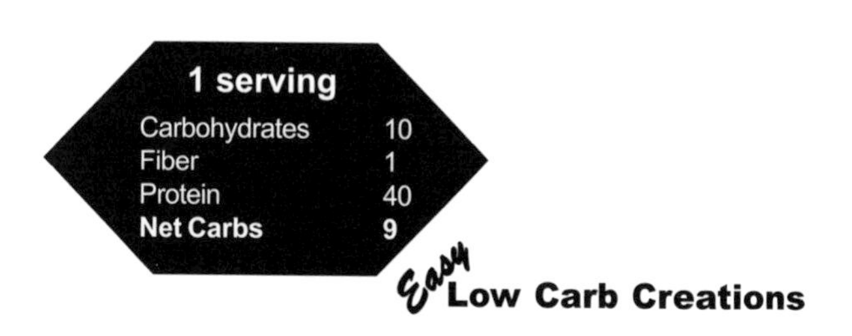

Grilled Beer Brats

Makes 12 servings

12 fresh bratwursts
4 12-ounce cans beer
2 green peppers, sliced
1 large onion, sliced

Directions

1. In large pot, combine all ingredients, making sure beer covers brats. Over medium heat, cook 20 minutes or until brats are cooked through.
2. Spray outdoor grill grates with non-stick cooking spray.
3. Over medium-hot coals, cook brats 5 minutes on each side. For gas grill, follow instructions for grilling brats.

Pork

Nutritional Information

Entire Recipe

Carbohydrates	30
Fiber	5
Protein	171
Net Carbs	**25**

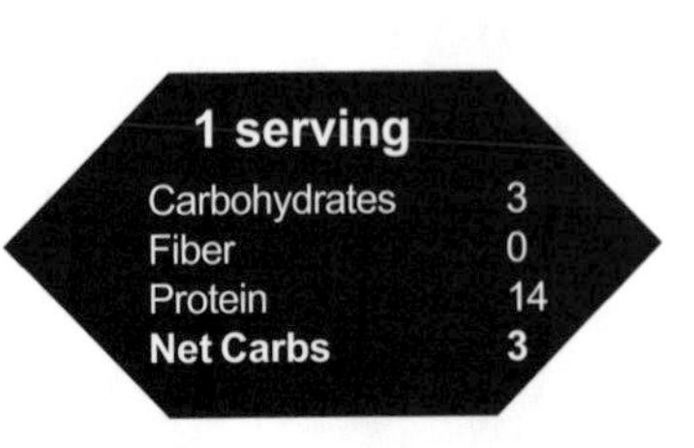

Ham and Cheese Rolls

Makes 8 servings

2 10-ounce packages frozen broccoli spears
8 1-ounce slices Swiss cheese
8 1/8-inch thick slices cooked ham (1 pound)
Toothpicks

1 10.75-ounce can condensed cream of mushroom soup
1/2 cup sour cream
2 teaspoons Dijon mustard

2 tablespoons sliced almonds

Net Carbs 5

Directions

1. Preheat oven to 350 degrees.
2. In microwave-safe dish, place broccoli; cover and microwave on high 2 to 3 minutes.
3. Rearrange spears; cover and microwave on high additional 3 to 4 minutes; drain.
4. On each ham slice, place 1 slice cheese.
5. Divide broccoli into 8 portions; arrange portion on each ham slice.
6. Roll up each ham slice and secure with toothpick. In prepared 9 x 13-inch baking dish, place secured rolls.
7. In medium bowl, combine next 3 ingredients. Over ham rolls, pour soup mixture.
8. Sprinkle ham rolls with almonds.
9. Bake 20 minutes or until hot and bubbly.

Nutritional Information

Entire Recipe

Carbohydrates	53
Fiber	16
Protein	172
Net Carbs	**37**

1 serving

Carbohydrates	7
Fiber	2
Protein	22
Net Carbs	**5**

Ham Roll-Ups

Makes 8 servings

2 pounds fresh asparagus spears, bottom inch removed
2 tablespoons water

8 1/8-inch thick slices cooked ham (1 pound)
Toothpicks

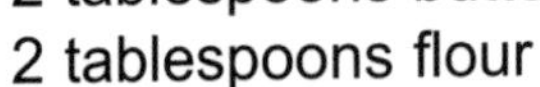

2 tablespoons butter
2 tablespoons flour
1/4 teaspoon salt
Dash pepper

1/2 cup chicken broth
1/2 cup milk

Pork

2 egg yolks, slightly beaten

1/2 cup shredded cheddar cheese
1 tablespoon lemon juice

Nutritional Information

Entire Recipe

Carbohydrates	57
Fiber	2
Protein	114
Net Carbs	**55**

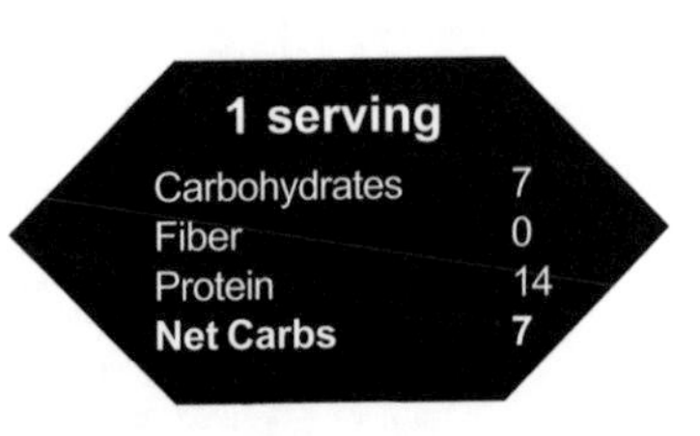

1 serving	
Carbohydrates	7
Fiber	0
Protein	14
Net Carbs	**7**

Directions

1. Preheat oven to 325 degrees.
2. In microwave-safe dish, place asparagus and 2 tablespoons water. Cover and microwave on high 5 to 6 minutes or until tender.
3. In center of each ham slice, place 5 or 6 asparagus spears.
4. Fold ham slice around asparagus to form roll; secure with toothpick; on prepared sheet cake pan, place rolls. Bake 20 minutes or until ham is hot.
5. Meanwhile, in heavy saucepan over medium heat, melt butter. Blend in next 3 ingredients; heat until bubbly.
6. In same saucepan, add broth and milk; bring to boil, stirring constantly. Cook 2 minutes.
7. Into egg yolks, stir 3 tablespoons of hot mixture and immediately blend yolks back into hot mixture. Over low heat, cook and stir 3 to 5 minutes.
8. Remove saucepan from heat; add cheese; stir until cheese melts. Stir in lemon juice.
9. On platter, place Roll-Ups; remove toothpicks; spoon sauce over them.

Oriental Grilled Chops

Makes 6 servings

3/4 cup soy sauce
1/4 cup lemon juice
1 tablespoon chili sauce
1 tablespoon brown sugar substitute, equivalent measure
1/4 teaspoon garlic powder

6 pork chops

Net Carbs 3

Directions

1. In large bowl, combine first 5 ingredients to make marinade.
2. To marinade, add pork chops; chill 2 to 3 hours, turning twice.
3. Spray outdoor grill grates with non-stick spray.
4. Over medium-hot coals, cook pork chops 15 to 20 minutes on each side until desired doneness. For gas grill, follow instructions for grilling pork chops.

Nutritional Information

Entire Recipe

Carbohydrates	20
Fiber	0
Protein	168
Net Carbs	**20**

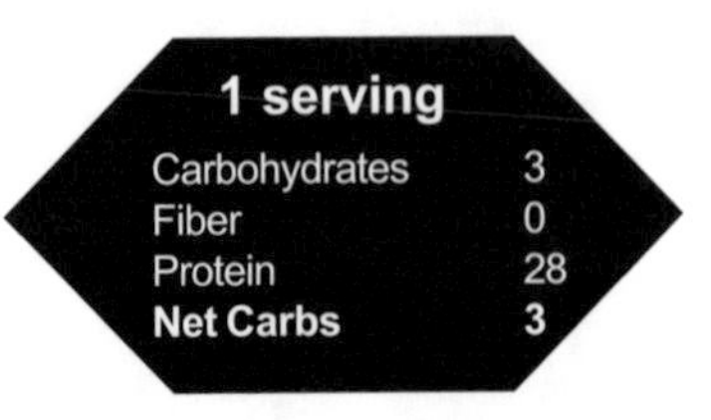

1 serving

Carbohydrates	3
Fiber	0
Protein	28
Net Carbs	**3**

Oven Bar-B-Cue Ribs

Makes 6 servings

4 pounds pork ribs, cut into serving-sized pieces
1 teaspoon salt
1/2 teaspoon pepper

1 lemon, chopped
1/3 cup onions, chopped

1 teaspoon chili powder
2 teaspoons celery seeds
1/3 cup brown sugar substitute, equivalent measure
1/3 cup vinegar
1/4 cup Worcestershire sauce
1 cup ketchup
2 cups water

Net Carbs 8

Directions

1. Preheat oven to 400 degrees.
2. In prepared 9 x 13-inch baking dish, place ribs; sprinkle meat with salt and pepper.
3. Over meat, layer lemon and onion. Bake 45 minutes.
4. In medium saucepan, combine remaining ingredients. Over medium-high heat, bring to boil; set aside.
5. Drain cooked ribs; over ribs, pour sauce.
6. Reduce oven temperature to 325 degrees; bake additional 1 to 1 1/2 hours.

Nutritional Information

Entire Recipe

Carbohydrates	48
Fiber	2
Protein	278
Net Carbs	**46**

1 serving

Carbohydrates	8
Fiber	0
Protein	46
Net Carbs	**8**

Pork Kabobs

Makes 8 servings

Net Carbs 3

Pork

1/2 teaspoon salt
1/4 teaspoon pepper
1/2 teaspoon garlic powder
1/4 cup vegetable oil
1/4 cup sugar substitute*
1/4 cup cider vinegar
1/4 cup soy sauce
1/2 cup diet lemon-lime soda or beer

3 pounds pork loin, cut into 1 1/2-inch cubes

1/4 cup butter
1 teaspoon minced garlic
2 large onions, cut into eighths

1 8-ounce package fresh mushrooms

2 green peppers, cut into eighths

1 pint cherry tomatoes

Nutritional Information

Entire Recipe

Carbohydrates	26
Fiber	1
Protein	322
Net Carbs	**25**

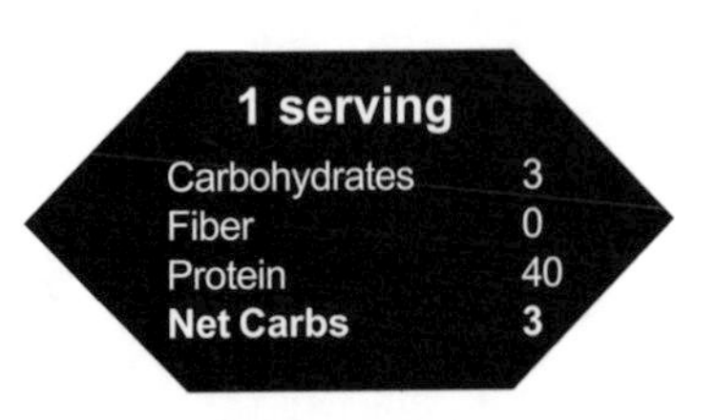

1 serving

Carbohydrates	3
Fiber	0
Protein	40
Net Carbs	**3**

Directions

1. In large bowl, combine first 8 ingredients to make marinade.
2. To marinade, add pork pieces; cover and chill 4 hours.
3. In skillet over medium heat, melt butter; stir in garlic and onions. Cook 3 to 4 minutes or until onions are tender; remove onions from skillet.
4. In same skillet, add mushrooms. Cook 3 to 4 minutes; remove mushrooms from skillet.
5. In same skillet, add green pepper. Cook 2 to 3 minutes; remove green pepper from skillet.
6. Alternating meat with vegetables, thread pieces onto 8 skewers.
7. Coat outdoor grill grates with non-stick spray.
8. Over hot coals, cook kabobs 10 to 15 minutes on each side until desired doneness. For gas grill, follow instructions for grilling pork.
9. On end of skewers, place cherry tomatoes the last 5 minutes of cooking.

Salads

Net Carbs	Recipe	Page
4	7-Layer Salad	141
6	Broccoli Salad	142
7	Cabbage Salad	143
5	Cauliflower Lettuce Layer Salad	144
5	Cheese Apple Salad	145
2	Dilled Cucumber Salad	146
5	Green Bean Salad	147
2	Italian Cucumber Tomato Salad	148
11	Italian Salad	149
2	Layered Spinach Salad	150
5	Mandarin Orange Salad	151
3	Mushroom Salad	152
1	Overnight Slaw	153
3	Pickled Cucumbers	154
1	Red Cabbage Salad	155
1	Slaw	156
6	Spinach Salad	157
1	Summer Salad	158
1	Wilted Lettuce Salad	159

7-Layer Salad

Makes 12 servings

1 pound bacon, cut into 1/2-inch pieces

1 medium head lettuce, torn into bite-sized pieces
1/2 cup celery, chopped
1/2 cup green onions, chopped
1 10-ounce package frozen baby peas, thawed, drained

1 1/2 cups mayonnaise or salad dressing
2 cups shredded cheddar cheese

Directions

1. In skillet over medium-high heat, cook bacon until crisp; drain; store in refrigerator until ready to use.
2. In 9 x 13-inch glass dish or large bowl, layer lettuce and next 3 ingredients.
3. Over peas, spread mayonnaise evenly.
4. Over mayonnaise, sprinkle grated cheese.
5. Cover and chill 2 hours.
6. Add bacon to salad before serving.

Nutritional Information

Entire Recipe

Carbohydrates	56
Fiber	14
Protein	116
Net Carbs	**42**

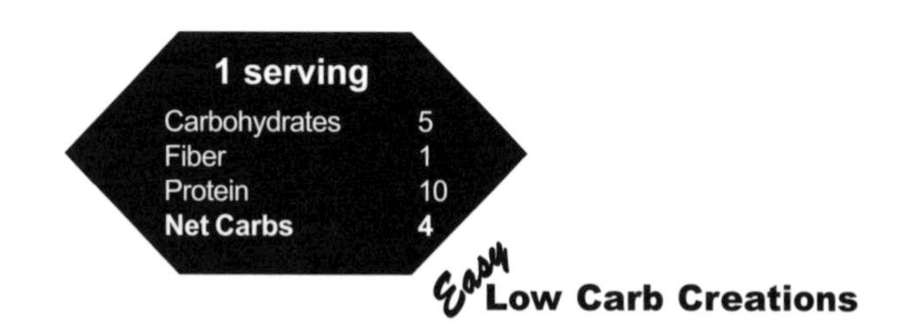

1 serving

Carbohydrates	5
Fiber	1
Protein	10
Net Carbs	**4**

Broccoli Salad

Makes 6 servings

1 pound bacon, cut into 1/2-inch pieces

1 bunch fresh broccoli, cut into florets
1/3 cup raisins
1/2 small onion, chopped

2/3 cup mayonnaise or salad dressing
2 tablespoons sugar substitute*
1 tablespoon cider vinegar

1/2 cup shelled, roasted sunflower seeds

Directions

1. In skillet over medium-high heat, cook bacon until crisp; drain; set aside.
2. In medium bowl, combine broccoli and next 2 ingredients.
3. In small bowl, combine next 3 ingredients.
4. Over broccoli, pour mayonnaise mixture; mix well. Cover and chill.
5. Add crumbled bacon and sunflower seeds to salad before serving.

Nutritional Information

Entire Recipe

Carbohydrates	55
Fiber	18
Protein	56
Net Carbs	**37**

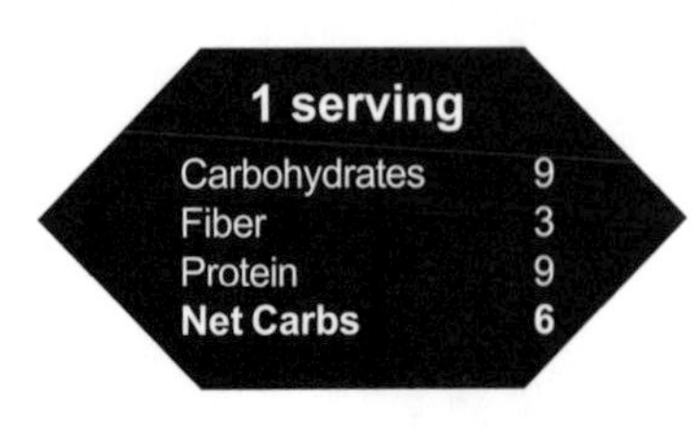

Cabbage Salad

Makes 14 servings

1 head cabbage, chopped into 1-inch pieces
3/4 cup sliced almonds, toasted
2 tablespoons sesame seeds, toasted

1/2 package ramen noodles, chicken flavored (reserve seasoning package)

1/2 cup vegetable oil
3 1/2 tablespoons cider vinegar
1 teaspoon salt
1/4 teaspoon pepper

Directions

1. In large bowl, combine first 3 ingredients.
2. Into cabbage mixture, break ramen noodles.
3. In small bowl, combine remaining ingredients and reserved chicken flavored seasoning packet. Chill 30 minutes; pour over salad before serving. Toss well.

Nutritional Information

Entire Recipe

Carbohydrates	121
Fiber	31
Protein	44
Net Carbs	**90**

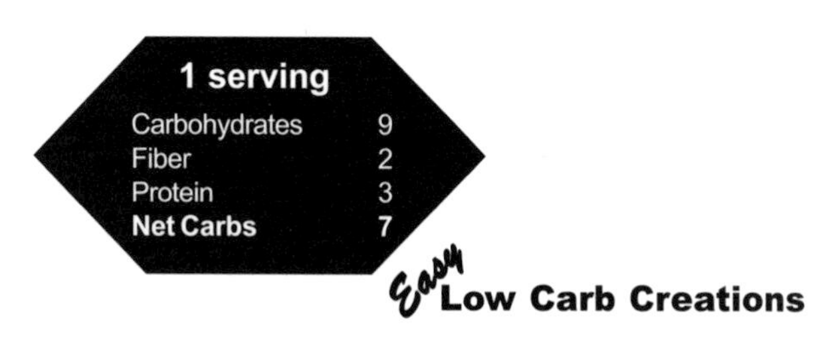

Cauliflower Lettuce Layer Salad

Makes 12 servings

1 pound bacon, cut into 1/2-inch pieces

1 head cauliflower, coarsely chopped
1 head lettuce, torn into bite-sized pieces
1 red onion, chopped

1 1/2 cups mayonnaise or salad dressing
2 cups shredded cheddar cheese

Directions

Net Carbs 5

1. In skillet over medium-high heat, cook bacon until crisp; drain. Store in refrigerator until ready to use.
2. In 9 x 13-inch glass dish or large bowl, layer first 3 ingredients in order given.
3. Over onions, spread salad dressing evenly.
4. Over salad dressing, sprinkle cheese.
5. Cover and chill 2 hours.
6. Add bacon to salad before serving.

Nutritional Information

Entire Recipe

Carbohydrates	64
Fiber	2
Protein	81
Net Carbs	**62**

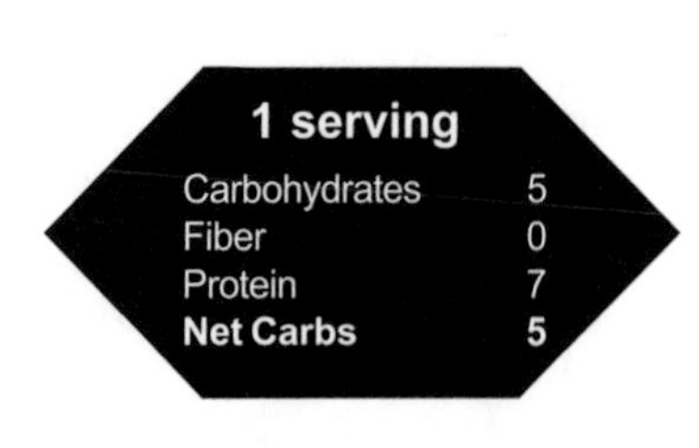

1 serving

Carbohydrates	5
Fiber	0
Protein	7
Net Carbs	**5**

Cheese Apple Salad

Makes 10 servings

2 medium apples, chopped
1 teaspoon lemon juice

1/2 cup shredded cheddar cheese
1/2 cup shredded Swiss cheese
1/3 cup red seedless grapes, halved
1/2 cup celery, chopped
1/4 cup walnut pieces

3/4 cup mayonnaise or salad dressing
2 tablespoons sugar substitute*
1/2 cup whipped topping

Net Carbs 5

Directions

1. In medium bowl, toss apples with lemon juice.
2. To same bowl, add next 5 ingredients; toss.
3. Before serving, in small bowl, combine next 3 ingredients. Pour over apple mixture and stir.

Nutritional Information

Entire Recipe

Carbohydrates	63
Fiber	13
Protein	39
Net Carbs	**50**

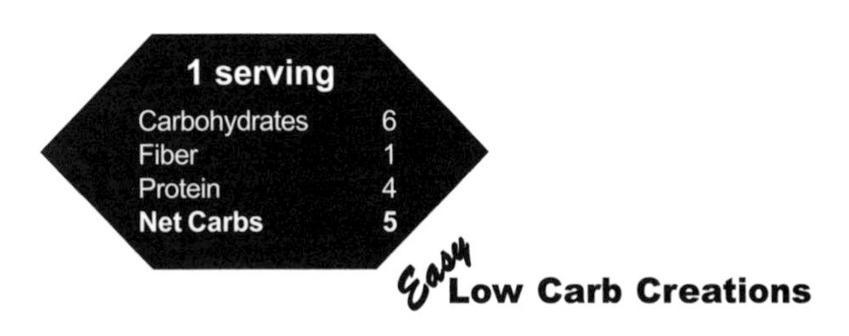

Dilled Cucumber Salad

Makes 8 servings

2 medium cucumbers, peeled, thinly sliced

3/4 cup sour cream
1/4 teaspoon minced garlic
1 tablespoon vegetable oil
1 teaspoon sugar substitute*
1/2 teaspoon salt
1/2 teaspoon cider vinegar

1/4 teaspoon dill weed

Directions

1. In medium bowl, place cucumbers.
2. In small bowl, combine next 6 ingredients.
3. Over cucumbers, pour sour cream mixture; mix gently.
4. Over salad, sprinkle dill weed; cover and chill 1 hour.
5. Mix lightly before serving.

Nutritional Information

Entire Recipe

Carbohydrates	19
Fiber	0
Protein	8
Net Carbs	**19**

1 serving	
Carbohydrates	2
Fiber	0
Protein	1
Net Carbs	**2**

Green Bean Salad

Makes 6 servings

1 pound bacon, cut into 1/2-inch pieces

2 14.5-ounce cans French-style green beans, drained
1 medium onion, thinly sliced, separated into rings
1 4-ounce can sliced mushrooms, drained

1/2 cup Italian salad dressing

2 medium tomatoes, cut into wedges

Directions

1. In skillet over medium-high heat, cook bacon until crisp; drain; set aside.
2. In large bowl, combine next 3 ingredients.
3. To same bowl, add salad dressing and toss; cover and chill 2 hours.
4. Before serving, stir bacon into salad; top with tomatoes.

Net Carbs 5

Nutritional Information

Entire Recipe

Carbohydrates	45
Fiber	17
Protein	54
Net Carbs	**28**

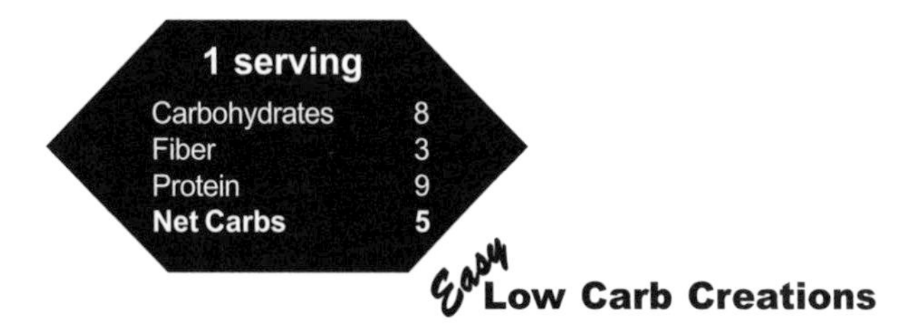

1 serving	
Carbohydrates	8
Fiber	3
Protein	9
Net Carbs	**5**

Italian Cucumber Tomato Salad

Makes 12 servings

2 cucumbers, peeled, thinly sliced
2 14.5-ounce cans diced tomatoes
1 onion, thinly sliced, separated into rings
1/2 large green pepper, chopped
1/2 teaspoon basil
1 teaspoon oregano
1/2 teaspoon parsley
3/4 teaspoon garlic salt
1/4 teaspoon pepper
1/4 cup olive oil
1/4 cup plus 1 tablespoon cider vinegar

1 cup fresh sliced mushrooms (optional)
1 cup broccoli florets (optional)
1 cup cauliflower florets (optional)

Directions

1. In large bowl, combine all ingredients.
2. Cover and chill 1 hour. Stir before serving.

Nutritional Information

Entire Recipe

Carbohydrates	41
Fiber	11
Protein	19
Net Carbs	**30**

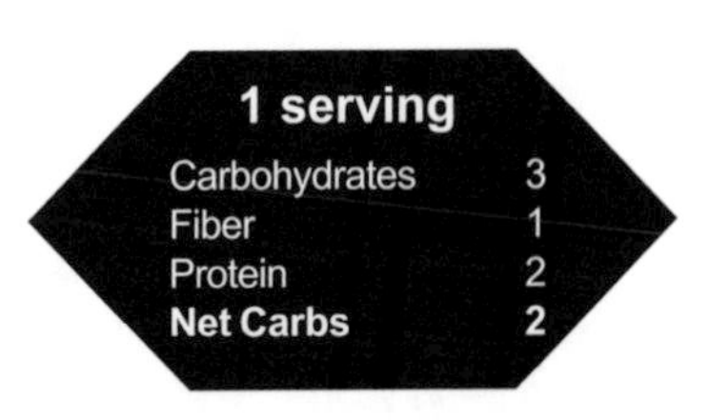

1 serving	
Carbohydrates	3
Fiber	1
Protein	2
Net Carbs	**2**

Italian Salad

Makes 8 servings

1 bunch leaf lettuce, torn into bite-sized pieces
1 equal bunch spinach, torn into bite-sized pieces
1 pint cherry tomatoes, sliced into halves
1 small red onion, thinly sliced, separated into rings
1 15-ounce can pitted black olives, drained

1 16-ounce bottle Italian salad dressing

8 to10 canned banana peppers (optional)

Directions

1. In large bowl, layer first 5 ingredients.
2. To same bowl, add salad dressing; toss. Cover and chill.
3. May garnish salad with peppers before serving.

Net Carbs 11

Nutritional Information

Entire Recipe

Carbohydrates	97
Fiber	8
Protein	39
Net Carbs	**89**

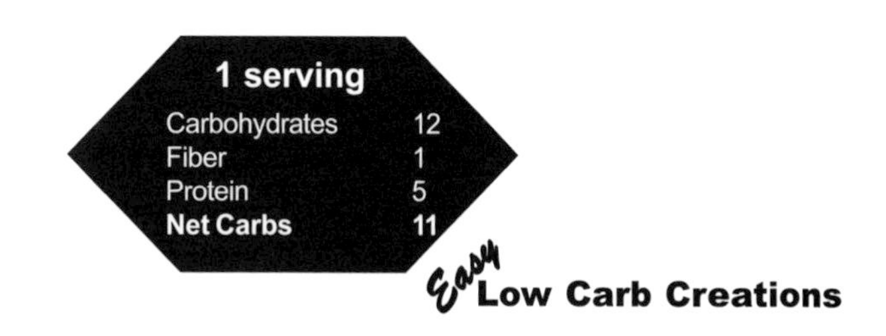

Layered Spinach Salad

Makes 10 servings

1 pound fresh spinach, torn into bite-sized pieces
1/2 head leaf lettuce, torn into bite-sized pieces
4 eggs, hard-cooked, sliced
1 onion, chopped
1 8-ounce package fresh sliced mushrooms
1 cup grated Parmesan cheese

Hot Bacon Dressing (see recipe page 164)

Directions

1. On individual plates, layer first 6 ingredients in order given.
2. Over each salad before serving, drizzle 2 tablespoons Hot Bacon Dressing.

Nutritional Information

Entire Recipe

Carbohydrates	42
Fiber	16
Protein	77
Net Carbs	**26**

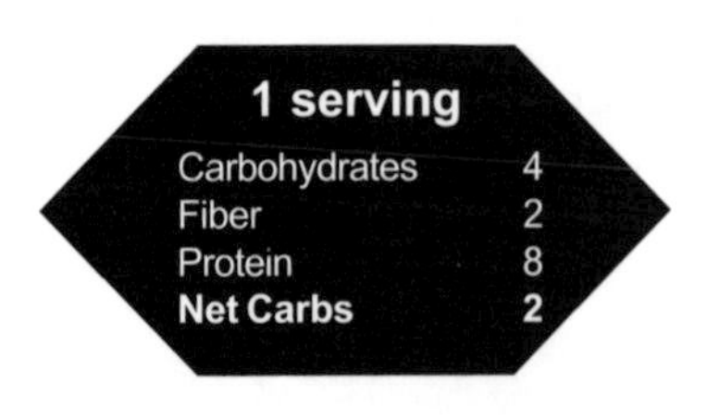

1 serving	
Carbohydrates	4
Fiber	2
Protein	8
Net Carbs	**2**

Mandarin Orange Salad

Makes 12 servings

1 bunch romaine lettuce, torn into bite-sized pieces
1/2 head iceberg lettuce, torn into bite-sized pieces
3 green onions, sliced
2 ribs celery, chopped
1 16-ounce can mandarin oranges, drained

2 tablespoons sugar substitute*
2 tablespoons white vinegar
1 teaspoon parsley
1/4 teaspoon salt
1/8 teaspoon pepper

1/2 cup sliced almonds
3 tablespoons sugar substitute*

Net Carbs 5

Directions

1. In large bowl, combine first 5 ingredients.
2. In small bowl, combine next 5 ingredients. Cover and chill.
3. In small skillet, toast almonds with sugar substitute*.
4. Over salad, add dressing and toasted almonds; mix lightly before serving.

Nutritional Information

Entire Recipe

Carbohydrates	77
Fiber	16
Protein	15
Net Carbs	**61**

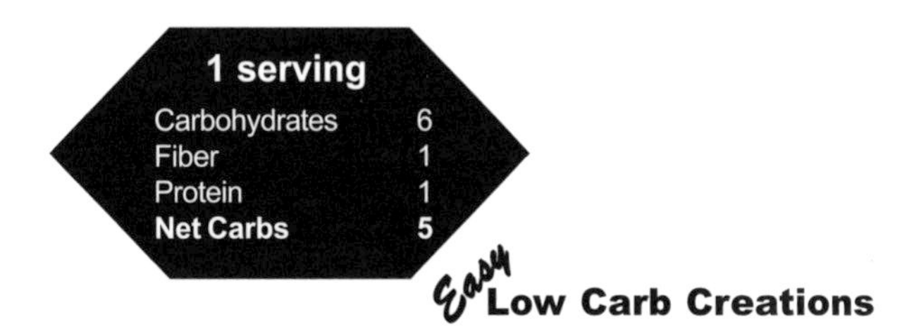

1 serving

Carbohydrates	6
Fiber	1
Protein	1
Net Carbs	**5**

Mushroom Salad

Makes 10 servings

1 16-ounce package fresh sliced mushrooms
3 green onions, sliced
1/2 cup olive oil
1/4 cup red wine vinegar
1 tablespoon sugar substitute*
1 1/2 tablespoons Greek seasoning

1 cup shredded cheddar cheese
1 cup shredded Swiss cheese
1/2 cup grated Parmesan cheese

Directions

Net Carbs 3

1. In large bowl, combine first 6 ingredients. Cover and chill.
2. To salad before serving, add cheeses; mix well.

Nutritional Information

Entire Recipe

Carbohydrates	27
Fiber	0
Protein	110
Net Carbs	**27**

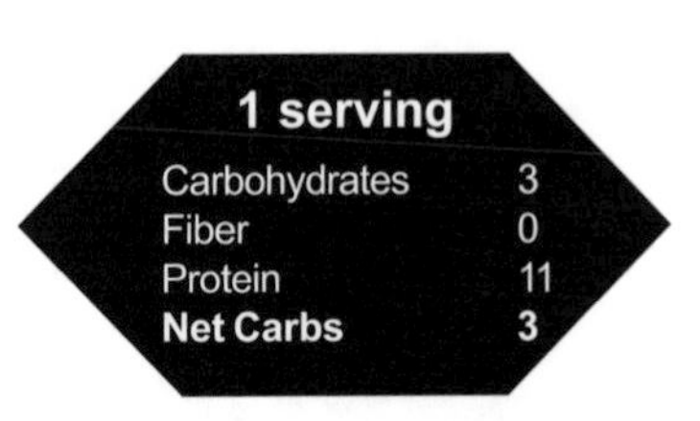

1 serving	
Carbohydrates	3
Fiber	0
Protein	11
Net Carbs	**3**

Overnight Slaw

Makes 12 servings

1 medium head cabbage, shredded
1 small red onion, thinly sliced, separated into rings

3/4 cup plus 2 tablespoons sugar substitute*, divided

1 cup red wine vinegar
3/4 cup vegetable oil
1 teaspoon celery seeds
1 teaspoon salt

Directions

1. In large bowl, layer first 2 ingredients.
2. Sprinkle cabbage with 3/4 cup sugar substitute*; do not mix.
3. In small saucepan, combine 2 tablespoons sugar substitute* and next 4 ingredients. Over medium heat, bring to boil.
4. Over cabbage and onions, pour sauce; do not mix.
5. Cover slaw and chill 12 hours. Drain to serve.

Nutritional Information

Entire Recipe

Carbohydrates	34
Fiber	19
Protein	10
Net Carbs	**15**

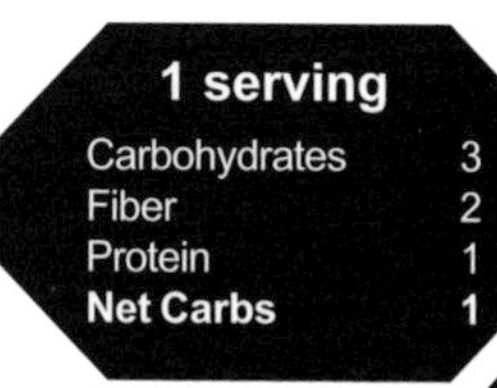

Pickled Cucumbers

Makes 8 servings

2 medium cucumbers, peeled, thinly sliced
1 medium onion, thinly sliced, separated into rings

1/4 cup cider vinegar
1/4 cup sugar substitute*
1/2 teaspoon salt
1/4 teaspoon pepper

Directions

1. In medium bowl with tight fitting lid, place cucumber and onion slices.
2. In small bowl, combine remaining ingredients; pour over cucumbers and onions.
3. Place lid on bowl; shake to combine mixture.
4. Chill 1 hour.

Nutritional Information

Entire Recipe

Carbohydrates	20
Fiber	2
Protein	6
Net Carbs	**18**

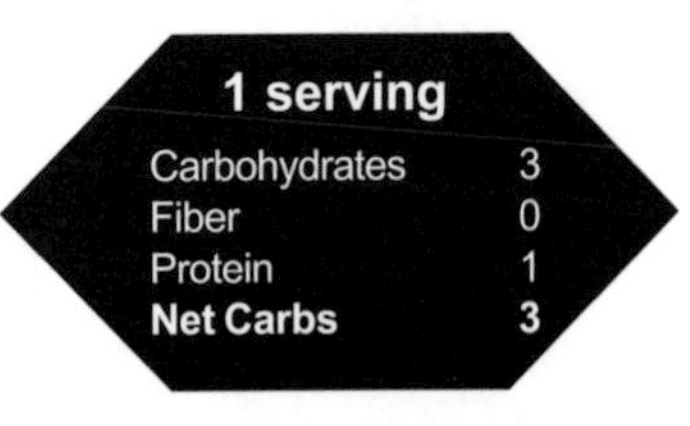

1 serving	
Carbohydrates	3
Fiber	0
Protein	1
Net Carbs	**3**

Red Cabbage Salad

Makes 10 servings

3 cups red cabbage, finely shredded
1 cup cauliflower, broken into florets
1/2 cup green pepper, chopped
1/4 cup onion, finely chopped

2 tablespoons sugar substitute*
3 tablespoons cider vinegar
2 tablespoons vegetable oil
1 teaspoon salt

Directions

1. In medium bowl, combine vegetables.
2. In small bowl, combine remaining ingredients; add to vegetables; mix lightly.
3. Cover and chill 1 hour.

Nutritional Information

Entire Recipe

Carbohydrates	42
Fiber	25
Protein	14
Net Carbs	**17**

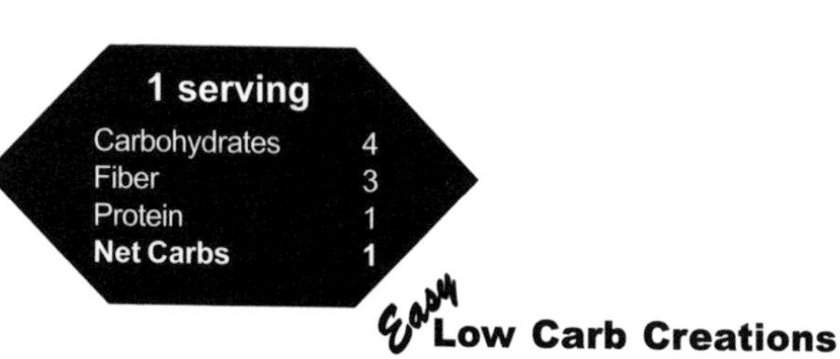

1 serving	
Carbohydrates	4
Fiber	3
Protein	1
Net Carbs	**1**

Slaw

12 servings

4 cups cabbage, shredded
1 small onion, chopped
1/4 cup green pepper, chopped
1/4 cup carrots, shredded

1/2 cup vegetable oil
1 cup sugar substitute*
1/2 cup cider vinegar
1/2 cup water
1 teaspoon salt
1 teaspoon celery seeds

Net Carbs 1

Directions

1. In large bowl, combine first 4 ingredients.
2. In medium bowl, combine remaining ingredients.
3. Over cabbage mixture, pour dressing; stir well.
4. Cover and chill 6 hours.

Nutritional Information

Entire Recipe

Carbohydrates	37
Fiber	20
Protein	10
Net Carbs	**17**

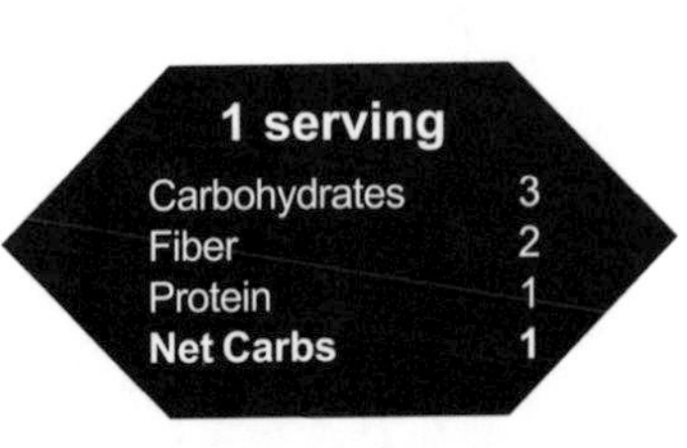

Spinach Salad

Makes 8 servings

1 pound bacon, cut into 1/2-inch pieces

1 pound fresh spinach, torn into bite-sized pieces
1 8-ounce can sliced water chestnuts, drained
4 eggs, hard-cooked, sliced

1/2 cup vegetable oil
1 onion, quartered
1/4 cup plus 2 tablespoons ketchup
2 tablespoons Worcestershire sauce
1/4 cup sugar substitute*
2 tablespoons vinegar

Directions

1. In skillet over medium-high heat, cook bacon until crisp; drain; set aside.
2. In large bowl, layer next 3 ingredients.
3. In electric blender, combine next 6 ingredients; blend 3 minutes.
4. Over salad, pour dressing; add crumbled bacon; toss.

Net Carbs 6

Nutritional Information

Entire Recipe

Carbohydrates	69
Fiber	21
Protein	108
Net Carbs	**48**

1 serving

Carbohydrates	9
Fiber	3
Protein	14
Net Carbs	**6**

Summer Salad

Makes 8 Servings

1 cucumber, peeled, quartered, sliced
1 cup broccoli, cut into florets
4 green onions, sliced
1 cup cauliflower, cut into florets
1/2 cup green pepper, chopped

1/2 cup vegetable oil
1/2 cup plus 2 tablespoons cider vinegar
1/4 cup plus 2 tablespoons sugar substitute*
1/8 teaspoon pepper
1/2 teaspoon salt

Directions

1. In large bowl, place first 5 ingredients.
2. In small bowl, combine next 5 ingredients.
3. Over vegetables, pour dressing; stir well to coat.
4. Cover and chill 2 hours.

Nutritional Information

Entire Recipe

Carbohydrates	21
Fiber	14
Protein	16
Net Carbs	**7**

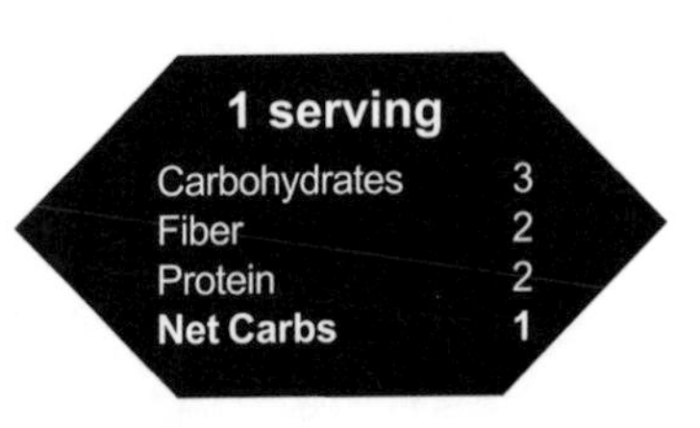

1 serving	
Carbohydrates	3
Fiber	2
Protein	2
Net Carbs	**1**

Wilted Lettuce Salad

Makes 4 servings

1 bunch leaf lettuce, torn into bite-sized pieces
3 green onions, chopped

1/2 pound bacon, cut into 1/2-inch pieces

1/4 cup cider vinegar
1/4 teaspoon salt
1/8 teaspoon pepper
3 tablespoons sugar substitute*

Directions

1. In large bowl, place lettuce and onions; set aside.
2. In large skillet over medium-high heat, cook bacon until crisp; remove bacon with slotted spoon.
3. In skillet with reserved drippings, add remaining ingredients. Cook and stir until mixture boils; remove from heat.
4. Into skillet, stir lettuce and onions until lettuce wilts.
5. Top each serving with bacon.

Nutritional Information

Entire Recipe

Carbohydrates	2
Fiber	0
Protein	16
Net Carbs	**2**

1 serving

Carbohydrates	1
Fiber	0
Protein	4
Net Carbs	**1**

Sauces and Dressings

Net Carbs	Recipe	Page
2	BBQ Sauce	161
0	Bleu Cheese Salad Dressing	162
2	French Dressing	163
1	Hot Bacon Dressing	164
3	Hot Bacon-Mustard Dressing	165
3	Microwave Cheese Sauce	166
1	Roquefort Dressing	167
0	Sesame Dressing	168

BBQ Sauce

Makes 2 3/4 cups (22, 2 tablespoon servings)

1 16-ounce bottle ketchup
3/4 cup sugar substitute*
3 tablespoons Worcestershire sauce
1 tablespoon cider vinegar
2 tablespoons mustard
1/2 cup dill pickle juice
2 tablespoons onion, finely chopped

Directions

1. In medium saucepan, combine all ingredients. Over medium heat, cook and stir; bring to boil.
2. Into container, pour sauce; cover and chill.

Nutritional Information

Entire Recipe

Carbohydrates	54
Fiber	0
Protein	0
Net Carbs	**54**

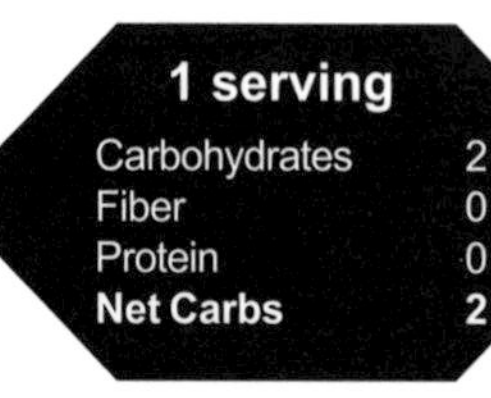

1 serving	
Carbohydrates	2
Fiber	0
Protein	0
Net Carbs	**2**

Bleu Cheese Salad Dressing

Makes 9 servings (2 tablespoons each)

1 cup mayonnaise
2 tablespoons buttermilk
1 tablespoon crumbled bleu cheese
1/8 teaspoon coarse ground pepper
1/8 teaspoon onion powder
1/8 teaspoon garlic powder

Directions

1. In small bowl, combine all ingredients until smooth.
2. Into container, pour salad dressing; cover and chill.

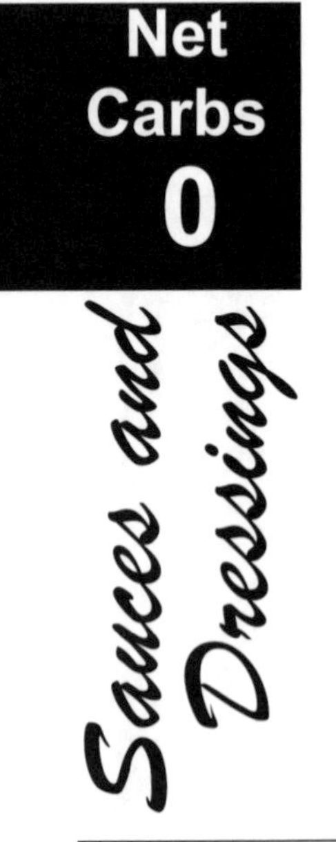

Nutritional Information

Entire Recipe

Carbohydrates	2
Fiber	0
Protein	2
Net Carbs	**2**

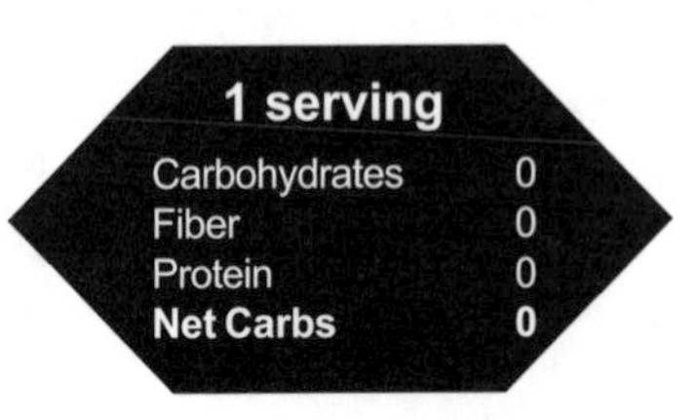

French Dressing

Makes 16 servings (2 tablespoons each)

1 cup vegetable oil
3/4 cup sugar substitute*
1/3 cup ketchup
1 teaspoon salt
1 small onion, quartered

1/3 cup vinegar
1 teaspoon celery seeds

Directions

1. In electric blender, place first 5 ingredients; blend 3 minutes.
2. To blender, add remaining ingredients; blend additional 2 minutes.
3. Into container, pour salad dressing; cover and chill.

Net Carbs 2

Nutritional Information

Entire Recipe

Carbohydrates	26
Fiber	2
Protein	1
Net Carbs	**24**

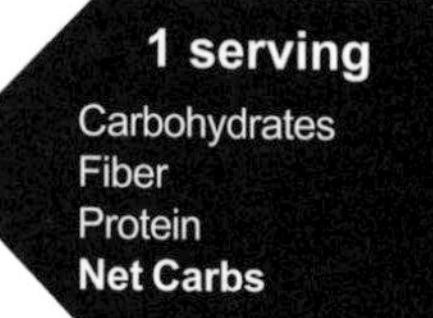

Hot Bacon Dressing

Makes 16 servings (2 tablespoons each)

1 1/2 pounds bacon, cut into 1/2-inch pieces

1/2 cup onion, finely chopped

Vegetable oil

2 teaspoons cornstarch
2 teaspoons water

1/2 cup cider vinegar
1/2 cup water
1/4 cup sugar substitute*
1/4 teaspoon salt
1/8 teaspoon pepper

Directions

1. In large skillet over medium-high heat, cook bacon until crisp; remove bacon with slotted spoon; set aside.
2. To bacon drippings, add onion; cook 5 minutes or until onion is tender.
3. Into measuring cup, pour bacon drippings with onion; add vegetable oil to equal 1 cup.
4. In small bowl, combine cornstarch and water; stir until dissolved. Stir into bacon dripping mixture.
5. In medium saucepan, combine next 5 ingredients. Over medium-high heat, cook and stir; bring to boil.
6. To same saucepan, add bacon dripping/cornstarch mixture; cook and stir 1 to 2 minutes or until thickened.
7. Remove saucepan from heat; add cooked bacon.
8. While warm, pour over salad of your choice.

Nutritional Information

Entire Recipe

Carbohydrates	10
Fiber	1
Protein	21
Net Carbs	**9**

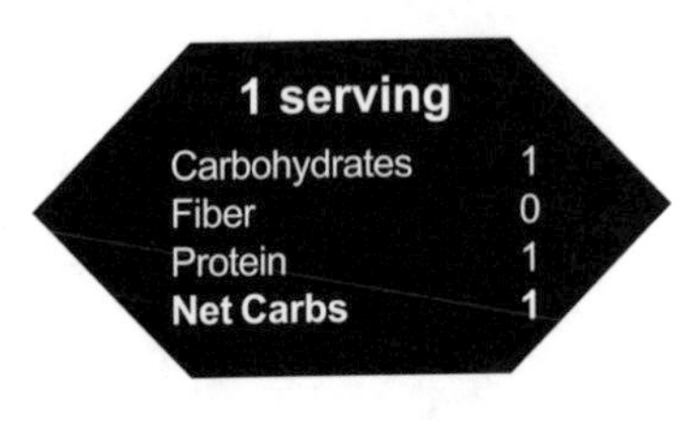

1 serving	
Carbohydrates	1
Fiber	0
Protein	1
Net Carbs	**1**

Hot Bacon-Mustard Dressing

Makes 16 servings (2 tablespoons each)

1/2 pound bacon, cut into 1/2-inch pieces

2 cups honey-Dijon mustard
1/2 cup sugar substitute*
1/3 cup orange juice
1 tablespoon cider vinegar
1/4 teaspoon ground mustard

2 tablespoons honey

Directions

1. In skillet over medium-high heat, cook bacon until crisp; remove bacon with slotted spoon; set aside.
2. In same skillet to bacon drippings, add next 5 ingredients; bring to boil. Remove from heat.
3. To skillet, stir in honey and bacon.
4. While warm, pour over salad of your choice.

Nutritional Information

Entire Recipe

Carbohydrates	43
Fiber	0
Protein	21
Net Carbs	**43**

1 serving

Carbohydrates	3
Fiber	0
Protein	1
Net Carbs	**3**

Microwave Cheese Sauce

Makes 6 servings (2 tablespoons each)

1 tablespoon butter

1 tablespoon flour
1/2 teaspoon dry mustard
1/8 teaspoon salt
Dash pepper

1/4 cup half-and-half
1/4 cup dry white wine (may substitute chicken broth)

1/2 cup shredded cheddar cheese

Directions

1. In small microwave-safe bowl, place butter; microwave on high 10 to 20 seconds or until butter melts.
2. To butter, blend next 4 ingredients.
3. To same glass bowl, gradually stir in half-and-half and wine (or broth). Microwave on high 2 to 3 minutes, stirring every minute, until mixture thickens and boils.
4. To same glass bowl, stir in cheese; microwave on high 1 minute or until cheese melts.

Great served over cooked cauliflower, broccoli, cabbage or zucchini.

Nutritional Information

Entire Recipe

Carbohydrates	19
Fiber	0
Protein	10
Net Carbs	**19**

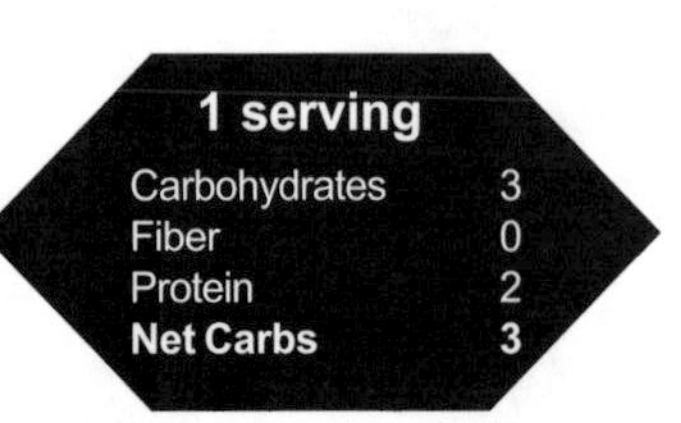

1 serving	
Carbohydrates	3
Fiber	0
Protein	2
Net Carbs	**3**

Roquefort Dressing

Makes 16 servings (2 tablespoons each)

1 cup mayonnaise or salad dressing
1/2 cup sour cream
1/2 cup crumbled Roquefort cheese
1/8 teaspoon garlic powder
1/4 medium onion
1 tablespoon lemon juice

Directions

1. In electric blender, place all ingredients. Blend 2 minutes.
2. Into container, pour salad dressing; cover and chill.

Nutritional Information

Entire Recipe

Carbohydrates	8
Fiber	0
Protein	15
Net Carbs	**8**

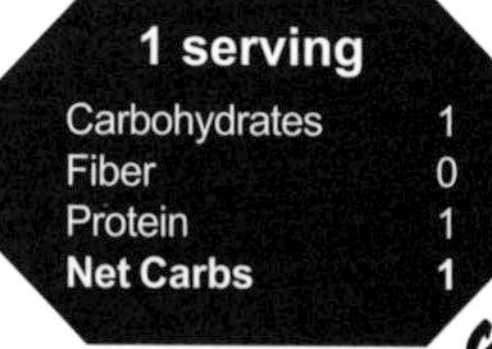

1 serving	
Carbohydrates	1
Fiber	0
Protein	1
Net Carbs	**1**

Sesame Dressing

Makes 20 servings (2 tablespoons each)

1/2 cup sugar substitute*
2 teaspoons salt
2 teaspoons dry mustard (or 2 tablespoons prepared)
2/3 cup cider vinegar
2 teaspoons soy sauce

1/4 medium onion

2 cups vegetable oil

3 tablespoons sesame seeds, toasted

Directions

1. In electric blender, add first 5 ingredients; blend mixture 1 minute.
2. To blender, add onion; blend until smooth.
3. With motor running on low speed, add oil slowly in a thin, steady stream; blend until thickened.
4. Into container, pour dressing and stir in sesame seeds.
5. Cover tightly and chill.

Net Carbs 0

Nutritional Information

Entire Recipe

Carbohydrates	5
Fiber	1
Protein	2
Net Carbs	**4**

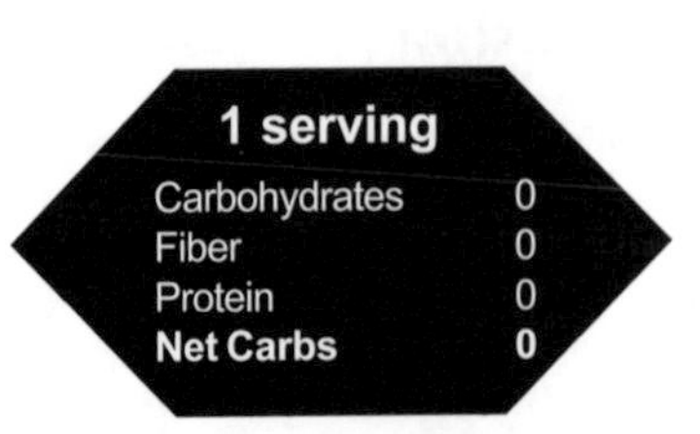

1 serving	
Carbohydrates	0
Fiber	0
Protein	0
Net Carbs	**0**

Seafood Main Dishes

Net Carbs	Recipe	Page
4	Baked Dilled Fish	170
4	Dilled Seafood Casserole	171
1	Elegant Fish	172
0	Grilled Tuna Steak	173
10	Seafood Au Gratin	174
7	Seafood Supreme	175
8	Tuna Casserole	176

Seafood

Baked Dilled Fish

Makes 4 servings

2 medium lemons, thinly sliced
5 green onions, sliced, divided
2 1/4 teaspoons dill weed, divided

4 6-ounce fish fillets (snapper, cod, orange roughy, mahi mahi, etc.)
1/4 teaspoon salt
1/8 teaspoon pepper

2/3 cup mayonnaise or salad dressing
1 teaspoon minced garlic
1/4 teaspoon dill weed
1 teaspoon lemon juice

Directions

1. Preheat oven to 350 degrees.
2. In foil-lined 9 x 13-inch pan, place lemon slices, 4 sliced onions and 2 teaspoons dill weed.
3. Top lemon and onions with fish fillets; sprinkle with salt and pepper.
4. Fold foil around fish and seal tightly.
5. Bake 35 minutes or until fish flakes easily with fork.
6. Meanwhile, in small saucepan, combine remaining ingredients including sliced onion and dill weed. Over medium-low heat, cook sauce until hot and bubbly.
7. Over fish, pour sauce; bake additional 5 minutes.

Nutritional Information

Entire Recipe

Carbohydrates	20
Fiber	2
Protein	170
Net Carbs	**18**

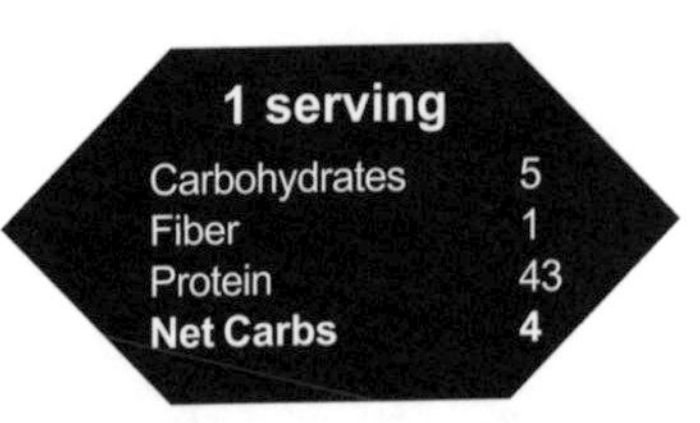

1 serving	
Carbohydrates	5
Fiber	1
Protein	43
Net Carbs	**4**

Net Carbs 4

Dilled Seafood Casserole

Makes 8 servings

4 tablespoons butter
1 pound medium shrimp, shelled, deveined and tail removed
8 ounces white fish fillets, cubed (cod, flounder, haddock, etc.) or crabmeat (imitation works fine)
4 ounces bay scallops
1 8-ounce package fresh sliced mushrooms
1 medium onion, chopped

2 tablespoons flour
1 cup half-and half

1/4 cup Parmesan cheese
1 tablespoon Dijon-style mustard
1/4 teaspoon dill weed
1/4 teaspoon salt
1/8 teaspoon pepper

Directions

1. Preheat oven to 350 degrees.
2. In large skillet over medium-high heat, melt butter; add next 5 ingredients. Cook 5 minutes or until onions are tender.
3. Remove seafood and vegetables with slotted spoon and place in prepared 2-quart casserole dish.
4. To liquid in skillet, add flour; stir and cook over medium heat 2 minutes. Add half-and-half slowly; cook and stir until sauce begins to thicken.
5. To skillet, add remaining ingredients; cook and stir until cheese melts.
6. Over seafood in casserole dish, spoon sauce.
7. Bake casserole 30 minutes or until hot and bubbly.

Nutritional Information

Entire Recipe

Carbohydrates	35
Fiber	2
Protein	159
Net Carbs	**33**

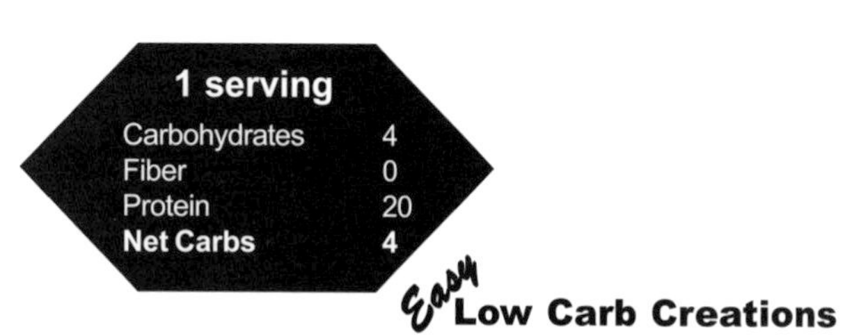

1 serving	
Carbohydrates	4
Fiber	0
Protein	20
Net Carbs	**4**

Net Carbs 1

Elegant Fish

Makes 9 servings

3 pounds fish filets (snapper, halibut, flounder, haddock, cod, etc.)
Juice of 1 lemon

1 cup mayonnaise
1 cup flaked crabmeat (imitation works fine)
1 cup grated Parmesan cheese

1/2 cup sliced almonds

Directions

1. Preheat oven to 350 degrees.
2. In bottom of foil covered broiler pan, place fish in single layer. Over fish, sprinkle lemon juice.
3. Bake 20 to 30 minutes until fish is white and flakes easily with fork.
4. Remove fish from oven; drain. Set broiler on high.
5. In medium bowl, combine next 3 ingredients; spread over fish. Top fish with almonds.
6. Place fish under broiler 3 to 5 minutes or until lightly browned.

Nutritional Information

Entire Recipe

Carbohydrates	19
Fiber	9
Protein	327
Net Carbs	**10**

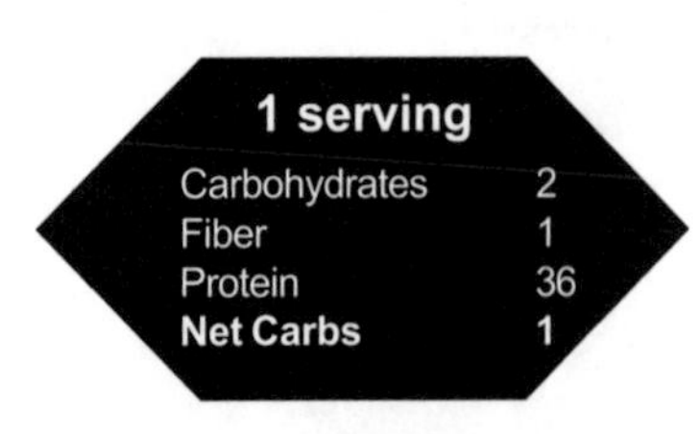

1 serving

Carbohydrates	2
Fiber	1
Protein	36
Net Carbs	**1**

Grilled Tuna Steak

Makes 4 servings

4 tuna steaks
1 tablespoon blackened seasoning

1/4 cup butter, melted

Directions

1. Over tuna steaks, evenly sprinkle blackened seasoning.
2. Coat outdoor grill grates with non-stick spray.
3. Over hot coals, cook tuna 8 minutes on each side or until it flakes easily with fork. For gas grill, follow instructions for grilling tuna steaks.
4. Serve steaks with melted butter for dipping.

Nutritional Information

Entire Recipe

Carbohydrates	0
Fiber	0
Protein	100
Net Carbs	**0**

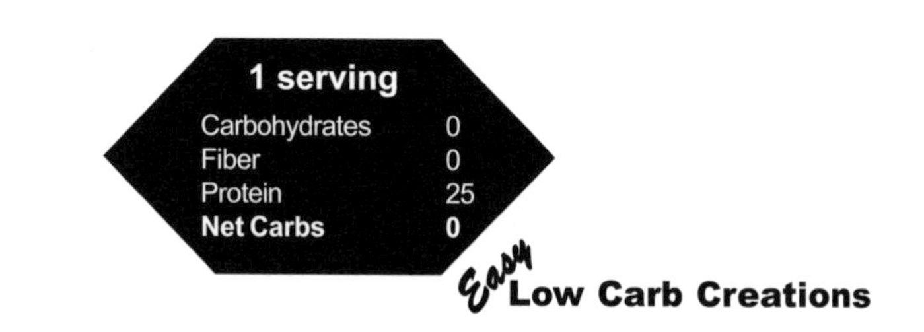

1 serving	
Carbohydrates	0
Fiber	0
Protein	25
Net Carbs	**0**

Seafood Au Gratin

Makes 6 servings

1/3 cup butter
1/2 cup onion, chopped

2 tablespoons flour
7/8 cup milk

2 teaspoons mustard
2 tablespoons dry sherry
3 green onions, sliced
1/4 teaspoon salt
1/8 teaspoon pepper
1/2 cup Monterey Jack cheese, shredded
2 pounds fresh crabmeat (imitation works fine), or 2 pounds cleaned, boiled shrimp, or a combination of the two

1 cup shredded cheddar cheese

Directions

1. Preheat oven to 350 degrees.
2. In large pan over medium heat, melt butter. Add onion and cook 5 minutes or until onion is tender
3. Into same pan, add flour; cook and stir 1 minute. Add milk slowly; continue to cook and stir; bring to boil. Remove pan from heat.
4. In same pan, combine next 7 ingredients.
5. Into prepared 2-quart casserole dish, pour seafood mixture; top with cheddar cheese.
6. Bake casserole 30 minutes or until hot and bubbly.

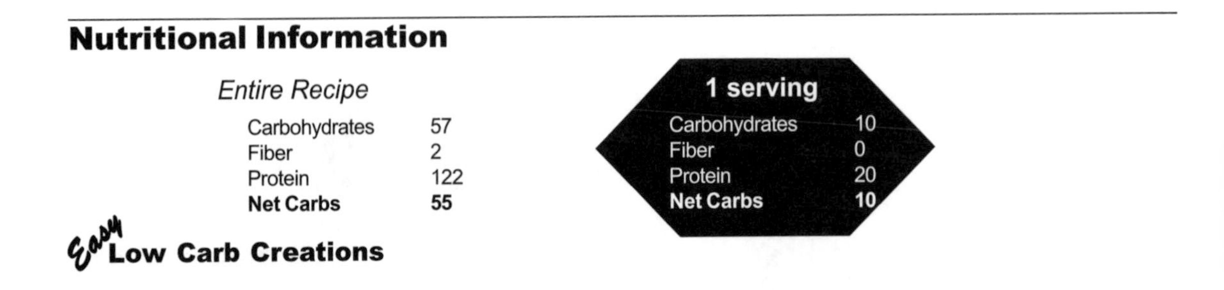

Nutritional Information

Entire Recipe

Carbohydrates	57
Fiber	2
Protein	122
Net Carbs	**55**

1 serving

Carbohydrates	10
Fiber	0
Protein	20
Net Carbs	**10**

Net Carbs 7

Seafood Supreme

Makes 6 servings

1 10.5-ounce can condensed cream of celery soup
1/2 cup milk
2 eggs, beaten
1 cup grated Parmesan cheese, divided

1 pound flaked crabmeat (imitation works fine)
8 ounces salad shrimp, thawed
1 8-ounce package fresh sliced mushrooms

1/2 cup sliced almonds

Directions

1. Preheat oven to 350 degrees.
2. In medium saucepan over low heat, combine first 3 ingredients and 1/2 cup cheese; stir until cheese melts.
3. To same pan, stir in next 3 ingredients.
4. Into prepared 2-quart casserole dish, pour seafood mixture; sprinkle with remaining cheese and almonds.
5. Bake casserole 30 minutes or until hot and bubbly.

Nutritional Information

Entire Recipe

Carbohydrates	51
Fiber	10
Protein	135
Net Carbs	**41**

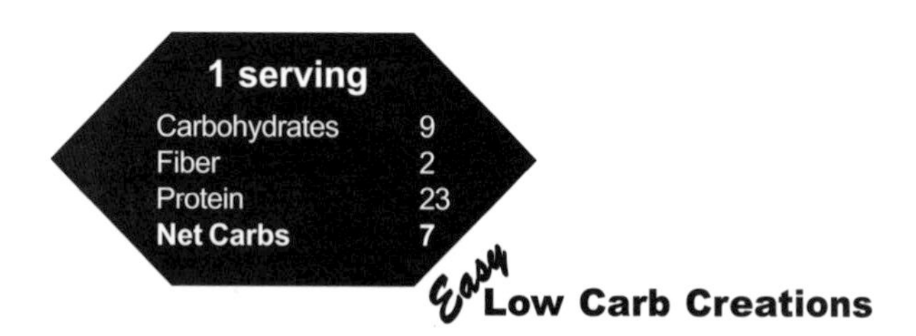

1 serving	
Carbohydrates	9
Fiber	2
Protein	23
Net Carbs	**7**

Tuna Casserole

Makes 6 servings

1 cup sour cream
1/4 teaspoon oregano
2 6.5-ounce cans water-packed tuna, drained
1/4 cup sliced, ripe black olives
1 8-ounce package fresh sliced mushrooms
1/2 cup cashews

1 cup shredded cheddar cheese

Directions

1. Preheat oven to 350 degrees.
2. In medium bowl, combine first 6 ingredients.
3. Into prepared 1 1/2-quart casserole dish, pour tuna mixture.
4. On top of casserole, evenly sprinkle cheese.
5. Bake casserole 25 to 30 minutes or until hot and bubbly.

Nutritional Information

Carbohydrates	47
Fiber	2
Protein	117
Net Carbs	**45**

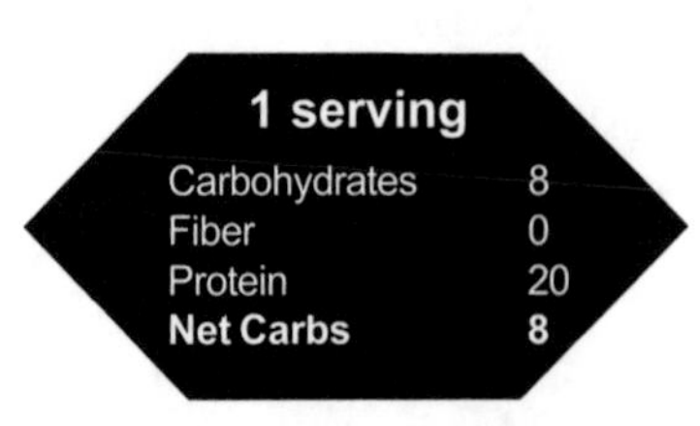

1 serving	
Carbohydrates	8
Fiber	0
Protein	20
Net Carbs	**8**

Net Carbs	Recipe	Page
13	Arizona Beans	178
3	Asparagus Casserole	179
4	Baked Swiss Vegetables	180
3	Broccoli Casserole	181
4	Cabbage Au Gratin	182
2	Cauliflower Stir-Fry	183
8	Company Cauliflower Casserole	184
4	Creamy Mushrooms	185
1	Deviled Eggs	186
1	Garden Skillet	187
4	Garlic Green Beans	188
3	Grandma's Green Beans	189
4	Green Bean Casserole	190
4	Green Beans with Almonds	191
6	Green Bean Swiss Cheese Crunch	192
3	Green Peppers with Tomatoes	193
1	Mediterranean Green Beans	194
4	Microwave Cauliflower with Cheese Sauce	195
5	Microwaved Dilled Vegetables	196
5	Oriental Green Beans	197
1	Oriental Vegetables	198
4	Slow Cooker Broccoli	199
5	Snow Peas and Almonds	200
4	Snow Peas with Water Chestnuts	201
7	Special Baked Green Beans	202
3	Stir Fries	203
4	Wilted Cabbage with Cheese	204
4	Zucchini Italian	205

Arizona Beans

Makes 9 servings

Net Carbs 13

1/2 pound lean ground beef
1 small onion, chopped

1/2 pound bacon, cut into 1/2-inch pieces

2 15-ounce cans pork and beans, partially drained
1/2 cup BBQ Sauce (see recipe page 161)

1/4 medium green pepper, cut into strips

Directions

1. Preheat oven to 350 degrees.
2. In large skillet over medium-high heat, cook ground beef and onion, stirring until meat is brown and crumbly; drain. Pour cooked meat into large bowl; set aside.
3. In same skillet, cook bacon until crisp. Remove bacon with slotted spoon and add to bowl with cooked beef.
4. To same bowl, add next 2 ingredients; stir to blend.
5. Into prepared 8 x 8-inch baking dish, pour bean mixture.
6. Top bean mixture with green pepper strips. Bake 45 minutes.

Nutritional Information

Entire Recipe

Carbohydrates	152
Fiber	38
Protein	93
Net Carbs	**114**

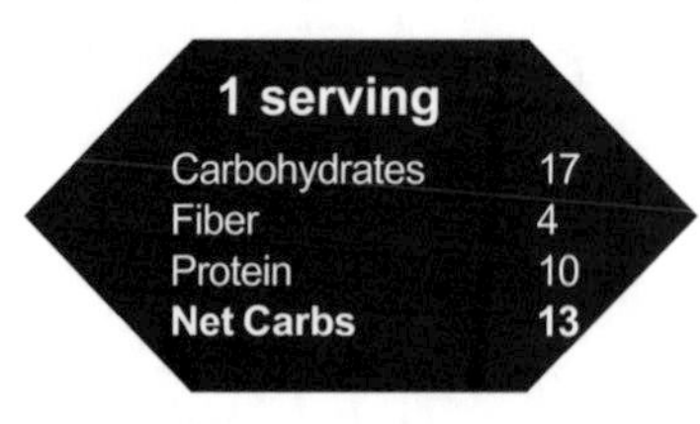

1 serving	
Carbohydrates	17
Fiber	4
Protein	10
Net Carbs	**13**

Asparagus Casserole

Makes 8 servings

1 1/2 pounds fresh asparagus or 16 ounces frozen
3 tablespoons water

1 12-ounce can condensed cream of mushroom soup
3 eggs, hard-cooked, sliced
2 tablespoons butter, thinly sliced
1 cup shredded cheddar cheese
1/2 cup sliced almonds

Directions

1. Preheat oven to 350 degrees.
2. Remove and discard bottom inch of fresh asparagus; cut asparagus into 1-inch pieces.
3. In 1 1/2-quart microwave-safe casserole dish, combine asparagus and water. Cover and microwave 4 to 5 minutes or until tender; drain.
4. Dry and prepare same casserole dish; return cooked asparagus.
5. Over asparagus, layer next 5 ingredients in order given.
6. Bake casserole 25 minutes or until hot and bubbly.

Nutritional Information

Entire Recipe

Carbohydrates	58
Fiber	29
Protein	87
Net Carbs	**29**

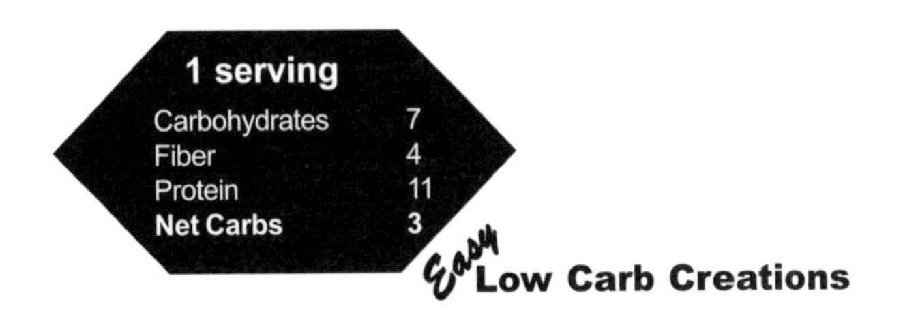

1 serving	
Carbohydrates	7
Fiber	4
Protein	11
Net Carbs	3

Baked Swiss Vegetables

Makes 8 servings

1 16-ounce package California blend vegetables

1 10.75-ounce can condensed cream of mushroom soup
1/3 cup sour cream
1/4 teaspoon salt
1/8 teaspoon pepper
1 cup shredded Swiss cheese

1/2 cup sliced almonds

Directions

1. Preheat oven to 350 degrees.
2. Cook and drain vegetables according to package directions.
3. In large bowl, combine cooked vegetables and next 5 ingredients.
4. Into prepared 1 1/2-quart casserole dish, pour vegetable mixture. Top with almonds.
5. Bake casserole 25 minutes or until hot and bubbly.

Nutritional Information

Entire Recipe

Carbohydrates	49
Fiber	19
Protein	67
Net Carbs	**30**

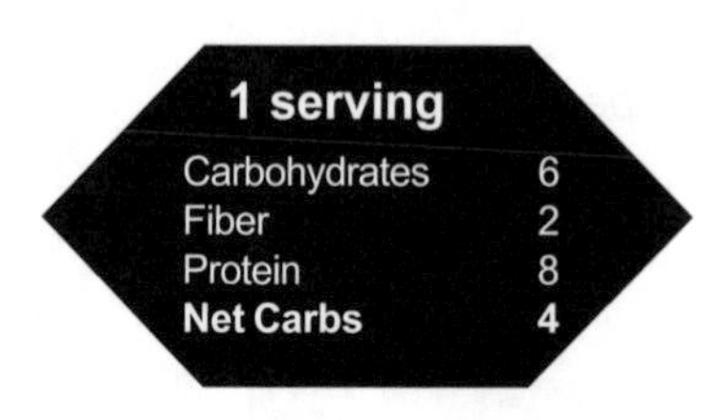

1 serving	
Carbohydrates	6
Fiber	2
Protein	8
Net Carbs	**4**

Broccoli Casserole

Makes 8 servings

1 16-ounce package frozen chopped broccoli

1/2 cup mayonnaise
1 cup shredded cheddar cheese
1 10.75-ounce can condensed cream of mushroom soup
1 tablespoon lemon juice

1/4 cup sliced almonds

Directions

1. Preheat oven to 350 degrees.
2. Cook and drain broccoli according to package directions. In prepared 1 1/2-quart casserole dish, place broccoli.
3. In medium bowl, combine next 4 ingredients.
4. Over cooked broccoli, spoon cheese mixture. Top with almonds.
5. Bake casserole 25 minutes or until hot and bubbly.

Nutritional Information

Entire Recipe

Carbohydrates	41
Fiber	15
Protein	48
Net Carbs	**26**

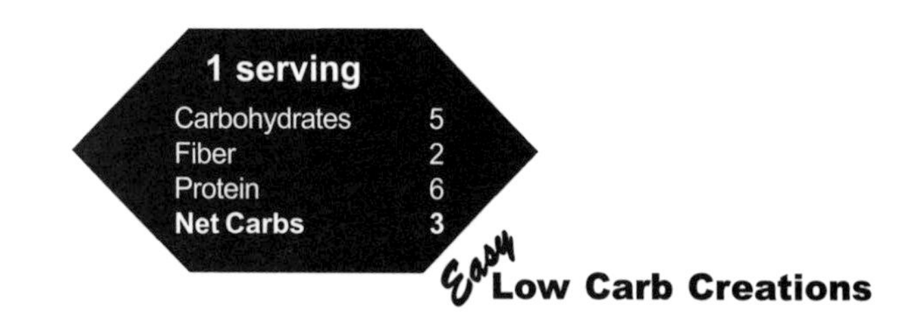

Cabbage Au Gratin

Makes 9 servings

Net Carbs 4

Side Dishes

1 head cabbage, cut into bite-sized pieces
1 teaspoon salt, divided

2 tablespoons butter
2 tablespoons flour

1 cup milk
1 cup shredded cheddar cheese

Directions

1. Preheat oven to 350 degrees.
2. In large saucepan over medium-high heat, combine cabbage and 1/2 teaspoon salt; cover with water. Bring to boil; reduce heat and simmer 6 to 8 minutes. Drain.
3. In prepared 1 1/2-quart baking dish, place cabbage.
4. In medium saucepan over medium heat, melt butter; stir in flour. Cook and stir 1 to 2 minutes.
5. To same saucepan, add milk and remaining salt; cook and stir until mixture thickens. Add grated cheese; cook and stir until cheese melts.
6. Over cabbage, pour cheese mixture.
7. Bake casserole 25 minutes or until hot and bubbly.

Nutritional Information

Entire Recipe

Carbohydrates	41
Fiber	11
Protein	27
Net Carbs	**30**

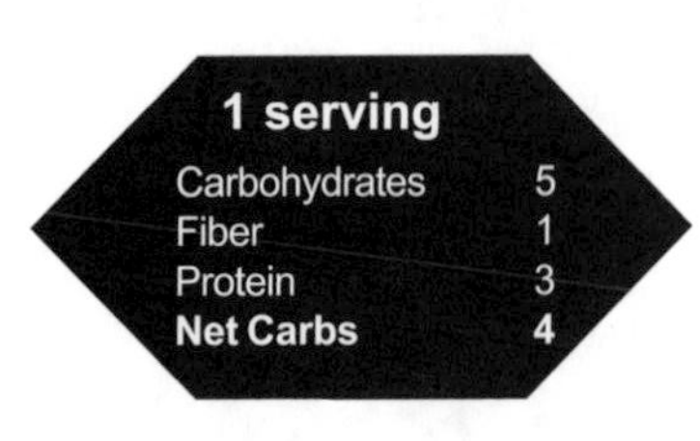

1 serving

Carbohydrates	5
Fiber	1
Protein	3
Net Carbs	**4**

Cauliflower Stir-Fry

Makes 8 servings

3 tablespoons butter
1 large head cauliflower, broken into florets
1 teaspoon minced garlic
1 teaspoon parsley
1 1/2 teaspoons lemon-pepper seasoning

Directions

1. In large skillet over medium-high heat, melt butter; add next 4 ingredients.
2. Cook and stir 12 to 15 minutes or until tender.

Nutritional Information

Entire Recipe

Carbohydrates	30
Fiber	12
Protein	13
Net Carbs	**18**

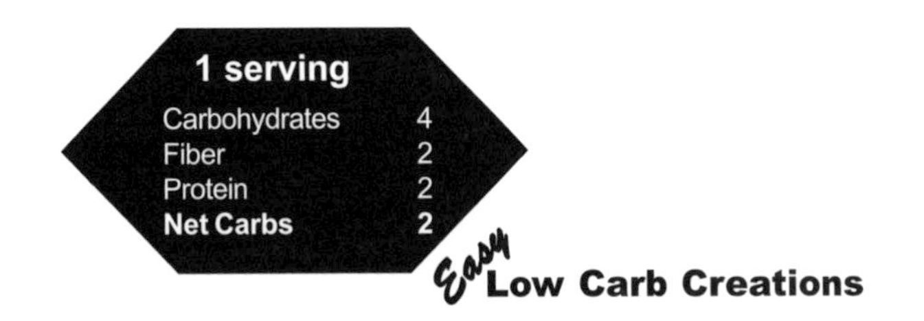

Company Cauliflower Casserole

Makes 9 servings

Net Carbs 8

Side Dishes

1 head cauliflower, broken into florets
3 tablespoons water

2 tablespoons vegetable oil
1 8-ounce package fresh sliced mushrooms
1/2 cup green onions, sliced

2 tablespoons flour
1/2 teaspoon salt
1/4 teaspoon pepper

1 1/2 cups milk

1 cup shredded cheddar cheese

Directions

1. Preheat oven to 375 degrees.
2. In 2-quart microwave-safe casserole dish, combine cauliflower and water; cover and microwave 4 to 5 minutes or until tender. Drain and set aside.
3. In small skillet over medium-high heat, heat vegetable oil. Add mushrooms and green onions; cook 2 to 3 minutes or until tender.
4. Remove vegetables from skillet; set aside.
5. Into remaining oil in skillet over medium-high heat, blend next 3 ingredients. Add milk slowly; cook and stir until mixture thickens.
6. In prepared 2-quart casserole dish, layer half of vegetables with half of cheese. Repeat layers.
7. Over cheese, pour milk mixture.
8. Bake casserole 25 minutes or until hot and bubbly.

Nutritional Information

Entire Recipe

Carbohydrates	78
Fiber	11
Protein	57
Net Carbs	**67**

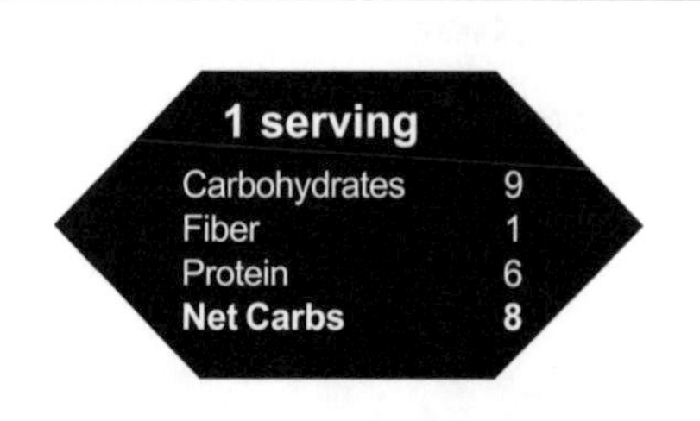

1 serving

Carbohydrates	9
Fiber	1
Protein	6
Net Carbs	**8**

Creamy Mushrooms

Makes 6 servings

3 tablespoons butter
1 8-ounce package fresh sliced mushrooms
2 tablespoons onion, finely chopped

1 tablespoon flour
1/8 teaspoon salt
Dash pepper

1 cup half-and-half
2 tablespoons grated Parmesan cheese
1 tablespoon lemon juice

2 egg yolks, slightly beaten

Directions

1. In skillet over medium heat, melt butter. Add mushrooms and onions; cook and stir 3 minutes.
2. Over vegetables, sprinkle next 3 ingredients; toss to coat. Reduce to low heat; cook 15 minutes.
3. To same skillet, add next 3 ingredients; cook and stir until cheese melts.
4. To egg yolks, add small amount of hot cream mixture; mix and return to hot mixture in skillet.
5. Over medium heat, cook and stir additional 1 minute.

Nutritional Information

Entire Recipe

Carbohydrates	23
Fiber	0
Protein	22
Net Carbs	**23**

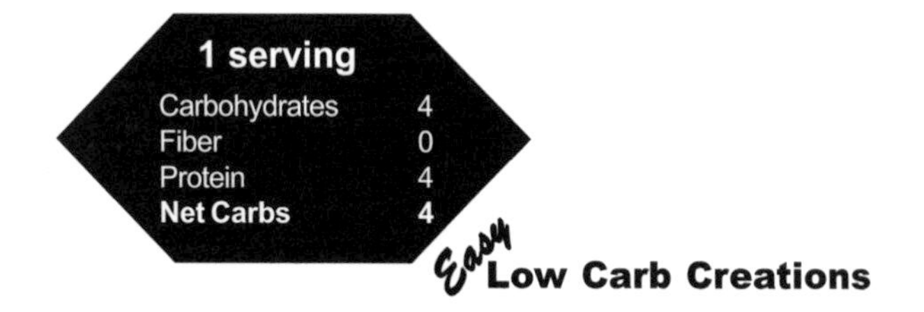

1 serving

Carbohydrates	4
Fiber	0
Protein	4
Net Carbs	**4**

Deviled Eggs

Makes 12 servings (2 halves each)

12 eggs, hard-cooked

1/4 cup plus 1 tablespoon salad dressing or mayonnaise
1/8 teaspoon cider vinegar
1/8 teaspoon mustard
3 tablespoons sweet pickle relish
1/8 teaspoon salt
Dash pepper
1 teaspoon sugar substitute*

Directions

1. Slice eggs in half length-wise.
2. Into medium bowl, place egg yolks as they are removed from whites; set whites aside.
3. Mash yolks with fork until fine and crumbly.
4. To same bowl, stir in remaining ingredients.
5. Fill egg white halves with yolk mixture; cover and chill.

Nutritional Information

Entire Recipe

Carbohydrates	13
Fiber	0
Protein	48
Net Carbs	**13**

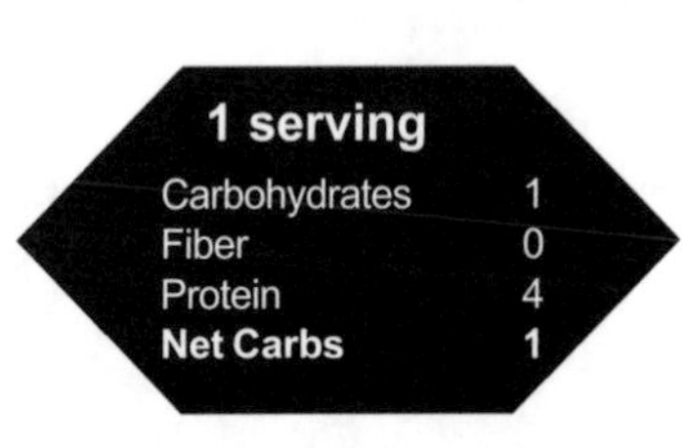

1 serving	
Carbohydrates	1
Fiber	0
Protein	4
Net Carbs	**1**

Garden Skillet

Makes 14 servings

Net Carbs 1

Side Dishes

2 1/2 cups cauliflower, cut into florets
1/4 cup water

1/3 cup butter
2 cups zucchini, cut into 1/8-inch rounds
1 1/2 cups green pepper, cut into strips
2 tablespoons onion, chopped
1 teaspoon salt
1 teaspoon basil
1 teaspoon oregano
1/2 teaspoon garlic powder
1/4 teaspoon pepper

2 medium tomatoes, chopped
2/3 cup grated Parmesan cheese

Directions

1. In large skillet over medium-high heat, cook cauliflower in water 5 minutes or until crisp-tender. Drain and set aside.
2. To same skillet, add butter and next 8 ingredients. Cook 3 minutes or until vegetables are crisp-tender, stirring occasionally.
3. To same skillet, add cooked cauliflower; cook additional 2 minutes or until cauliflower is hot.
4. To cauliflower mixture, add tomatoes and cheese; toss.

Nutritional Information

Entire Recipe

Carbohydrates	30
Fiber	16
Protein	16
Net Carbs	**14**

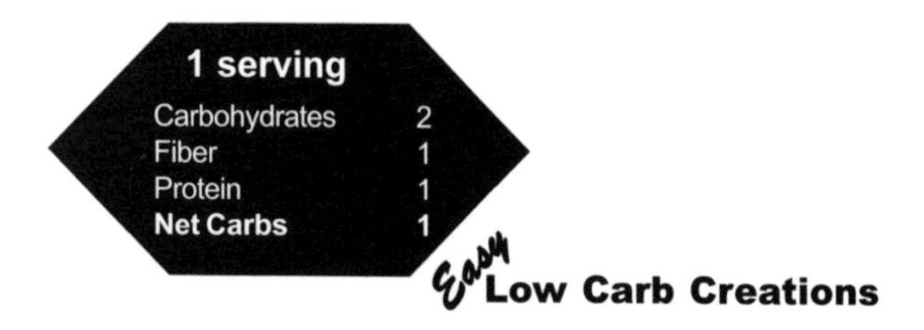

1 serving

Carbohydrates	2
Fiber	1
Protein	1
Net Carbs	**1**

Garlic Green Beans

Makes 8 servings

2 pounds fresh green beans, ends removed
1/2 cup water
1/4 cup butter
1/2 teaspoon salt
1/4 teaspoon lemon-pepper seasoning

2 teaspoons minced garlic

Directions

1. In large skillet over medium-high heat, combine first 4 ingredients; bring to boil. Cover and cook, with lid tilted slightly so steam escapes, 4 minutes or until liquid is nearly gone.
2. To same skillet over high heat, add garlic; cook green beans uncovered 4 minutes until garlic is lightly browned and liquid is gone.

Nutritional Information

Entire Recipe

Carbohydrates	52
Fiber	24
Protein	20
Net Carbs	**28**

Grandma's Green Beans

Makes 5 servings

Net Carbs 3

Side Dishes

4 slices bacon, cut into 1/2-inch pieces

2 tablespoons onion, finely chopped

2 cans green beans, partially drained
1/8 teaspoon salt
Dash pepper

Directions

1. In saucepan over medium-high heat, cook bacon 5 minutes or until almost done.
2. To same saucepan, add onion; cook and stir 2 to 3 minutes or until onion is tender.
3. To bacon mixture, stir in next 3 ingredients. Cook additional 10 to 12 minutes or until liquid evaporates.

Nutritional Information

Entire Recipe

Carbohydrates	28
Fiber	14
Protein	15
Net Carbs	**14**

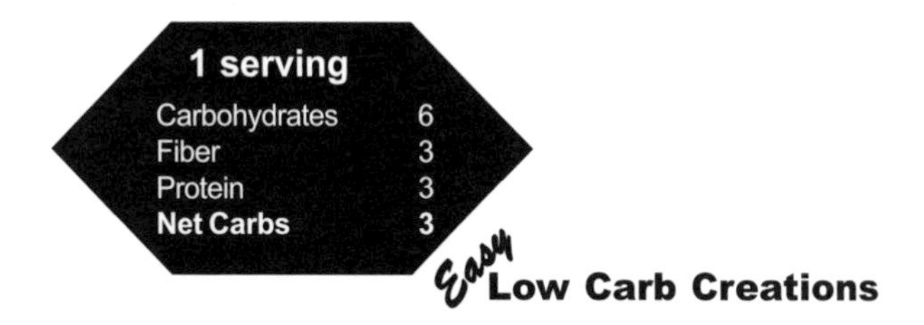

1 serving	
Carbohydrates	6
Fiber	3
Protein	3
Net Carbs	**3**

Green Bean Casserole

Makes 12 servings

1 tablespoon butter
1 tablespoon flour
1/2 cup milk

1 tablespoon Worcestershire sauce
1 10.75-ounce can condensed cream of mushroom soup
1 cup shredded cheddar cheese

3 16-ounce cans green beans, drained

1/2 cup sliced almonds

Directions

1. Preheat oven to 350 degrees.
2. In large saucepan over medium heat, melt butter; stir in flour; cook 1 minute. Add milk slowly; cook and stir until mixture thickens. Remove from heat.
3. To same saucepan, stir in next 3 ingredients.
4. In bottom of prepared 2-quart casserole dish, place green beans.
5. Over beans, pour cheese sauce; top with almonds.
6. Bake 30 minutes or until hot and bubbly.

Nutritional Information

Entire Recipe

Carbohydrates	86
Fiber	32
Protein	60
Net Carbs	**54**

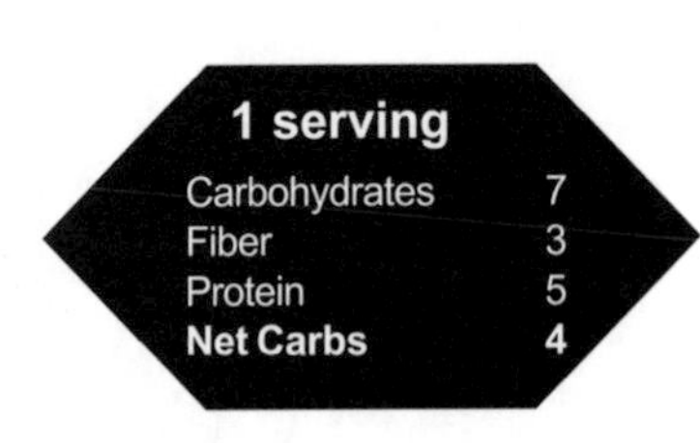

1 serving	
Carbohydrates	7
Fiber	3
Protein	5
Net Carbs	**4**

Green Beans with Almonds

Makes 5 servings

2 tablespoons butter
2 14.5-ounce cans French-style green beans, drained

1/2 cup chicken broth
1/4 teaspoon salt
1/4 teaspoon pepper

1 teaspoon cornstarch
1 tablespoon water

1 1/2 teaspoons lemon juice
1/4 cup sliced almonds, toasted

Directions

1. In large skillet over high heat, melt 2 tablespoons butter. Add green beans; cook and stir 3 minutes.
2. To same skillet, combine next 3 ingredients; bring to boil.
3. Reduce heat; cover and simmer 5 minutes.
4. Meanwhile, in cup, combine cornstarch and water; stir into beans. Cook and stir additional 1 minute.
5. To bean mixture, stir in lemon juice; sprinkle with toasted almonds.

Nutritional Information

Entire Recipe

Carbohydrates	36
Fiber	16
Protein	13
Net Carbs	**20**

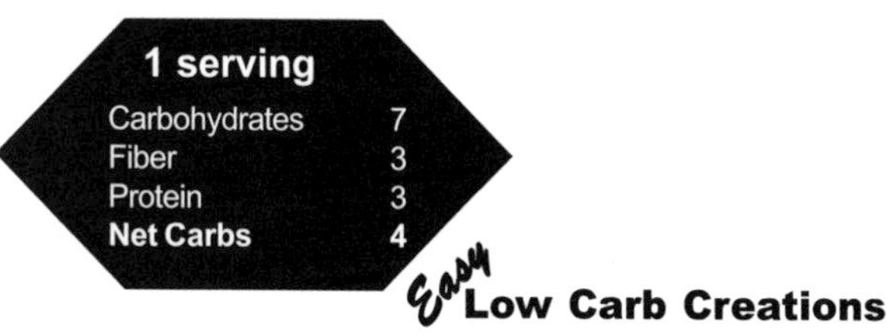

1 serving	
Carbohydrates	7
Fiber	3
Protein	3
Net Carbs	**4**

Green Bean Swiss Cheese Crunch

Makes 15 servings

4 tablespoons butter
2 tablespoons flour
1 tablespoon dried, minced onion
1/4 teaspoon salt
1/4 teaspoon pepper

2 cups sour cream
1 teaspoon sugar substitute*

6 14.5-ounce cans green beans, drained
1 cup shredded Swiss cheese

1/2 cup sliced almonds, toasted

Directions

1. Preheat oven to 350 degrees.
2. In medium saucepan over medium heat, melt butter. Add next 4 ingredients; cook and stir 1 minute.
3. Remove saucepan from heat; stir in next 2 ingredients.
4. In prepared 9 x 13-inch baking dish, layer 3 cans green beans and half cheese; repeat layers.
5. Over green beans, pour sauce; bake 30 minutes or until hot and bubbly.
6. Sprinkle green bean mixture with toasted almonds.

Nutritional Information

Entire Recipe

Carbohydrates	141
Fiber	50
Protein	89
Net Carbs	**91**

1 serving

Carbohydrates	9
Fiber	3
Protein	6
Net Carbs	**6**

Green Peppers with Tomatoes

Makes 10 servings

3 tablespoons olive oil, divided
1/2 cup onion, thinly sliced
1 teaspoon minced garlic

1 14.5-ounce can chopped tomatoes, undrained
2 teaspoons sugar substitute*
3/4 teaspoon salt
Dash pepper
1/2 teaspoon basil

4 large green peppers, cut into strips

Directions

1. In large skillet over medium-high heat, heat 1 tablespoon olive oil. Add onion and garlic; cook and stir 2 to 3 minutes or until onion is tender.
2. To same skillet, add next 5 ingredients; simmer 20 minutes.
3. Meanwhile, in separate skillet over medium-high heat, heat 2 tablespoons olive oil. Add green peppers; cook and stir 5 minutes or until crisp-tender.
4. Into skillet with tomato sauce, stir in green peppers.

Nutritional Information

Entire Recipe

Carbohydrates	35
Fiber	8
Protein	9
Net Carbs	**27**

1 serving

Carbohydrates	4
Fiber	1
Protein	1
Net Carbs	**3**

Mediterranean Green Beans

Makes 10 servings

2 tablespoons olive oil
1 medium onion, chopped

1 teaspoon minced garlic

1 14.5-ounce can chopped tomatoes
2 pounds fresh green beans, ends removed, snapped into 2-inch pieces
1/2 cup water
1 tablespoon oregano
1 1/2 teaspoons basil
1 teaspoon sugar substitute*
1 teaspoon salt
1/4 teaspoon pepper

1/4 cup grated Parmesan cheese

Directions

1. In large saucepan over medium-high heat, heat oil. Add onion; cook and stir 2 to 3 minutes or until tender.
2. To same saucepan, add garlic; cook additional 1 minute.
3. To onion mixture, add next 8 ingredients; bring to boil. Reduce heat and simmer 10 minutes or until beans are crisp-tender.
4. To green beans, add cheese; cook and stir until cheese melts.

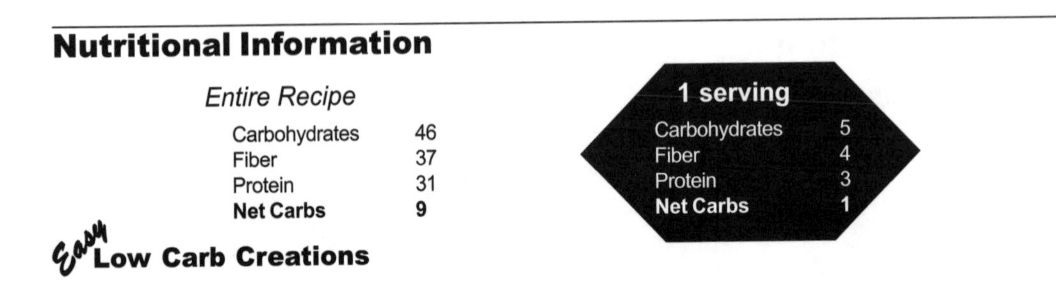

Nutritional Information

Entire Recipe

Carbohydrates	46
Fiber	37
Protein	31
Net Carbs	**9**

1 serving

Carbohydrates	5
Fiber	4
Protein	3
Net Carbs	**1**

Microwave Cauliflower with Cheese Sauce

Makes 6 servings

Net Carbs 4

1 medium head cauliflower

Microwave Cheese Sauce (see recipe page 166)

Directions

1. Cut core from head of cauliflower or separate into florets.
2. In 2-quart microwave-safe casserole dish, place cauliflower and 1/4 cup water.
3. Cover and microwave on high 10 to 12 minutes.
4. Let stand covered 1 minute; drain.
5. Pour Microwave Cheese Sauce over cauliflower.

Nutritional Information

Entire Recipe

Carbohydrates	35
Fiber	11
Protein	21
Net Carbs	**24**

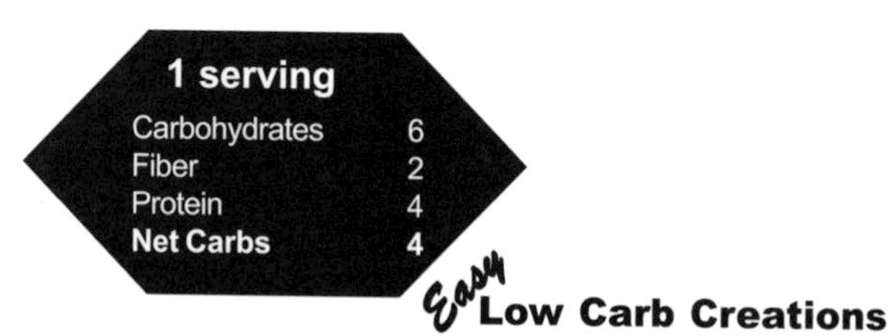

1 serving	
Carbohydrates	6
Fiber	2
Protein	4
Net Carbs	**4**

Microwave Dilled Vegetables

Makes 8 servings

Side Dishes

4 ounces fresh small mushrooms
4 baby carrots, cut into 1/8-inch rounds
1 small yellow squash, cut into 1/8-inch rounds (2 cups)
2 cups broccoli, cut into florets
2 cups cauliflower, cut into florets

1/2 teaspoon dill weed
2 tablespoons water

Microwave Cheese Sauce (see recipe page 166)

Directions

1. In center of microwave-safe 10-inch pie plate, mound mushrooms; arrange next 4 ingredients around mushrooms.
2. To pie plate, add water; sprinkle vegetables with dill weed.
3. Cover vegetables and microwave on high 7 to 11 minutes or until crisp-tender.
4. Let stand covered 5 minutes; drain.
5. Pour Microwave Cheese Sauce over vegetables.

Nutritional Information

Entire Recipe

Carbohydrates	57
Fiber	14
Protein	23
Net Carbs	**43**

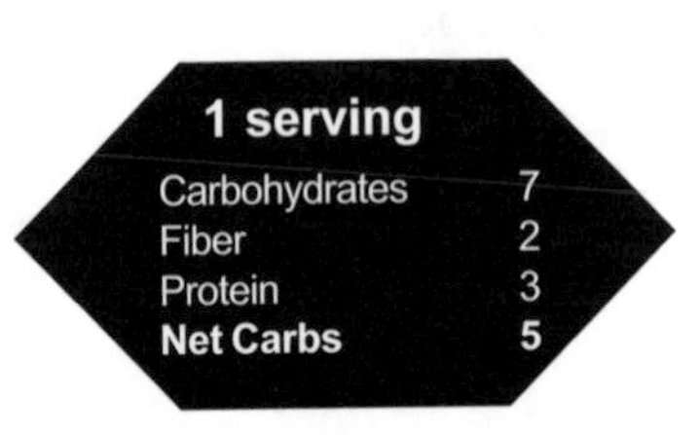

Oriental Green Beans

Makes 6 servings

1/2 pound bacon, cut into 1/2-inch pieces

2 tablespoons onion, chopped

2 14.5-ounce cans green beans, drained
1 8-ounce can sliced water chestnuts, drained

Net Carbs 5

Directions

1. In skillet over medium-high heat, cook bacon until crisp. Remove bacon and set aside.
2. To drippings in skillet, add onion and cook 2 to 3 minutes.
3. To same skillet, add next 2 ingredients; continue cooking 8 to 10 minutes.
4. To bean mixture, add bacon and stir.

Nutritional Information

Entire Recipe

Carbohydrates	47
Fiber	20
Protein	27
Net Carbs	**27**

1 serving

Carbohydrates	8
Fiber	3
Protein	5
Net Carbs	**5**

Oriental Vegetables

Makes 12 servings

3 tablespoons butter
1 cup green onions, chopped

1 8-ounce package fresh sliced mushrooms
1 cup celery, diagonally sliced

3 cups fresh bean sprouts
2 tablespoons soy sauce
1/2 teaspoon beef bouillon granules

Directions

1. In large skillet or wok over high heat, melt butter. Add onions; cook and stir 2 to 3 minutes or until tender.
2. To same skillet, add mushrooms and celery; cook and stir 3 minutes.
3. To vegetables, add bean sprouts and soy sauce; sprinkle bouillon granules over vegetables. Reduce to medium heat; cook and stir additional 2 to 3 minutes or until sprouts are hot.

Nutritional Information

Entire Recipe

Carbohydrates	17
Fiber	0
Protein	12
Net Carbs	**17**

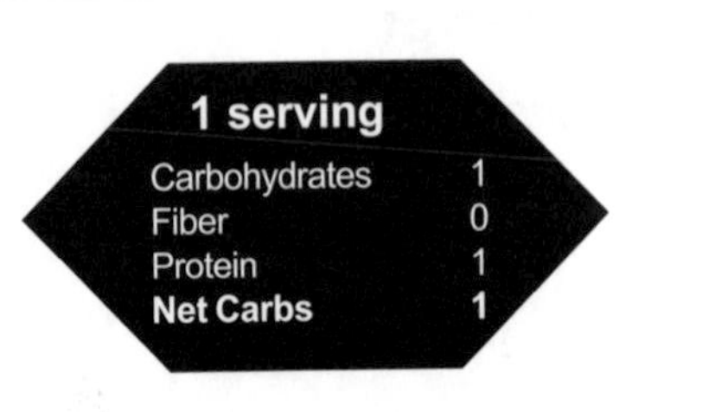

Slow Cooker Broccoli

Makes 12 servings

2 10-ounce packages frozen chopped broccoli, partially thawed
1 10.75-ounce can condensed cream of celery soup
2 cups shredded cheddar cheese, divided
1/4 cup onion, finely chopped
1/2 teaspoon Worcestershire sauce
1/4 teaspoon pepper

2 tablespoons butter, thinly sliced

1 cup sliced almonds, toasted

Directions

1. In large bowl, combine broccoli, soup, 1 cup cheese, and next 3 ingredients.
2. Into prepared slow cooker, pour broccoli mixture. Over mixture, place sliced butter.
3. Cover and cook on high 1 to 1 1/2 hours or on low 2 to 2 1/2 hours.
4. Sprinkle broccoli with remaining cheese; cook additional 10 minutes or until cheese melts.
5. Top casserole with toasted almonds before serving.

Nutritional Information

Entire Recipe

Carbohydrates	82
Fiber	32
Protein	102
Net Carbs	**50**

1 serving

Carbohydrates	7
Fiber	3
Protein	9
Net Carbs	**4**

Snow Peas and Almonds

Makes 6 servings

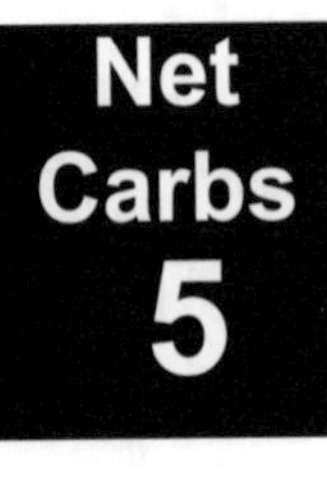

2 tablespoons vegetable oil
1/2 cup green onions, sliced

1 16-ounce package frozen snow peas, thawed
1 8-ounce package fresh sliced mushrooms

1/2 cup boiling water
2 chicken bouillon cubes

2 teaspoons cornstarch
2 teaspoons cold water
1 tablespoon soy sauce

1/2 cup sliced almonds, toasted

Directions

1. In large skillet over high heat, heat oil. Add onion; cook and stir 2 to 3 minutes or until tender.
2. To same skillet, add snow peas and mushrooms; cook and stir additional 1 to 2 minutes.
3. In cup, combine boiling water and bouillon cubes; stir until dissolved.
4. In separate cup, combine next 3 ingredients; stir until dissolved.
5. Into peas, stir chicken broth and cornstarch liquid. Over medium-high heat, cook until mixture thickens.
6. To snow peas, add almonds and toss.

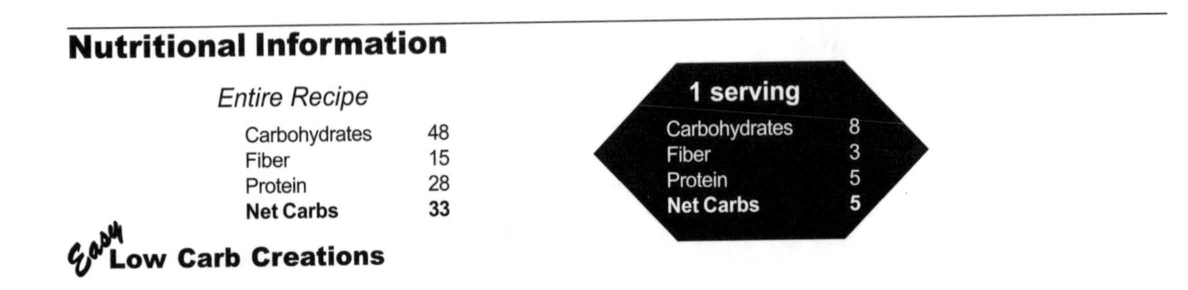

Nutritional Information

Entire Recipe	
Carbohydrates	48
Fiber	15
Protein	28
Net Carbs	**33**

1 serving	
Carbohydrates	8
Fiber	3
Protein	5
Net Carbs	**5**

Snow Peas with Water Chestnuts

Makes 6 servings

Net Carbs 4

1/2 pound bacon, cut into 1/2-inch pieces

1 16-ounce package frozen snow peas, thawed
1 8-ounce can sliced water chestnuts, drained
1/4 teaspoon salt

1/2 cup boiling water
2 chicken bouillon cubes

Directions

1. In large skillet over medium-high heat, cook bacon until crisp. Remove bacon; reserve 2 tablespoons drippings in skillet.
2. To skillet over high heat, add next 3 ingredients; cook and stir 2 to 3 minutes.
3. In small bowl, combine boiling water and bouillon cubes; stir until dissolved.
4. Into vegetables, stir chicken broth; cook additional 3 minutes.
5. To vegetables, add bacon and stir.

Nutritional Information

Entire Recipe

Carbohydrates	40
Fiber	17
Protein	31
Net Carbs	**23**

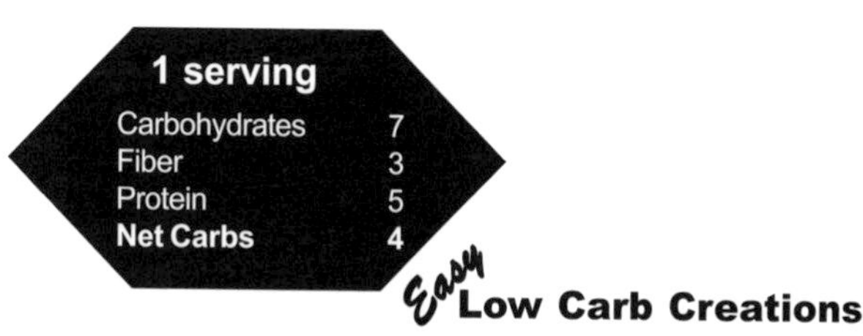

1 serving	
Carbohydrates	7
Fiber	3
Protein	5
Net Carbs	**4**

Special Baked Green Beans

Makes 9 servings

1 pound bacon, cut into 1/2-inch pieces

1/2 cup onions, sliced into rings

2 teaspoons flour
1/4 teaspoon salt
Dash pepper

1/2 cup milk

1 cup sour cream
3 cans green beans, drained

6 slices American cheese singles

Directions

1. Preheat oven to 350 degrees.
2. In skillet over medium-high heat, cook bacon until crisp. Remove bacon with slotted spoon; set aside.
3. To skillet with 3 tablespoons drippings, add onions; cook 2 to 3 minutes or until tender.
4. To same skillet, blend next 3 ingredients; cook 1 minute.
5. To onion mixture, add 1/2 cup milk; cook and stir until mixture boils.
6. To onion/milk mixture, blend in sour cream.
7. To same skillet, add green beans and heat thoroughly, stirring gently.
8. Into prepared 2-quart casserole dish, pour green bean mixture; top with cheese slices and cooked bacon.
9. Bake 20 minutes or until hot and bubbly.

Nutritional Information

Entire Recipe

Carbohydrates	79
Fiber	22
Protein	136
Net Carbs	**57**

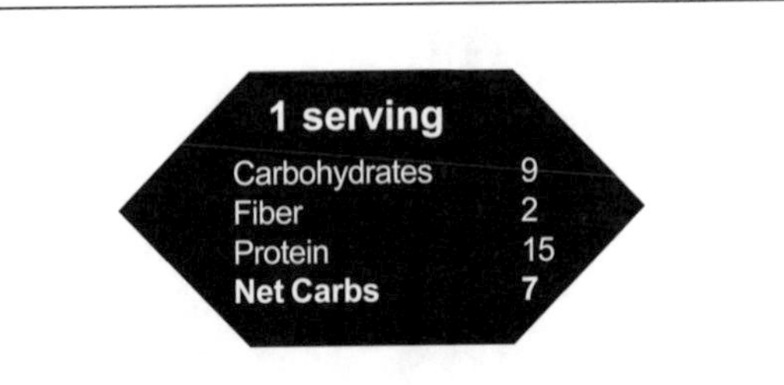

1 serving	
Carbohydrates	9
Fiber	2
Protein	15
Net Carbs	**7**

Stir Fries

Makes 8 servings

2 tablespoons vegetable oil

1 16-ounce package fresh sliced mushrooms
1 medium zucchini, cut into 1/8-inch rounds
1 large onion, thinly sliced, separated into rings
1 teaspoon seasoned salt

1/2 cup grated Parmesan cheese

Directions

1. In large skillet over high heat, heat oil. Add next 4 ingredients; cook and stir 3 minutes or until crisp-tender.
2. Top vegetables with Parmesan cheese; cover and remove from heat.
3. Serve after cheese melts.

Nutritional Information

Entire Recipe

Carbohydrates	23
Fiber	3
Protein	26
Net Carbs	**20**

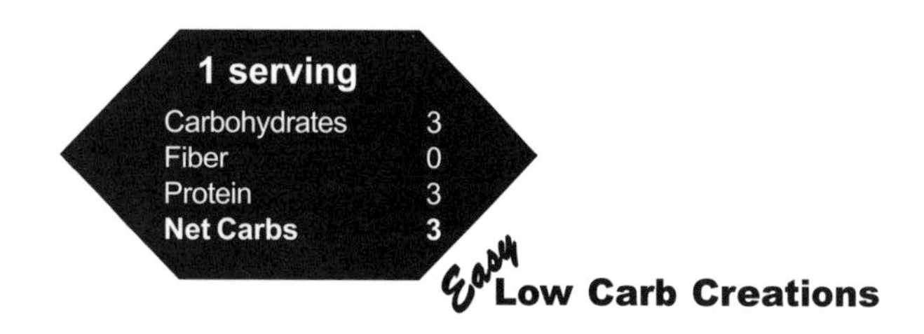

1 serving

Carbohydrates	3
Fiber	0
Protein	3
Net Carbs	**3**

Wilted Cabbage with Cheese

Makes 9 servings

2 cups water
9 cups cabbage, chopped

1 10.75-ounce can condensed cream of celery soup
1 1/2 cups shredded cheddar cheese
1 teaspoon caraway seeds

1/2 cup sliced almonds, toasted

Directions

1. Preheat oven to 350 degrees.
2. In large pan, add first 2 ingredients. Over high heat, bring to boil; cook 5 minutes or until cabbage is wilted. Drain.
3. To cabbage in pan, combine next 3 ingredients.
4. Into prepared 9 x 13-inch baking dish, pour cabbage mixture; bake 25 minutes or until hot and bubbly.
5. Sprinkle cabbage with toasted almonds.

Nutritional Information

Entire Recipe

Carbohydrates	67
Fiber	28
Protein	70
Net Carbs	**39**

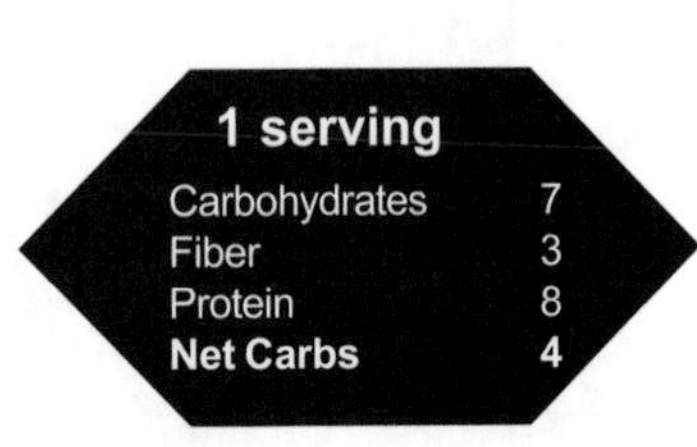

1 serving	
Carbohydrates	7
Fiber	3
Protein	8
Net Carbs	**4**

Zucchini Italian

Makes 8 servings

2 medium zucchini, sliced into 1/8-inch rounds
1 15-ounce can Italian tomato sauce
1/4 teaspoon oregano

1 cup mozzarella cheese

Directions

1. In large skillet, combine first 3 ingredients. Over medium-high heat, cook until zucchini is tender.
2. Top zucchini with mozzarella cheese; cover and remove from heat.
3. Serve after cheese melts.

Nutritional Information

Entire Recipe

Carbohydrates	36
Fiber	10
Protein	69
Net Carbs	**26**

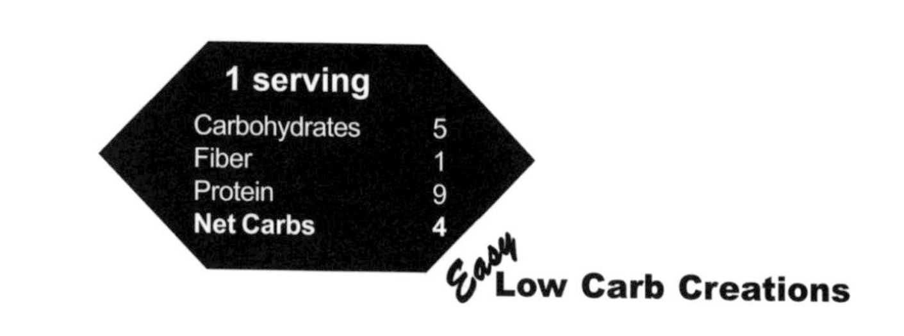

1 serving

Carbohydrates	5
Fiber	1
Protein	9
Net Carbs	**4**

Skillet Dinners

Net Carbs	Recipe	Page
9	Chicken Almond Stir-Fry	207
7	Chicken Oriental	208
1	Chicken Walnut Sauté	209
5	Montana Goulash	210
1	Moo Goo Gai Pan	211
2	Pepper Steak with Oriental Gravy	212
5	Sub Gum	213
8	Szechuan Pork	214
6	Wilted Cabbage and Sausage	215

Chicken Almond Stir Fry

Makes 6 servings

2 tablespoons vegetable oil
4 boneless, skinless chicken breasts, cut into 1/4-inch strips
3/4 cup whole almonds

1 16-ounce package frozen broccoli, carrots, and water chestnuts

1 tablespoon cornstarch
1 tablespoon brown sugar substitute, equivalent measure
1/2 teaspoon ground ginger
1/2 cup soy sauce
1/3 cup pineapple juice

Net Carbs 9

Directions

1. In large skillet over high heat, heat vegetable oil. Add chicken and almonds; cook and stir 7 to 8 minutes.
2. To same skillet, add frozen vegetables. Cover and cook 4 minutes, stirring 2 or 3 times.
3. Meanwhile, in small bowl, combine remaining ingredients to make sauce.
4. Into chicken/vegetable mixture, stir sauce; cook 1 to 2 minutes or until mixture thickens.

Nutritional Information

Entire Recipe

Carbohydrates	72
Fiber	15
Protein	136
Net Carbs	**57**

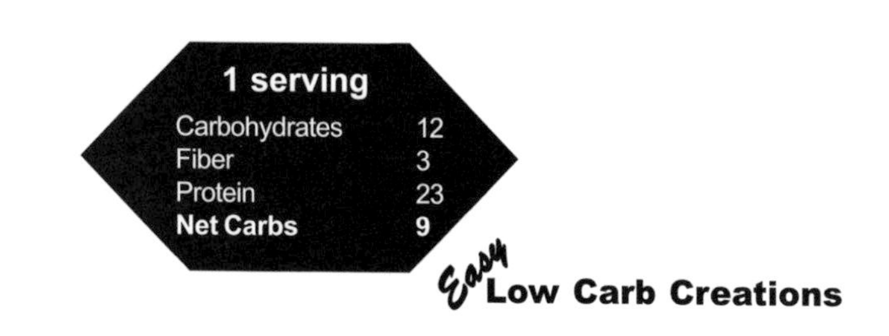

1 serving

Carbohydrates	12
Fiber	3
Protein	23
Net Carbs	**9**

Chicken Oriental

Makes 6 servings

Net Carbs 7

Skillet Dinners

1 tablespoon butter
1 tablespoon flour

2 teaspoons basil leaves, crushed
2 teaspoons garlic salt
1/2 teaspoon pepper
1 1/2 cups half-and-half
1/4 cup dry vermouth (may substitute chicken broth)

2 tablespoons olive oil, divided
4 boneless, skinless chicken breasts, cut into 1/4-inch strips

1 cup carrots, thinly sliced

2 cups snow peas
1 cup fresh sliced mushrooms

1/2 cup walnut pieces, toasted

Directions

1. In medium saucepan over medium heat, melt butter; blend in flour. Add next 5 ingredients; cook and stir until mixture thickens. Cover and keep warm.
2. In large skillet over high heat, heat 1 tablespoon oil. Add chicken strips; cook and stir 7 to 8 minutes until chicken is tender and no longer pink. Remove chicken and set aside.
3. To same skillet, add remaining oil and carrots; cook and stir 1 to 2 minutes.
4. To carrots, add next 2 ingredients; cook additional 2 to 3 minutes or until crisp-tender.
5. To vegetables in skillet, add cooked chicken.
6. Over chicken mixture, pour warm sauce and stir in walnuts.

Nutritional Information

Entire Recipe

Carbohydrates	53
Fiber	13
Protein	119
Net Carbs	**40**

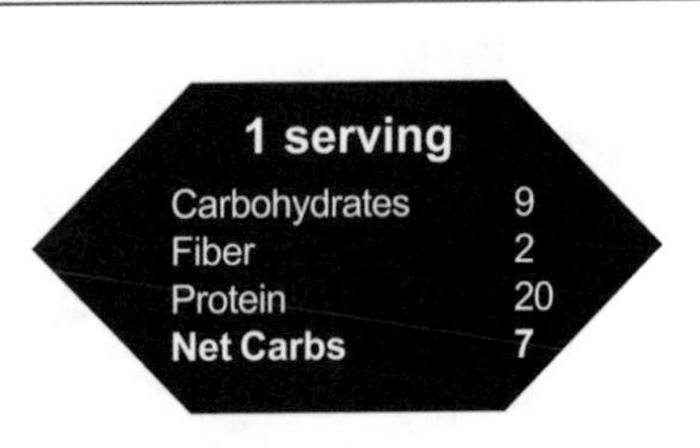

Chicken Walnut Sauté

Makes 6 servings

2 tablespoons vegetable oil

4 boneless, skinless chicken breasts, cut into 1/4-inch strips
1/4 teaspoon garlic salt
1/8 teaspoon pepper
1/4 cup green onions, sliced
4 ribs celery, chopped

1 tablespoon butter
1 cup walnut pieces
1 teaspoon grated lemon peel

2 tablespoons lemon juice
1/4 cup soy sauce

Net Carbs 1

Directions

1. In large skillet over high heat, heat vegetable oil. Add chicken and next 4 ingredients. Cook and stir 7 to 8 minutes until chicken is tender and no longer pink.
2. To same skillet, add next 3 ingredients; cook and stir 3 minutes.
3. To chicken mixture, add remaining ingredients; stir until chicken is well-coated.

Nutritional Information

Entire Recipe

Carbohydrates	21
Fiber	16
Protein	98
Net Carbs	**5**

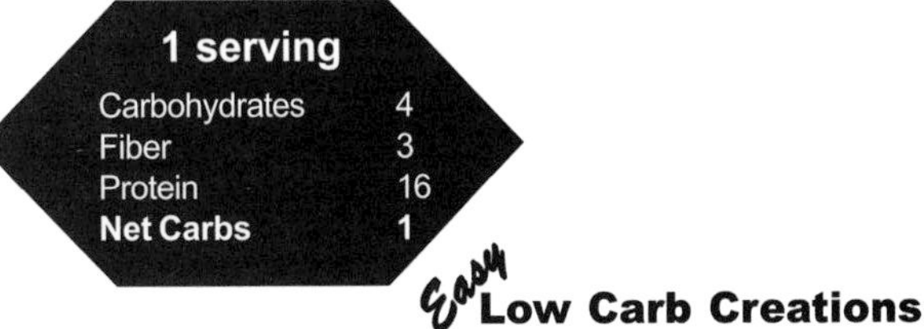

1 serving

Carbohydrates	4
Fiber	3
Protein	16
Net Carbs	**1**

Montana Goulash

Makes 12 servings

1 tablespoon vegetable oil

3 pounds sirloin steak, cut into cubes
2 large onions, chopped

1 10.75-ounce can cream of mushroom soup
2 cups sour cream
1 10.75-ounce can water
2 cups turnips, peeled, cubed
1 16-ounce package fresh sliced mushrooms
1/2 teaspoon salt
1/4 teaspoon pepper

Net Carbs 5

Directions

1. In large skillet over medium-high heat, heat vegetable oil. Add meat and onions; cook and stir until meat is no longer pink.
2. To same skillet, add remaining ingredients; simmer 2 hours, stirring occasionally, or until meat is tender.

Nutritional Information

Entire Recipe

Carbohydrates	74
Fiber	10
Protein	426
Net Carbs	**64**

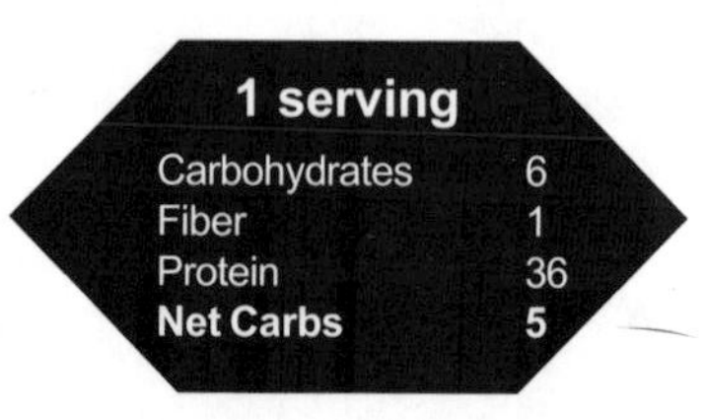

1 serving	
Carbohydrates	6
Fiber	1
Protein	36
Net Carbs	**5**

Moo Goo Gai Pan

Makes 12 servings

2 tablespoons vegetable oil
8 boneless, skinless chicken breasts, cut into small pieces
1/2 teaspoon minced garlic

2 4-ounce cans mushroom pieces and stems, drained
1 rib celery, chopped
4 tablespoons green onions, sliced

1/4 cup soy sauce
1 head leaf lettuce, chopped

Net Carbs 1

Directions

1. In large skillet over high heat, heat vegetable oil. Add chicken and garlic; cook and stir 7 to 8 minutes until chicken is tender and no longer pink. Remove chicken from skillet and set aside.
2. In same skillet, add next 3 ingredients; cook and stir 2 to 3 minutes until crisp-tender.
3. To vegetables, add soy sauce and chicken; cook and stir until hot and bubbly.
4. To chicken mixture, stir in lettuce.

Nutritional Information

Entire Recipe

Carbohydrates	9
Fiber	2
Protein	129
Net Carbs	**7**

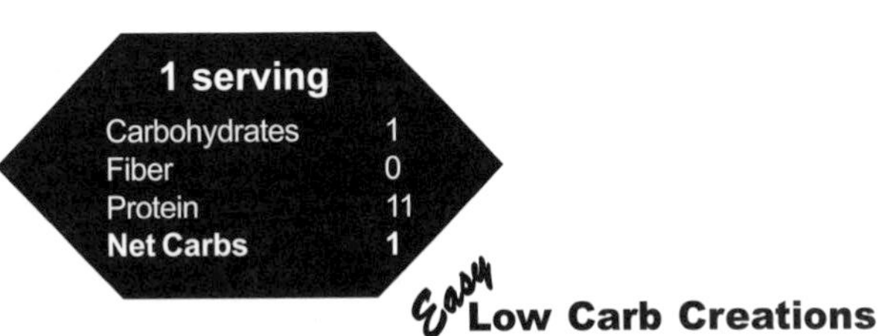

1 serving	
Carbohydrates	1
Fiber	0
Protein	11
Net Carbs	**1**

Pepper Steak with Oriental Gravy

Makes 8 servings

Net Carbs 2

1/4 cup olive oil
1 1/2 pounds sirloin steak, cut into 1/4-inch strips
1/2 teaspoon minced garlic
1 medium onion, sliced

2 large tomatoes, chopped
4 medium green peppers, cut into strips
1/4 cup soy sauce
1/4 teaspoon sugar substitute*
1 1/4 teaspoons ground ginger
1 1/4 cups beef bouillon, divided

2 teaspoons cornstarch

Directions

1. In large skillet over high heat, heat olive oil. Add next 3 ingredients; cook and stir until meat is no longer pink.
2. To same skillet, stir in next 5 ingredients and 3/4 cup beef bouillon. Bring to boil. Reduce heat to medium-low; cover and simmer 30 minutes or until meat is tender.
3. In small bowl, blend cornstarch with remaining 1/2 cup bouillon.
4. To meat mixture in skillet, stir cornstarch/bouillon mixture. Over medium-high heat, bring meat mixture to boil; reduce heat. Simmer and stir 2 minutes; serve in bowls.

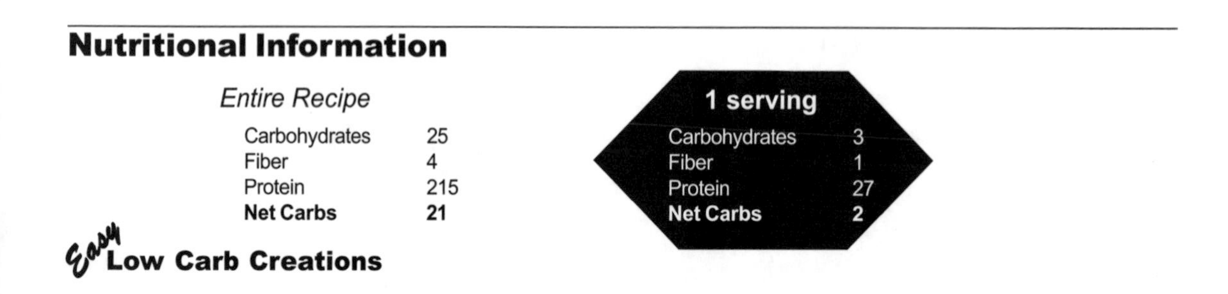

Nutritional Information

Entire Recipe	
Carbohydrates	25
Fiber	4
Protein	215
Net Carbs	**21**

1 serving	
Carbohydrates	3
Fiber	1
Protein	27
Net Carbs	**2**

Sub Gum

Makes 8 servings

2 tablespoons vegetable oil

1 8-ounce can sliced water chestnuts, drained
1 8-ounce can sliced bamboo shoots, drained
3 tablespoons green onions, sliced
2 cups celery, chopped
1 medium green pepper, chopped
1 teaspoon salt
1/2 teaspoon pepper
1 1/2 teaspoons sugar substitute*

2 cups chicken broth

3 tablespoons soy sauce
1 tablespoon cornstarch
1 tablespoon water

2 pounds cooked chicken, cubed
1/2 cup sliced almonds, toasted

Directions

1. In large skillet over high heat, heat oil. Add next 8 ingredients; cook and stir 2 to 3 minutes.
2. To same skillet, add broth and bring to boil. Reduce heat to medium; cook 8 to 10 minutes, stirring occasionally.
3. In small bowl, combine next 3 ingredients, blending thoroughly.
4. Into hot mixture, stir soy sauce mixture; cook 2 minutes or until thickened.
5. To skillet, add chicken and almonds; cook and stir until hot and bubbly.

Nutritional Information

Entire Recipe

Carbohydrates	57
Fiber	18
Protein	207
Net Carbs	**39**

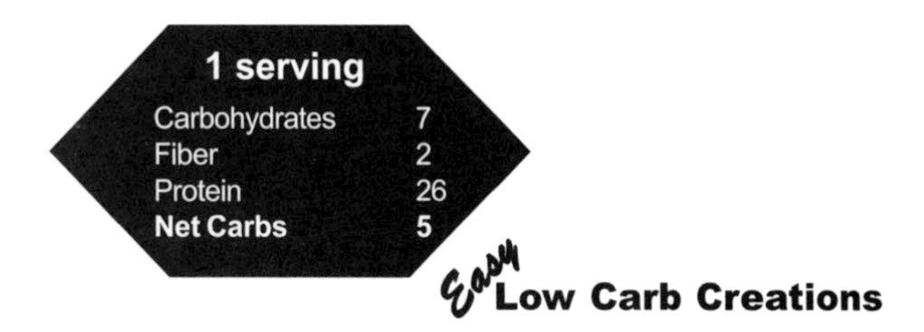

1 serving	
Carbohydrates	7
Fiber	2
Protein	26
Net Carbs	**5**

Szechuan Pork

Makes 6 servings

1 1/2 pounds boneless pork loin, cut into 1/8-inch strips
1 tablespoon soy sauce
1 tablespoon cornstarch
1/2 teaspoon ground red pepper (cayenne)
1/2 teaspoon minced garlic

2 tablespoons vegetable oil

1 16-ounce package frozen broccoli cuts, thawed, drained
2 small onions, cut into eighths
1 8-ounce can whole water chestnuts, drained
1/4 cup chicken broth

1/2 cup peanuts

Net Carbs 8

Directions

1. In large bowl, toss pork together with next 4 ingredients; cover and chill 20 minutes.
2. In large skillet over high heat, heat vegetable oil. Add pork strips; cook and stir 8 to 10 minutes until pork is no longer pink.
3. To same skillet, stir in next 4 ingredients; cook and stir additional 2 to 3 minutes or until broccoli is crisp-tender.
4. To pork mixture, stir in peanuts.

Nutritional Information

Entire Recipe

Carbohydrates	70
Fiber	24
Protein	195
Net Carbs	**46**

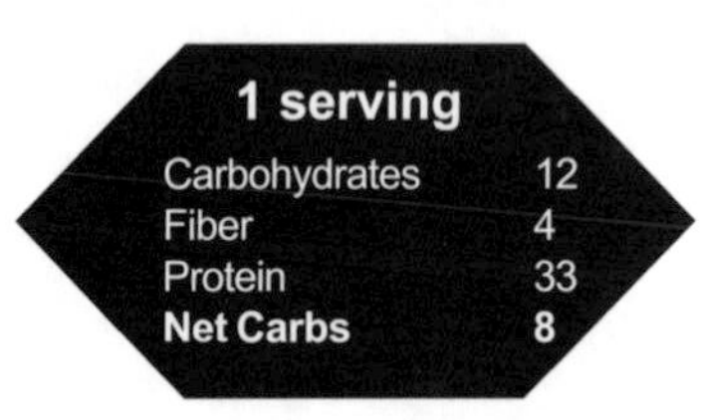

1 serving

Carbohydrates	12
Fiber	4
Protein	33
Net Carbs	**8**

Wilted Cabbage and Sausage

Makes 10 servings

1/2 pound bacon, cut into 1/2-inch pieces

2 quarts water
1/2 cup plus 2 tablespoons cider vinegar, divided
1 small head red cabbage, coarsely shredded

1/4 cup water
1 medium onion, thinly sliced, separated into rings
3 tablespoons brown sugar substitute, equivalent measure
1 tablespoon dry mustard
1 teaspoon salt
1/8 teaspoon pepper

6 fully-cooked bratwursts, cut into 1-inch pieces
1 medium pear, cut into lengthwise pieces

Directions

1. In large skillet over medium-high heat, cook bacon until crisp. Remove bacon and set aside; reserve 3 tablespoons drippings in skillet.
2. In large pan, combine next 3 ingredients. Over high heat, bring to boil; cook 1 minute; drain.
3. In skillet with bacon drippings, combine remaining vinegar and next 6 ingredients. Over medium heat, cook and stir 3 minutes.
4. To same skillet, add bratwurst and pear slices; cover and cook 10 minutes.
5. To bratwurst, add cabbage and bacon, stirring lightly to combine.

Nutritional Information

Entire Recipe

Carbohydrates	75
Fiber	22
Protein	114
Net Carbs	**53**

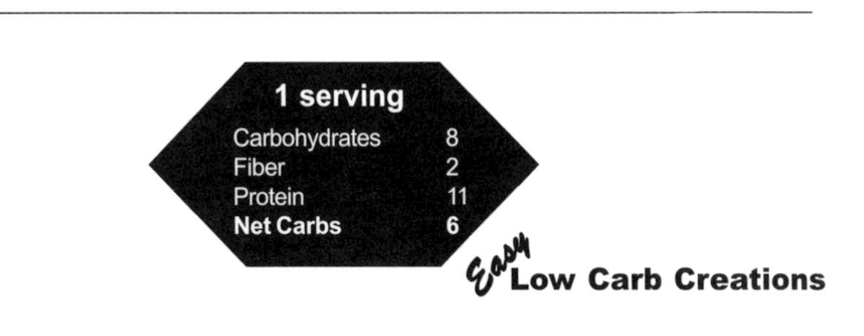

1 serving	
Carbohydrates	8
Fiber	2
Protein	11
Net Carbs	**6**

Slow Cooker Main Dishes

Net Carbs	Recipe	Page
0	Aunt Edith's Sauerkraut and Ribs	217
4	Cantonese Dinner	218
3	Dilled Rump Roast with Sauce	219
15	Pork Chops with Squash	220
1	Roast Pork Rosemary	221
2	Slow Cooked Beef with Mushrooms	222
12	Slow Cooked Chicken Italian	223
0	Slow Cooker Turkey	224
9	Stuffed Beef Rounds	225

Aunt Edith's Sauerkraut and Ribs

Makes 8 servings

4 pounds country-style pork ribs

2 16-ounce cans sauerkraut, undrained
1/2 cup water
1/4 teaspoon caraway seeds

Directions

1. In large slow cooker, place spare ribs.
2. Cover meat with remaining ingredients in order given.
3. Cook on high 4 to 5 hours or on low 7 to 8 hours.

Net Carbs 0

Nutritional Information

Entire Recipe

Carbohydrates	32
Fiber	32
Protein	277
Net Carbs	**0**

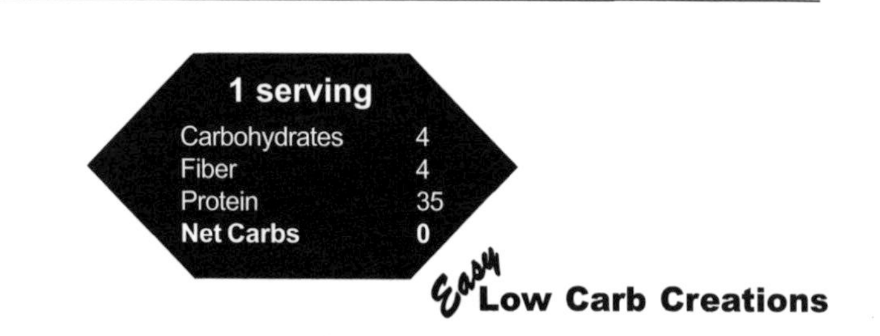

1 serving	
Carbohydrates	4
Fiber	4
Protein	35
Net Carbs	**0**

Cantonese Dinner

Makes 9 servings

1/4 cup vegetable oil
3 pounds boneless pork, cut into 1/2-inch strips

2 medium onions, sliced
2 green peppers, cut into strips
2 4-ounce cans mushrooms, drained

2 8-ounce cans tomato sauce
1/4 cup plus 2 tablespoons brown sugar substitute, equivalent measure
3 tablespoons cider vinegar
1 tablespoon salt
1/4 cup Worcestershire sauce

Directions

1. In large skillet over high heat, heat vegetable oil. Add pork and cook 8 to 10 minutes or until browned.
2. Into large slow cooker, place browned pork; layer next 3 ingredients in order given.
3. In small bowl, combine remaining ingredients; pour over meat and vegetables.
4. Cook on high 4 to 5 hours or on low 7 to 8 hours.

Nutritional Information

Entire Recipe

Carbohydrates	49
Fiber	12
Protein	370
Net Carbs	**37**

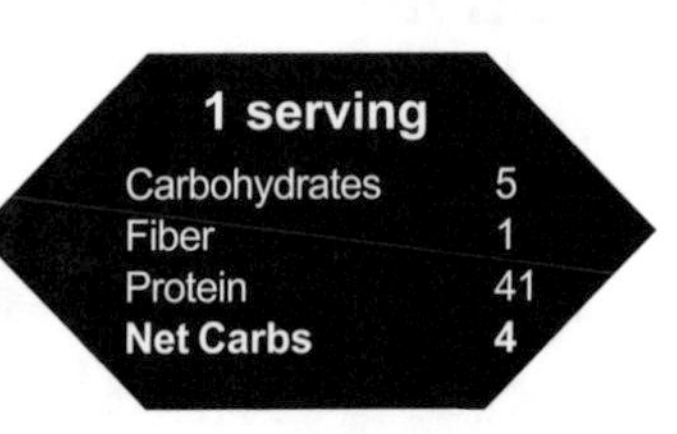

1 serving

Carbohydrates	5
Fiber	1
Protein	41
Net Carbs	**4**

Dilled Rump Roast with Sauce

Makes 9 servings

1 3-pound beef rump roast
1/2 teaspoon salt
1/4 teaspoon pepper
2 teaspoons dill weed, divided
1/4 cup water
1 tablespoon cider vinegar

1 tablespoon cornstarch
2 tablespoons water

1 cup sour cream

Net Carbs
3

Directions

1. In large slow cooker, place beef roast.
2. Sprinkle meat with salt, pepper, and 1 teaspoon dill weed; add water and vinegar.
3. Cook on high 4 to 5 hours or on low 7 to 8 hours.
4. Remove meat and turn slow cooker to high.
5. In cup, combine cornstarch and water; stir cornstarch/water mixture and remaining dill weed into drippings.
6. Cook sauce on high 10 to 15 minutes or until thickened. To slow cooker, stir in sour cream; cover and cook additional 10 to 15 minutes.
7. Meanwhile, slice meat; return it to sauce in slow cooker before serving.

Nutritional Information

Entire Recipe

Carbohydrates	27
Fiber	0
Protein	392
Net Carbs	**27**

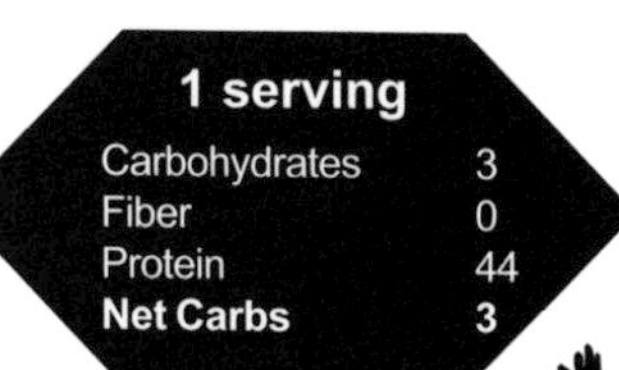

1 serving	
Carbohydrates	3
Fiber	0
Protein	44
Net Carbs	**3**

Pork Chops with Squash

Makes 6 servings

6 boneless pork chops, 1/2-inch thick
1 medium acorn squash, unpeeled

1/2 teaspoon salt
2 tablespoons butter, melted
3/4 cup brown sugar substitute, equivalent measure
3/4 teaspoon browning and seasoning sauce
1/8 teaspoon nutmeg
2 tablespoons orange juice
1 teaspoon grated orange peel

Directions

Net Carbs 15

1. Trim fat from edges of chops; discard fat.
2. Cut squash into 6 crosswise slices.
3. On bottom of slow cooker, arrange 3 chops; top with 3 slices squash and repeat layers.
4. In small bowl, combine remaining ingredients; pour over squash and chops.
5. Cook on high 3 to 4 hours or on low 6 to 7 hours or until pork is tender.
6. Serve slice of squash with each pork chop.

Nutritional Information

Entire Recipe

Carbohydrates	116
Fiber	23
Protein	90
Net Carbs	**93**

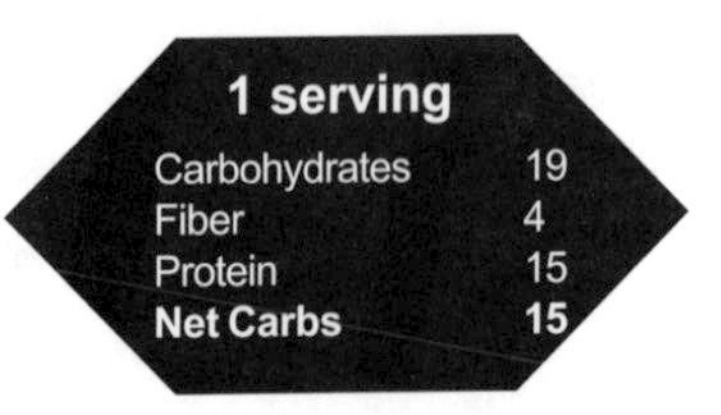

1 serving

Carbohydrates	19
Fiber	4
Protein	15
Net Carbs	**15**

Roast Pork Rosemary

Makes15 servings

5 pounds boneless pork loin

2 cups apple cider
1 teaspoon minced garlic
2 teaspoons rosemary
1 teaspoon bay leaves, crushed

Directions

1. In large slow cooker, place pork roast.
2. Combine remaining ingredients and pour over roast.
3. Cook on high 4 to 5 hours or on low 7 to 8 hours.
4. Remove roast and slice; dispose of liquid.

Net Carbs 1

Nutritional Information

Entire Recipe

Carbohydrates	14
Fiber	0
Protein	480
Net Carbs	**14**

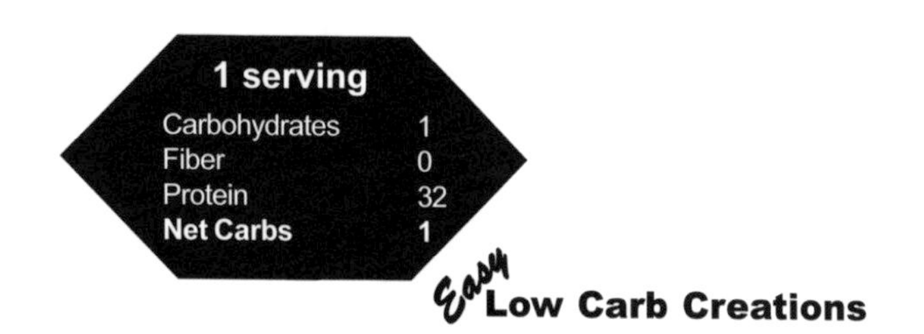

1 serving	
Carbohydrates	1
Fiber	0
Protein	32
Net Carbs	**1**

Slow Cooked Beef with Mushrooms

Makes 12 servings

4 pounds boneless beef loin, cut into 1-inch cubes
1 envelope onion soup mix
1 10.75-ounce can condensed cream of mushroom soup
1 4-ounce can whole mushrooms, undrained
1/2 cup red wine (may substitute beef broth)

Directions

1. In slow cooker, combine all ingredients. Mix well.
2. Cook on high 4 to 5 hours or on low 7 to 8 hours.

Net Carbs 2

Nutritional Information

Entire Recipe

Carbohydrates	24
Fiber	5
Protein	264
Net Carbs	**19**

1 serving

Carbohydrates	2
Fiber	0
Protein	22
Net Carbs	**2**

Slow Cooked Chicken Italian

Makes 6 servings

4 boneless, skinless chicken breasts, cut into pieces
1 cup chicken broth
1/2 cup dry white wine
1 onion, finely chopped
1/2 teaspoon salt
1/4 teaspoon pepper
1/4 teaspoon thyme
2 teaspoons parsley

1 8-ounce package fresh sliced mushrooms
3 tablespoons cornstarch
1/4 cup water

1/2 cup half-and-half
1/2 cup Parmesan cheese

Net Carbs 12

Directions

1. In slow cooker, combine chicken and next 7 ingredients.
2. Cook on high 3 to 4 hours or on low 6 to 7 hours.
3. Turn control to high; add mushrooms.
4. In cup, combine cornstarch and water; stir into slow cooker; cover and cook on high 20 minutes.
5. To slow cooker, stir in half-and-half and cheese; cover and heat 10 to 15 minutes or until hot.
6. Serve with extra Parmesan cheese.

Nutritional Information

Entire Recipe

Carbohydrates	71
Fiber	2
Protein	110
Net Carbs	**69**

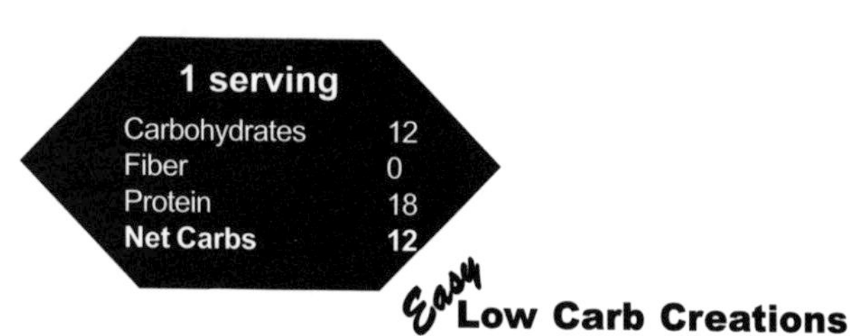

1 serving	
Carbohydrates	12
Fiber	0
Protein	18
Net Carbs	**12**

Slow Cooker Turkey

Makes 18 servings

1 6 pound turkey breast
1 stick butter
1 teaspoon salt

Directions

1. In slow cooker, place butter.
2. Sprinkle salt in turkey breast cavity and place breast side up in slow cooker.
3. Cook on high 4 to 5 hours or on low 8 to 9 hours.

Net Carbs 0

Nutritional Information

Entire Recipe

Carbohydrates	0
Fiber	0
Protein	528
Net Carbs	**0**

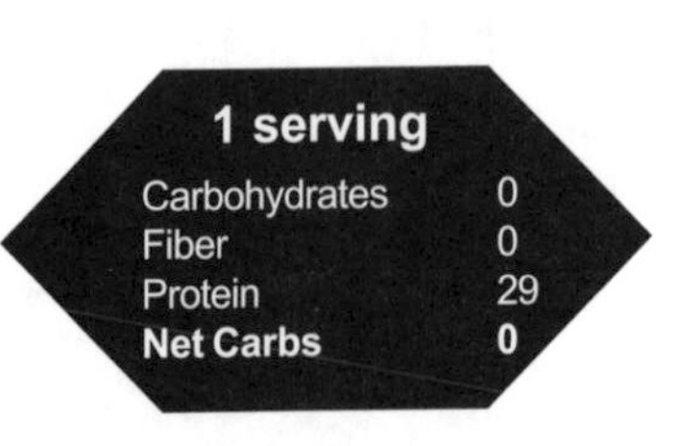

1 serving

Carbohydrates	0
Fiber	0
Protein	29
Net Carbs	**0**

Stuffed Beef Rounds

Makes 6 servings

2 pounds boneless chuck steak, cut into serving-sized pieces

1 cup shredded cheddar cheese
1/2 cup celery, chopped
1/2 cup fresh parsley, chopped

Toothpicks

1/4 cup plus 2 tablespoons flour, divided
1 teaspoon salt
1/8 teaspoon pepper

2 tablespoons vegetable oil

1 10.5-ounce can chicken broth
1/2 teaspoon mustard
1/4 cup water

Net Carbs 9

Directions

1. Pound steak to 1/4-inch thickness.
2. In medium bowl, combine next 3 ingredients.
3. Into center of each steak piece, place 1/4 cup cheese mixture; reserve remaining cheese mixture.
4. Roll up each steak, jelly-roll fashion; secure with toothpicks.
5. In medium bowl, combine 1/4 cup flour, salt, and pepper; roll meat in flour mixture to coat.
6. In large skillet over medium-high heat, heat vegetable oil; cook meat roll-ups 3 to 4 minutes on each side; set aside.
7. In slow cooker, combine remaining ingredients and 2 tablespoons flour. Add browned meat; sprinkle remaining cheese mixture over top of meat.
8. Cook on low 4 to 6 hours.

Nutritional Information

Entire Recipe

Carbohydrates	58
Fiber	6
Protein	344
Net Carbs	**52**

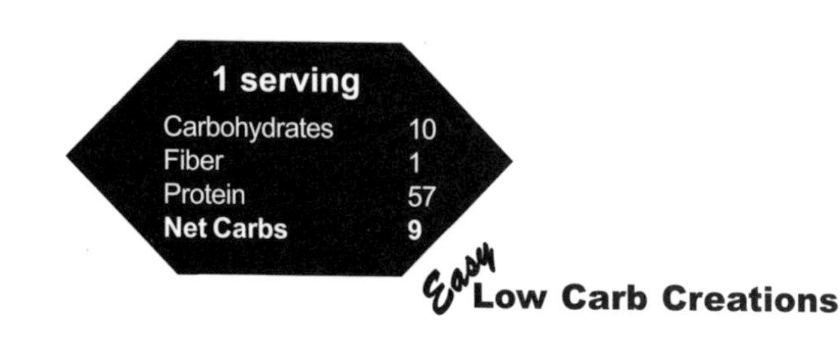

Soups

Net Carbs	Recipe	Page
10	Bacon Cheese Soup	227
5	Bacon Vegetable Soup	228
8	Broccoli Cheese Soup	229
7	Cabbage Soup	230
9	Cauliflower Soup	231
7	Chicken Soup with Almonds	232
9	Chili	233
10	Creamy Bacon, Lettuce, Tomato Soup	234
11	Taco Soup	235
10	Vegetable Soup	236

Bacon Cheese Soup

Makes 8 servings

1 pound bacon, cut into 1/2-inch pieces

1/2 cup carrots, grated
1/2 cup celery, finely chopped
1/2 cup onion, finely chopped
1/2 cup green pepper, finely chopped

3 tablespoons flour
4 cups chicken broth

1 cup sharp shredded cheddar cheese
2 cups processed cheese loaf, cut into small pieces
2 cups half-and-half
2 tablespoons dry sherry (may substitute chicken broth)
1/4 cup stuffed green olives, sliced
1/4 teaspoon pepper

Directions

1. In large pan over medium-high heat, cook bacon until crisp. Remove bacon; reserve 3 tablespoons drippings.
2. In drippings over low heat, cook next 4 ingredients 5 minutes or until tender.
3. To vegetables, blend in flour; cook and stir 1 minute.
4. To same pan, increase to medium heat; gradually add broth. Cook and stir; bring to boil. Simmer 8 minutes or until mixture thickens.
5. To same pan, stir in next 6 ingredients; cook 10 minutes or until hot and bubbly. Stir in cooked bacon.

Net Carbs 10

Nutritional Information

Entire Recipe

Carbohydrates	86
Fiber	6
Protein	123
Net Carbs	**80**

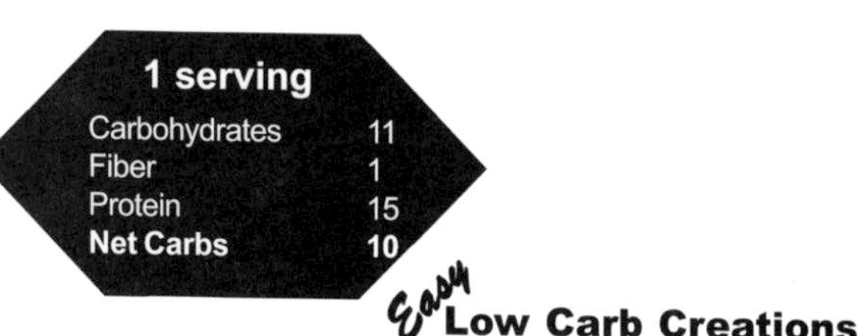

1 serving	
Carbohydrates	11
Fiber	1
Protein	15
Net Carbs	**10**

Bacon Vegetable Soup

Makes 5 servings

3 beef-flavored bouillon cubes
3 cups hot water

1 pound bacon, cut into 1/2-inch pieces

1/3 cup onion, chopped
1/3 cup celery, chopped

5 medium ripe tomatoes, coarsely chopped
1 tablespoon Worcestershire sauce
1/2 teaspoon garlic salt
1/2 teaspoon parsley
1/4 teaspoon whole thyme
1/4 teaspoon pepper
Dash hot sauce

2 cups lettuce, shredded

Net Carbs 5

Directions

1. Dissolve bouillon cubes in hot water; set aside.
2. In large pan over medium-high heat, cook bacon until crisp. Remove bacon, reserving 3 tablespoons drippings.
3. To bacon drippings over medium-high heat, add onion and celery. Cook and stir 3 to 4 minutes or until onion is tender.
4. To same pan, add bouillon, tomatoes and next 6 ingredients; bring to boil.
5. Reduce heat to medium-low and simmer 20 to 25 minutes.
6. To same pan, add lettuce; cook 2 minutes or until lettuce wilts. Stir in cooked bacon.

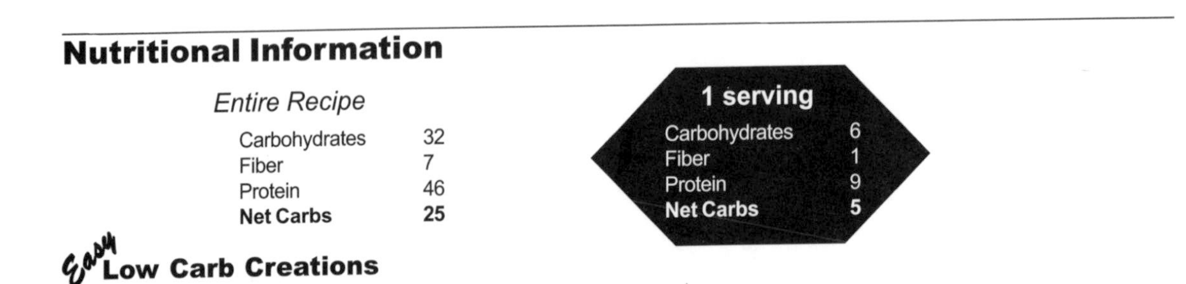

Nutritional Information

Entire Recipe

Carbohydrates	32
Fiber	7
Protein	46
Net Carbs	**25**

1 serving

Carbohydrates	6
Fiber	1
Protein	9
Net Carbs	**5**

Broccoli Cheese Soup

Makes 11 servings

1 stick butter
1 cup onion, chopped

2 pounds chopped broccoli, fresh or frozen
4 cups chicken broth

4 cups half-and-half
1 pound pasteurized processed cheese spread, cut into small pieces

1 tablespoon cornstarch
1 tablespoon water

Directions

1. In large pan over medium-high heat, melt butter. Add onion; cook and stir 3 to 4 minutes or until onion is tender.
2. To same pan, stir in broccoli and chicken broth; cook 8 to 10 minutes or until broccoli is tender.
3. To broccoli, add next 2 ingredients; cook and stir until cheese melts.
4. In cup, combine cornstarch and water.
5. To soup, add cornstarch mixture; cook and stir additional 1 to 2 minutes or until mixture thickens.

Nutritional Information

Entire Recipe

Carbohydrates	110
Fiber	18
Protein	113
Net Carbs	**92**

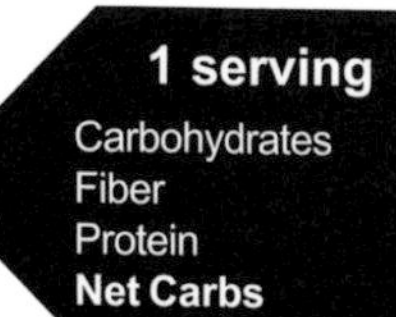

1 serving

Carbohydrates	10
Fiber	2
Protein	10
Net Carbs	**8**

Cabbage Soup

Makes 8 servings

1 pound lean ground beef
1 large onion, chopped
1/2 cup celery, sliced

1 16-ounce can diced tomatoes
2 cups water
1 large onion, chopped
1 16-ounce can chili beans, undrained
1 teaspoon salt
1 1/2 teaspoons chili powder
1/4 teaspoon pepper
2 cups cabbage, shredded

Directions

1. In large pan over medium-high heat, cook first 3 ingredients, stirring until meat is brown and crumbly; drain.
2. To same pan, stir in remaining ingredients; bring to boil. Reduce heat to low; simmer 1 hour.

Nutritional Information

Entire Recipe

Carbohydrates	98
Fiber	40
Protein	103
Net Carbs	**58**

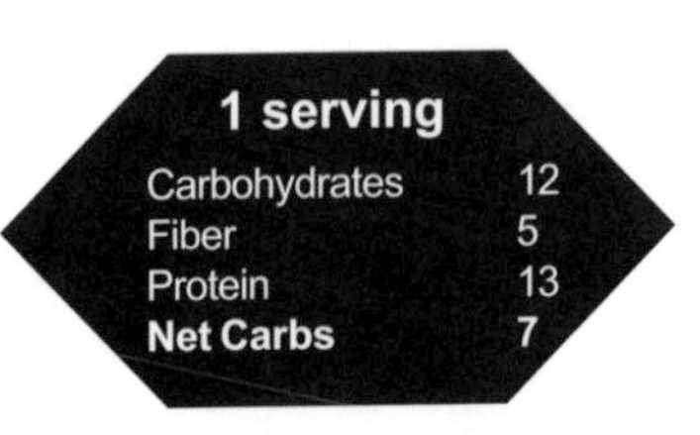

1 serving	
Carbohydrates	12
Fiber	5
Protein	13
Net Carbs	**7**

Cauliflower Soup

Makes 6 servings

2 tablespoons butter
1/2 cup onion, chopped

3 cups cauliflower, coarsely chopped
1 cup chicken broth

2 tablespoons flour
2 1/2 cups half-and-half

2 cups shredded cheddar cheese
1/2 teaspoon salt
1/4 teaspoon pepper

Directions

1. In large pan over medium-high heat, melt butter. Add onion; cook and stir 3 to 4 minutes or until onion is tender.
2. To same pan, stir in next 2 ingredients; bring to boil. Cover and reduce heat to medium; simmer 12 minutes or until cauliflower is tender.
3. In small bowl, combine next 2 ingredients.
4. Into cauliflower mixture, add half-and-half/flour mixture; cook and stir; bring to boil.
5. Remove pan from heat. Add next 3 ingredients; stir until cheese melts.

Nutritional Information

Entire Recipe

Carbohydrates	67
Fiber	12
Protein	70
Net Carbs	**55**

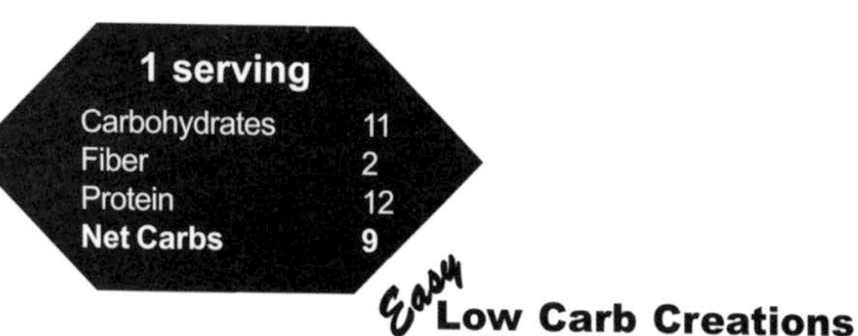

Chicken Soup with Almonds

Makes 4 servings

1 tablespoon butter
1 tablespoon flour
1/4 teaspoon salt

1 cup chicken broth

2 cups cooked chicken or turkey, cubed
1/2 cup sliced almonds, toasted
2 cups half-and-half
1 teaspoon cilantro

Directions

1. In large saucepan over medium heat, melt butter. Stir in flour and salt; cook and stir 1 to 2 minutes or until lightly browned.
2. Into same saucepan, gradually stir in chicken broth; cook and stir until mixture boils.
3. Reduce heat to medium-low; stir in remaining ingredients. Simmer and stir 10 to 20 minutes or until desired consistency.

Nutritional Information

Entire Recipe

Carbohydrates	36
Fiber	8
Protein	107
Net Carbs	**28**

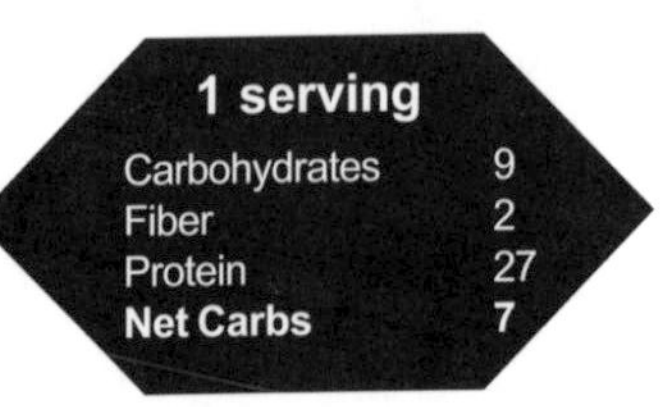

1 serving

Carbohydrates	9
Fiber	2
Protein	27
Net Carbs	**7**

Chili

Makes 6 servings

1 1/2 pounds lean ground beef
1 medium onion, chopped

1/2 medium green pepper, chopped

1 14.5-ounce can chili beans, undrained
3 cups tomato juice

Directions

1. In large pan over medium-high heat, cook ground beef and onion, stirring until meat is almost done.
2. To same pan, add green pepper; cook and stir until meat is brown and crumbly. Drain.
3. To beef in pan, stir in remaining ingredients; bring to boil.
4. Reduce heat to low. Simmer 1 hour, stirring occasionally.

Nutritional Information

Entire Recipe

Carbohydrates	82
Fiber	28
Protein	131
Net Carbs	**54**

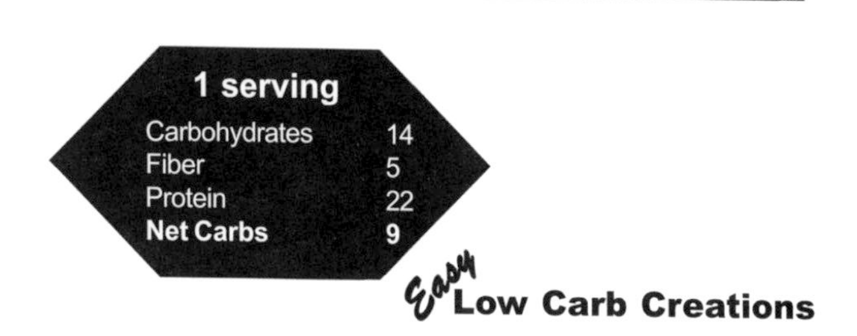

1 serving

Carbohydrates	14
Fiber	5
Protein	22
Net Carbs	**9**

Creamy Bacon, Lettuce, Tomato Soup

Makes 7 servings

1/2 cup boiling water
4 chicken bouillon cubes

1 pound bacon, cut into 1/2-inch pieces

1 head lettuce, shredded

3 tablespoons flour

1 14.5-ounce can diced tomatoes
1/4 teaspoon nutmeg
1/4 teaspoon pepper

4 cups half-and-half

Directions

Soups

1. In glass measuring cup, combine boiling water and bouillon cubes; stir until dissolved. Set aside.
2. In large pan over medium-high heat, cook bacon until crisp.
3. To bacon and drippings, add lettuce. Reduce heat to medium; cook and stir 2 minutes.
4. To same pan, stir in flour; cook and stir additional 2 to 3 minutes.
5. To lettuce mixture, stir in chicken broth and next 3 ingredients; bring to boil. Reduce heat to low.
6. To same pan, gradually stir in half-and-half; cook and stir until hot and bubbly.

Nutritional Information

Entire Recipe

Carbohydrates	70
Fiber	3
Protein	48
Net Carbs	**67**

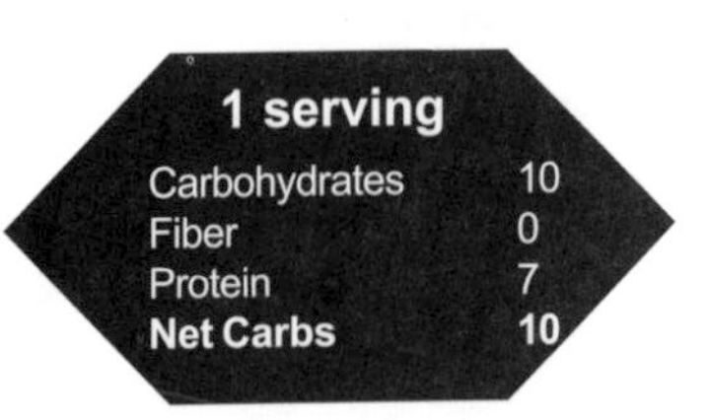

1 serving

Carbohydrates	10
Fiber	0
Protein	7
Net Carbs	**10**

Taco Soup

Makes 8 servings

1 pound lean ground beef
1 large onion, chopped

1 16-ounce can Mexican-style chili beans, undrained
1 16-ounce can chopped tomatoes, undrained
3 8-ounce cans tomato sauce
1 1/2 cups water
1 4 1/2-ounce can chopped green chilies, drained
1 package taco seasoning mix
1 package ranch salad dressing mix

Toppings: 2 cups shredded Mexican 4-blend cheese, 1 cup shredded lettuce, 1 chopped avocado, 1/2 cup sour cream and 2 ounces corn chips*

Directions

1. In large pan over medium-high heat, cook ground beef and onion, stirring until meat is brown and crumbly; drain.
2. To beef in pan, stir in next 7 ingredients. Bring mixture to boil.
3. Reduce heat to low; simmer 30 to 40 minutes.
4. Serve with toppings.

*Without toppings subtract 5 net carbs per serving.

Nutritional Information

Entire Recipe

Carbohydrates	127
Fiber	43
Protein	110
Net Carbs	**84**

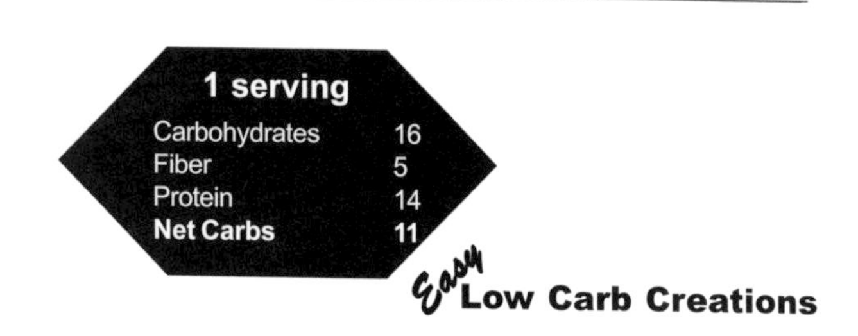

Vegetable Soup

Makes 16 servings

4 pounds boneless beef chuck roast
2 teaspoons salt
3/4 teaspoon pepper

1 medium head cabbage, cut into bite-sized pieces
1 stalk celery, chopped (use ribs and leaves)
1 16-ounce package baby carrots, chopped
1 16-ounce package frozen peas
3 14.5-ounce cans green beans, undrained
1 46-ounce can tomato juice

Directions

1. In large pot, place first 3 ingredients; cover roast with water. Over high heat, bring water to boil.
2. Reduce heat to medium-low; simmer 1 1/2 to 2 hours or until beef is tender.
3. Remove meat from broth; add remaining ingredients to broth. Cut meat into bite-sized pieces; return to pan.
4. Bring soup to boil; reduce heat to medium-low; simmer additional 1 to 2 hours.

Nutritional Information

Entire Recipe

Carbohydrates	219
Fiber	71
Protein	563
Net Carbs	**148**

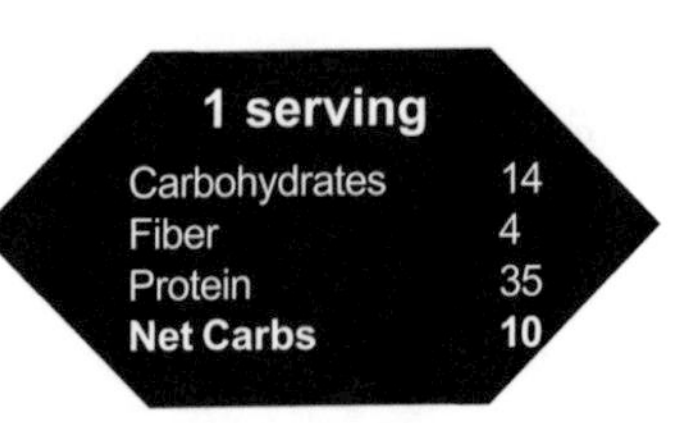

Menus

The next pages of dinner menus were prepared with the following advantages:

20 or fewer carbs per serving per meal
Delicious taste the entire family will enjoy
Pleasing variety of textures, colors, temperatures and food combinations
Packed with nutrients
Easy preparation
Dessert with every meal

The total carb count for each meal is based on the serving size indicated in each recipe.

	Net Carbs	Protein	Page
Stuffed Mushrooms w/ Parmesan Cheese	1	2	39
Green Bean Salad	5	9	147
Elegant Fish	1	36	172
Baked Swiss Vegetables	4	8	180
Chocolate Silk Pie	7	3	97

Totals
18 net carbs
58 proteins

	Net Carbs	Protein	Page
Bleu Cheese Dip w/Celery	2	2	19
Chicken Drumettes	1	21	22
Bacon Vegetable Soup	5	9	228
Chocolate Peanut Butter Mousse	9	2	89

Totals
17 net carbs
34 proteins

	Net Carbs	Protein	Page
Pepperoni-Cheese-Spinach Mini Cups	2	7	33
Side Salad w/Bleu Cheese Dressing	5	1	162
Lasagna	11	37	67
Chocolate Peanut Pops	2	1	95

Totals
20 net carbs
46 proteins

	Net Carbs	Protein	Page
Cheese Apple Salad	5	4	145
Aunt Edith's Sauerkraut and Ribs	0	35	217
Special Baked Green Beans	7	15	202
Vanilla Silk Pie	7	4	115

Totals
19 net carbs
58 proteins

	Net Carbs	Protein	Page
Stuffed Cherry Tomatoes (4)	1	4	37
Slaw	1	1	156
Ham and Cheese Rolls	5	22	133
Butterscotch Peanut Butter Mousse	7	2	89

Totals
14 net carbs
29 proteins

	Net Carbs	Protein	Page
Beef Stuffed Mushrooms (2)	4	6	17
7 Layer Salad	4	10	141
Roast Pork Rosemary	1	32	221
Asparagus Casserole	3	11	179
Cheesecake Pie	7	6	90

Totals
19 net carbs
65 proteins

	Net Carbs	Protein	Page
Dried Beef Dip w/Celery (2)	2	2	25
Layered Spinach Salad	2	8	150
Seafood AuGratin	10	20	174
Stir Fries	3	3	203
Cherry-Diet Cola Dessert	3	3	92

Totals
20 net carbs
36 proteins

	Net Carbs	Protein	Page
Cabbage Salad	7	3	143
Lemon-Dilled Chicken	1	23	80
Green Bean Casserole	4	5	190
Cream Cheese Puffs	8	2	98

Totals
20 net carbs
33 proteins

Easy Low Carb Creations Menus

	Net Carbs	Protein	Page
Cauliflower Lettuce Layer Salad	5	7	144
Italian Meatballs	6	22	47
Broccoli Casserole	3	6	181
Chocolate Pie	6	4	96

Totals
20 net carbs
39 proteins

	Net Carbs	Protein	Page
Peanut Pineapple Bites (2)	2	1	32
Spinach Salad	6	14	157
Cantonese Dinner	4	41	218
Grandma's Green Beans	3	3	189
Chocolate Cheesecake Singles	2	3	94

Totals
17 net carbs
62 proteins

	Net Carbs	Protein	Page
Pickle Pick-Ups	1	2	34
Red Cabbage Salad	1	1	155
Beef Kabobs	2	49	43
Microwave Cauliflower w/ Cheese Sauce	4	4	195
Four Layer Dessert	9	3	99

Totals
17 net carbs
59 proteins

	Net Carbs	Protein	Page
Stuffed Mushrooms w/ Bacon (2)	2	6	38
Tossed Salad w/ Sesame Dressing	5	0	168
Bourbon Chicken and Gravy	6	15	75
Cauliflower Stir-Fry	2	2	183
Strawberry White Chocolate Mousse	5	1	114

Totals
20 net carbs
24 proteins

Easy Low Carb Creations *Menus*

	Net Carbs	Protein	Page
Deviled Eggs	1	4	186
Broccoli Salad	6	9	142
Marinated Chuck Roast	1	33	48
Creamy Mushrooms	4	4	185
Lime Dessert	7	2	106

Totals
19 net carbs
52 proteins

	Net Carbs	Protein	Page
Italian Cucumber Tomato Salad	2	2	148
Marinated Grilled Chicken	0	26	81
Cabbage Au Gratin	4	3	182
Peanut Butter Pie	13	8	109

Totals
19 net carbs
39 proteins

	Net Carbs	Protein	Page
Cheese Dip on Celery	3	3	20
Mandarin Orange Salad	5	1	151
Slow Cooker Turkey	0	29	224
Green Bean Swiss Cheese Crunch	6	6	192
Pumpkin Chiffon Dessert	6	5	110

Totals
20 net carbs
44 proteins

	Net Carbs	Protein	Page
Italian Salad	11	5	149
Parmesan Chicken	0	26	82
Zucchini Italian	4	9	205
Layered Gelatin Dessert	4	0	104

Totals
19 net carbs
40 proteins

	Net Carbs	Protein	Page
Bacon Wrapped Shrimp (2)	4	4	14
Dilled Cucmber Salad	2	1	146
Baked Steak	5	33	42
Strawberry Pecan Dessert	7	7	113

Totals
18 net carbs
45 proteins

	Net Carbs	Protein	Page
Summer Salad	1	2	158
Pineapple Chicken	3	16	83
Oriental Vegetables	1	1	198
Frozen Peanut Butter Dessert	13	12	100

Totals
18 net carbs
31 proteins

	Net Carbs	Protein	Page
Wilted Lettuce Salad	1	4	159
Grilled Tuna Steak	0	100	173
Slow Cooker Broccoli	4	9	199
Fruit Fluff	12	10	102

Totals
17 net carbs
123 proteins

	Net Carbs	Protein	Page
Mushroom Salad	3	11	152
Pepper Steak w/Oriental Gravy	3	36	212
Oriental Green Beans	5	5	197
Chilled Cheesecake	9	3	93

Totals
20 net carbs
55 proteins

	Net Carbs	Protein	Page
Overnight Slaw	1	1	153
Dilled Rump Roast w/ Sauce	3	44	219
Company Cauliflower Casserole	8	6	184
Lemon Cream Nutty Delight	5	4	105

Totals
17 net carbs
55 proteins

	Net Carbs	Protein	Page
Dill Dip w/Celery (2)	1	0	24
Montana Goulash	5	36	210
Snow Peas w/ Water Chestnuts	4	5	201
Pumpkin Cream Pie	7	4	111

Totals
17 net carbs
45 proteins

Easy Low Carb Creations *Menus*

	Net Carbs	Protein	Page	
Stuffed Mushrooms w/ Parmesan Cheese	1	2	39	**Totals 20 net carbs 21 proteins**
Layered Tex-Mex Salad	9	13	126	
Margueritaville Pecan Pie	10	6	107	

	Net Carbs	Protein	Page	
Bacon Wraps (2)	7	3	15	**Totals 18 net carbs 34 proteins**
Pickled Cucumbers	3	1	154	
Baked Ham	0	17		
Wilted Cabbage w/ Cheese	4	8	204	
Peanut Butter Cookies	4	5	108	

	Net Carbs	Protein	Page	
Pineapple Cheese Ball	3	1	35	**Totals 18 net carbs 27 proteins**
Slow-Cooked Beef w/ Mushrooms	2	22	222	
Garden Skillet	1	1	187	
Pumpkin Fluff	12	3	112	

	Net Carbs	Protein	Page	
Tossed Salad w/French Dressing	7	0	163	**Totals 19 net carbs 25 proteins**
Chicken Walnut Sauté	1	16	209	
Garlic Green Beans	4	3	188	
Cheesecake Supreme	7	6	91	

	Net Carbs	Protein	Page	
Nichole's Stuffed Mushrooms	5	5	30	**Totals 19 net carbs 31 proteins**
Chicken Divan	4	21	76	
Mediterranean Green Beans	1	3	194	
Fruity Cheese Fluff	9	2	103	

Dairy

Dairy products are excellent sources of needed vitamins, minerals, and protein. Utilize the following carbohydrate counts to make informed choices.

Milk Product	Carbs per 8-ounces
Buttermilk, 1% milk fat	10
Buttermilk, skim	12
Evaporated milk, 2% milk fat	28
Evaporated milk, whole	24
Half-and-half	8
Heavy cream, liquid	0
Heavy cream, whipped	0
Light cream	8
Lowfat milk, 1% milk fat	13
Nonfat milk, skim	13
Reduced fat milk, 2% milk fat	12
Sour cream	(2 T. = 2) 16
Whole milk	12
Yogurt, plain whole milk	11

Cheese provides benefits of other dairy products in a compact package. Serving sizes are 1-ounce for hard cheese (makes about 1/4 cup grated) and 2 tablespoons for soft cheese.

Cheese	Carbs per serving
American	(1 slice, 3/4-ounce = .7) 1
American Processed Cheese Food	(1 slice, 3/4-ounce = 1) 1.5
Blue, crumbled	0
Brie	0
Camembert	0
Cheddar	0
Cottage, 4% milk fat, 1/2 cup	4
Cream, plain	1
Edam	1
Feta	1
Gouda	1
Havarti	0
Jarlsberg	0
Mozzarella, part skim	0
Mozzarella, whole milk	1
Muenster	0
Parmesan, chunk	0
Parmesan, grated, 1 tablespoon	0
Provolone	0
Ricotta, part skim, 1/4 cup	1
Ricotta, whole milk, 1/4 cup	2
Romano, chunk	1
Romano, grated, 2 tablespoon	1
Swiss	1

Vegetables

Filled with vitamins, minerals and antioxidants, these **vegetables, all having fewer than 4 net carbs per serving, should be eaten often.** Serving size is 1/2 cup fresh, frozen or canned unless a difference is noted.

Alfalfa sprouts
Artichoke hearts
Asparagus, 1/2 cup or 4 spears
Bamboo shoots
Bean sprouts
Broccoli
Cabbage
Cauliflower
Celery, 3/4 cup sliced or 1 rib
Cucumber
Eggplant
Green beans
Green onions
Green pepper
Lettuce
Mushrooms
Okra
Pea pods/Snow peas
Radishes
Red pepper
Sauerkraut
Spaghetti squash
Spinach
Summer squash
Tomato
Turnips
Zucchini

Although still important nutrient providers, these **vegetables containing 4-8 carbs should only be eaten occasionally.** Serving size is 1/2 cup fresh, frozen or canned unless a difference is noted.

Acorn squash, boiled
Artichoke, 1 whole
Beets
Brussel sprouts
Butternut squash, baked
"California Blend"
Carrots, 1/2 cup sliced or 1 whole 7" long
Cherry tomatoes, 10
Kohlrabi
Onion
Peas, frozen
Portabello mushrooms, 4-ounces
Pumpkin
Rutabaga
Waterchestnuts

Eating these vegetables provides too many carbs; therefore, consumption should be limited. Serving size is 1/2 cup fresh, frozen or canned unless a difference is noted.

Acorn squash, baked
Corn, 1/2 cup or 1 cob
Parsnips
Potatoes
Shallots
Sweet potatoes
Yams

Fruits

Fresh fruits are recommended for vitamins, fiber and the fact that no refined sugar has been added. **Eating protein with a serving of fruit will help stabilize blood sugar. The following fruits contain fewer than 6 net carbs per serving.** Serving size is 1/2 cup fresh or frozen unless otherwise noted.

Avocado, 1/2 of fruit
Blackberries
Boysenberries
Cherries, sour
Cranberries
Gooseberries
Loganberries
Plum, 1 fruit
Raspberries
Rhubarb
Strawberries
Watermelon

Fresh fruits still valuable for vitamins and fiber, but **contain 6-10 carbs per serving.** Serving size is 1/2 cup fresh or frozen unless otherwise noted.

Apple, 1/2 medium fruit
Apricots, 3 whole fruits
Blueberries
Cantaloupe balls
Cherries, sweet
Figs, 1 small
Grapefruit
Honeydew melon balls
Kiwifruit, 1 fruit
Kumquats, 4 fruits
Orange sections
Papaya, 1/2 small fruit
Passion fruit, 1/4 cup
Peach, 1 small fruit
Pineapple chunks
Pomegranate, 1/4 fruit
Purple grapes
Tangerine, 1 small fruit

Fresh fruits containing **11-15 carbs per serving and should be eaten sparingly.** Serving size is 1/2 cup fresh or frozen unless otherwise noted.

Green seedless grapes
Mango
Nectarine, 1 medium fruit
Persimmon, 1/2 large fruit
Red seedless grapes
Whole orange, 1 medium

Fresh fruits containing more than 15 carbs per serving and consumption should be limited.

Banana, 1 small fruit
Pear, 1 small fruit

Nuts and Seeds

Nuts and seeds provide a great snack and add flavor and crunch to many recipes. Being high in protein, fiber and fat, they are nutrient rich. Listed below are the net carbs per serving. A serving size measures 1/4 cup nuts or seeds unless otherwise noted.

Nuts or Seeds	Carbs per serving
Almonds, sliced or slivered	2
Almonds, whole, roasted	3
Brazil nuts, whole, roasted (12 nuts)	4
Cashews, whole, roasted	6
Chestnuts, whole, roasted (12 nuts)	12
Coconut, dried, shredded, sweetened	5
Coconut, dried, shredded, unsweetened	2
Hazelnuts, whole, roasted	5
Macadamia nuts, whole, roasted	1
Peanut butter, 2 tablespoons	5
Peanuts, dry-roasted	4
Peanuts, oil-roasted	4
Pecans	2
Pistachios	6
Pumpkin seeds, hulled	11
Sesame seeds (2 tablespoons)	0
Sunflower seeds, hulled	6
Walnuts	0

What to buy

Fruit

1 medium apple ____ 1 cup diced
1 pound berries (except strawberries) ____ 2 cups
1 pound grapes ____ 2 1/2 cups
1 medium lemon ____ 1 teaspoon grated lemon rind,
____ 2 tablespoons lemon juice
1 medium orange ____ 4 teaspoons grated orange rind,
____ 1/3 cup orange juice
1 medium peach ____ 1/2 cup sliced
1 pound peaches (4 medium) ____ 2 cups sliced
2 pounds pineapple (1 medium) ____ 3 cups, cubed
1 pound strawberries ____ 1 3/4 cups sliced
1 pint strawberries ____ 2 cups sliced
1 quart strawberries ____ 4 cups sliced

Vegetables

1 pound fresh asparagus (16 - 20 thin spears) ____ 2 cups, cooked
1 pound broccoli ____ 4 1/2 cups chopped
1 small cabbage head ____ 4-5 cups shredded
1 medium cabbage head ____ 6-7 cups shredded
1 large cabbage head ____ 8-9 cups shredded
1 pound carrots ____ 4 cups sliced
2 large carrots ____ 1 cup sliced
1 pound cauliflower ____ 1 1/2 cups chopped
1 rib celery ____ 3/4 cup chopped
1 medium cucumber ____ 2 cups sliced
1 pound fresh green beans ____ 4 cups fresh cut
____ 2 1/2 cups cooked
4 green onions ____ 1 cup chopped
1 medium green pepper ____ 1/2 cup chopped
1 large green pepper ____ 1 cup chopped
1 pound lettuce, Iceberg, leaf or romaine ____
____ 8 cups torn into bite-sized pieces
8 ounces mushrooms ____ 3 cups sliced (1 cup cooked)
1 medium onion ____ 1/2 cup chopped
1 1/4 large onions ____ 1 cup chopped
1 pound onions (3 large) ____ 2 1/2 cups chopped

What to buy

1 pound spinach ____ 10 cups torn into bite-sized pieces
1 medium tomato ____ 1/2 cup chopped
1 large tomato ____ 1 cup chopped
1 pound tomatoes (3 large) ____ 3 cups chopped
2 medium zucchinis ____ 4 cups sliced

Other

1 pound bacon ____ 22 regular slices
1 stick butter ____ 1/2 cup, 1/4 pound, 8 tablespoons
4 ounces bleu cheese ____ 1 cup crumbled
8 ounces cheese, cheddar, mozzarella, etc. ____ 2 cups shredded
16 ounces cheese, cheddar, mozzarella, etc. ____ 4 cups shredded
2 medium boneless, skinless chicken breasts, cooked ____ 1 1/2 cups cubed
1 pound cottage cheese ____ 2 cups
28 saltine crackers ____ 1 cup fine crumbs
1 cup whipping cream ____ 2 cups whipped
8 ounce carton whipped topping ____ 3 cups

Substitutions

1 tablespoon cornstarch

Substitute: 2 tablespoons flour or quick-cooking tapioca

1 cup buttermilk

Substitute: 1 tablespoon lemon juice or vinegar plus milk equal to 1 cup or 1 cup plain yogurt

1 cup half-and-half

Substitute: 7/8 cup milk plus 3 tablespoons melted butter

1 cup heavy cream

Subsititute: 3/4 cup milk plus 1/3 cup melted butter

1 cup whole milk

Substitute: 1/2 cup evaporated milk plus 1/2 cup water or 1 cup reconstituted nonfat dry milk plus 2 1/2 teaspoons butter

1 cup sour cream

Substitute: 1 cup plain yogurt

1 ounce chocolate square

Substitute: 3 tablespoons unsweetened cocoa plus 1 tablespoon butter

1 tablespoon fresh snipped herbs

Substitute: 1 teaspoon dried herbs

1 clove garlic

Substitute: 1/8 teaspoon garlic powder or 1/2 teaspoon minced garlic

1 teaspoon dried mustard

Substitute: 1 tablespoon prepared mustard

1 small fresh onion, chopped

Substitute: 1 tablespoon minced dried onion
or 1 teaspoon onion powder

2 cups tomato sauce

Substitute: 3/4 cup tomato paste plus 1 cup water

1 tablespoon Worcestershire sauce

Substitute: 1 tablespoon soy sauce plus dash red pepper sauce

Index

Symbols

7-Layer Salad 141
8- Inch Nut Crust 9
9 x 13-Inch Nut Crust 11
9-Inch Nut Crust 10

A

Almond Chicken Salad 117
Appetizers and Snacks
- Bacon Horseradish Dip 13
- Bacon Wrapped Shrimp 14
- Bacon Wraps 15
- Beef Jerky 16
- Beef Stuffed Mushrooms 17
- Bleu Cheese Ball 18
- Bleu Cheese Dip 19
- Cheese Dip 20
- Chicken Balls 21
- Chicken Drumettes 22
- Chilled Ham Ball 23
- Dill Dip 24
- Dried Beef Dip 25
- Favorite Cheese Ball 26
- Guacamole Dip 27
- Ham and Cheese Nut Balls 28
- Hot Brats 29
- Nichole's Stuffed Mushrooms 30
- Party Beef Balls 31
- Peanut Pineapple Bites 32
- Pepperoni-Cheese-Spinach Mini-Cups 33
- Pickle Pick-Ups 34
- Pineapple Cheese Ball 35
- Spiced Pecans 36
- Stuffed Cherry Tomatoes 37
- Stuffed Mushrooms with Bacon 38
- Stuffed Mushrooms with Parmesan Cheese 39

Apple-Rosemary Chicken 74
Arizona Beans 178
Asparagus Casserole 179
Aunt Edith's Sauerkraut and Ribs 217
Avocado Chicken Salad 118

B

Bacon and Egg Casserole 50
Bacon and Egg Salad 119
Bacon Burgers 41
Bacon Cheese Soup 227
Bacon Horseradish Dip 13
Bacon Vegetable Soup 228
Bacon Wrapped Shrimp 14
Bacon Wraps 15
Baked Apples (Microwave) 87
Baked Bacon and Eggs 51
Baked Dilled Fish 170
Baked Ham and Cheese Omelet 52
Baked Ham and Eggs 53
Baked Ham Salad 58
Baked Sausage and Eggs 54
Baked Steak 42
Baked Swiss Vegetables 180
BBQ Sauce 161
Beef Main Dishes
- Bacon Burgers 41
- Baked Steak 42
- Beef Kabobs 43
- Chuck Roast with Sauce 44
- Cubed Steak Parmesan 45
- Grilled Teriyaki Burgers 46
- Italian Meatballs (Meatloaf) 47
- Marinated Chuck Roast 48

Beef Fajita Salad 120
Beef Jerky 16
Beef Kabobs 43
Beef Stuffed Mushrooms 17
Bing Cherry Supreme 88
Bleu Cheese Ball 18
Bleu Cheese Dip 19
Bleu Cheese Salad Dressing 162
Bourbon Chicken and Gravy 75
Breakfast Main Dishes
- Bacon and Egg Casserole 50
- Baked Bacon and Eggs 51
- Baked Ham and Cheese Omelet 52
- Baked Ham and Eggs 53
- Baked Sausage and Eggs 54
- Reuben Omelet 55
- Sausage Gravy 56

Broccoli Cheese Soup 229
Broccoli Casserole 181
Broccoli Salad 142
Butterscotch Peanut Butter Mousse 89

C

Cabbage Au Gratin 182
Cabbage Salad 143
Cabbage Soup 230
Cabbage Un-rolls 59
Cantonese Dinner 218
Casseroles
- Baked Ham Salad 58
- Cabbage Un-Rolls 59
- Cheese-Stuffed Beef Rolls 60
- Chicken Bacon Casserole 61
- Chicken Broccoli Casserole 62
- Creamy Chicken Broccoli Casserole 63

Crunchy Chicken Casserole 64
Green Bean Hamburger Casserole 65
Hot Chicken Salad 66
Lasagna 67
Nichole's Cabbage Casserole 68
Pizza Casserole 69
Sausage-Stuffed Eggplant 70
Stuffed Green Peppers 71
Taco-Filled Peppers 72
Cauliflower Lettuce Layer Salad 144
Cauliflower Soup 231
Cauliflower Stir-Fry 183
Cheese Apple Salad 145
Cheese-Stuffed Beef Rolls 60
Cheese Dip 20
Cheesecake Pie 90
Cheesecake Supreme 91
Cherry-Diet Cola Dessert 92
Chicken Almond Stir-Fry 207
Chicken and Turkey Main Dishes
Apple-Rosemary Chicken 74
Bourbon Chicken and Gravy 75
Chicken Divan 76
Chicken Rosé 77
Chicken with Artichokes 78
Grilled Chicken Patties 79
Lemon-Dilled Chicken 80
Marinated Grilled Chicken 81
Parmesan Chicken 82
Pineapple Chicken 83
Quick Chicken Cacciatore 84
Teriyaki Chicken Kabobs 85
Chicken Bacon Casserole 61
Chicken Balls 21
Chicken Broccoli Casserole 62
Chicken Divan 76
Chicken Drumettes 22
Chicken Oriental 208
Chicken Rosé 77
Chicken Soup with Almonds 232
Chicken Walnut Sauté 209
Chicken with Artichokes 78
Chili 233
Chili Salad 121
Chilled Cheesecake 93
Chilled Ham Ball 23
Chocolate Cheesecake Singles 94
Chocolate Peanut Pops 95
Chocolate Pie 96
Chocolate Silk Pie 97
Chuck Roast with Sauce 44
Company Cauliflower Casserole 184
Crabmeat Salad 122
Cream Cheese Puffs 98
Creamy Bacon, Lettuce, Tomato Soup 234
Creamy Chicken Broccoli Casserole 63
Creamy Mushrooms 185
Crunchy Chicken Casserole 64
Cubed Steak Parmesan 45

D

Dairy Net Carb Counts 243
Desserts
Baked Apples 87
Bing Cherry Supreme 88
Butterscotch Peanut Butter Mousse 89
Cheesecake Pie 90
Cheesecake Supreme 91
Cherry-Diet Cola Dessert 92
Chilled Cheesecake 93
Chocolate Cheesecake Singles 94
Chocolate Peanut Pops 95
Chocolate Pie 96
Chocolate Silk Pie 97
Cream Cheese Puffs 98
Four Layer Dessert 99
Frozen Peanut Butter Dessert 100
Frozen Pops 101
Fruit Fluff 102
Fruity Cheese Fluff 103
Layered Gelatin Dessert 104
Lemon Cream Nutty Delight 105
Lime Dessert 106
Margueritaville Pecan Pie 107
Peanut Butter Cookies 108
Peanut Butter Pie 109
Pumpkin Chiffon Dessert 110
Pumpkin Cream Pie 111
Pumpkin Fluff 112
Strawberry Pecan Dessert 113
Strawberry White Chocolate Mousse 114
Vanilla Silk Pie 115
Deviled Eggs 186
Dill Dip 24
Dilled Cucumber Salad 146
Dilled Rump Roast with Sauce 219
Dilled Seafood Casserole 171
Dried Beef Dip 25

E

Elegant Fish 172

F

Favorite Cheese Ball 26
Foodles (Pork Barbeque) 131
Four Layer Dessert 99
French Dressing 163
Frozen Peanut Butter Dessert 100
Frozen Pops 101
Fruit Fluff 102
Fruits: Net Carb Rankings 245
Fruity Cheese Fluff 103

G

Garden Skillet 187
Garlic Green Beans 188
Grandma's Green Beans 189
Green Bean Casserole 190
Green Bean Hamburger Casserole 65
Green Bean Salad 147
Green Bean Swiss Cheese Crunch 192
Green Beans with Almonds 191
Green Peppers with Tomatoes 193
Grilled Beer Brats 132
Grilled Chicken Caesar Salad 123
Grilled Chicken Patties 79
Grilled Teriyaki Burgers 46
Grilled Tuna Steak 173
Guacamole Dip 27

H

Ham and Cheese Nut Balls 28
Ham and Cheese Rolls 133
Ham Roll-Ups 134
Ham Salad 124
Hard-Cooked Eggs 8
Hot Bacon Dressing 164
Hot Bacon-Mustard Dressing 165
Hot Brats 29
Hot Chicken Salad 66

I

Italian Cucumber Tomato Salad 148
Italian Meatballs (or Meatloaf) 47
Italian Salad 149

J

Joni's Chicken Salad 125

L

Lasagna 67
Layered Gelatin Dessert 104
Layered Spinach Salad 150
Layered Tex-Mex Salad 126
Lemon Cream Nutty Delight 105
Lemon-Dilled Chicken 80
Lime Dessert 106

M

Margueritaville Pecan Pie 107
Main Dish Salads
- Almond Chicken Salad 117
- Avocado Chicken Salad 118
- Bacon and Egg Salad 119
- Beef Faijta Salad 120
- Chili Salad 121
- Crabmeat Salad 122
- Grilled Chicken Caesar Salad 123
- Ham Salad 124
- Joni's Chicken Salad 125
- Layered Tex-Mex Salad 126
- Oriental Crunch Salad 127
- Taco Salad 128
- Tuna Salad 129

Mandarin Orange Salad 151
Marinated Chuck Roast 48
Marinated Grilled Chicken 81
Mediterranean Green Beans 194
Microwave Cauliflower with Cheese Sauce 195
Microwave Cheese Sauce 166
Microwave Dilled Vegetables 196
Montana Goulash 210
Moo Goo Gai Pan 211
Mushroom Salad 152

N

Nichole's Cabbage Casserole 68
Nichole's Stuffed Mushrooms 30
Nuts and Seeds Net Carb Counts 246

O

Oriental Crunch Salad 127
Oriental Green Beans 197
Oriental Grilled Chops 136
Oriental Vegetables 198
Oven Bar-B-Cue Ribs 137
Overnight Slaw 153

P

Parmesan Chicken 82
Party Beef Balls 31
Peanut Butter Cookies 108
Peanut Butter Pie 109
Peanut Pineapple Bites 32
Pepper Steak with Oriental Gravy 212
Pepperoni-Cheese-

Spinach Mini-Cups 33
Pickled Cucumbers 154
Pickle Pick-Ups 34
Pineapple Cheese Ball 35
Pineapple Chicken 83
Pizza Casserole 69

Pork Main Dishes

Foodles (Pork Barbeque) 131
Grilled Beer Brats 132
Ham and Cheese Rolls 133
Ham Roll-Ups 134
Oriental Grilled Chops 136
Oven Bar-B-Cue Ribs 137
Pork Kabobs 138

Pork Chops with Squash 220
Pork Kabobs 138
Pumpkin Chiffon Dessert 110
Pumpkin Cream Pie 111
Pumpkin Fluff 112

Q

Quick Chicken Cacciatore 84

R

Red Cabbage Salad 155
Reuben Omelet 55
Roast Pork Rosemary 221
Roquefort Dressing 167

S

Salads

7-Layer Salad 141
Broccoli Salad 142
Cabbage Salad 143
Cauliflower Lettuce Layer Salad 144
Cheese Apple Salad 145
Dilled Cucumber Salad 146
Green Bean Salad 147
Italian Cucumber Tomato Salad 148
Italian Salad 149
Layered Spinach Salad 150
Mandarin Orange Salad 151
Mushroom Salad 152
Overnight Slaw 153
Pickled Cucumbers 154
Red Cabbage Salad 155
Slaw 156
Spinach Salad 157
Summer Salad 158
Wilted Lettuce Salad 159

Sauces and Dressings

BBQ Sauce 161
Bleu Cheese Salad Dressing 162
French Dressing 163
Hot Bacon Dressing 164
Hot Bacon-Mustard Dressing 165
Microwave Cheese Sauce 166
Roquefort Dressing 167
Sesame Dressing 168

Sausage-Stuffed Eggplant 70
Sausage Gravy 56

Seafood Main Dishes

Baked Dilled Fish 170
Dilled Seafood Casserole 171
Elegant Fish 172
Grilled Tuna Steak 173
Seafood Au Gratin 174
Seafood Supreme 175
Tuna Casserole 176

Seafood Au Gratin 174
Seafood Supreme 175
Sesame Dressing 168

Side Dishes

Arizona Beans 178
Asparagus Casserole 179
Baked Swiss Vegetables 180
Broccoli Casserole 181
Cabbage Au Gratin 182
Cauliflower Stir-Fry 183
Company Cauliflower Casserole 184
Creamy Mushrooms 185
Deviled Eggs 186
Garden Skillet 187
Garlic Green Beans 188
Grandma's Green Beans 189
Green Bean Casserole 190
Green Beans with Almonds 191
Green Bean Swiss Cheese Crunch 192
Green Peppers with Tomatoes 193
Mediterranean Green Beans 194
Microwave Cauliflower with Cheese Sauce 195
Microwaved Dilled Vegetables 196
Oriental Green Beans 197
Oriental Vegetables 198
Slow Cooker Broccoli 199
Snow Peas and Almonds 200
Snow Peas with Water Chestnuts 201
Special Baked Green Beans 202
Stir Fries 203
Wilted Cabbage with Cheese 204
Zucchini Italian 205

Skillets

Chicken Almond Stir Fry 207
Chicken Oriental 208
Chicken Walnut Sauté 209
Montana Goulash 210
Moo Goo Gai Pan 211

Pepper Steak with Oriental Gravy 212
Sub Gum 213
Szechuan Pork 214
Wilted Cabbage and Sausage 215

Slaw 156
Slow Cooked Beef with Mushrooms 222
Slow Cooked Chicken Italian 223

Slow Cooker Main Dishes

Aunt Edith's Sauerkraut and Ribs 217
Cantonese Dinner 218
Dilled Rump Roast with Sauce 219
Pork Chops with Squash 220
Roast Pork Rosemary 221
Slow Cooked Beef with Mushrooms 222
Slow Cooked Chicken Italian 223
Slow Cooker Turkey 224
Stuffed Beef Rounds 225

Slow Cooker Broccoli 199
Slow Cooker Turkey 224
Snow Peas and Almonds 200
Snow Peas with Water Chestnuts 201

Soups

Bacon Cheese Soup 227
Bacon Vegetable Soup 228
Broccoli Cheese Soup 229
Cabbage Soup 230
Cauliflower Soup 231
Chicken Soup with Almonds 232
Chili 233
Creamy Bacon, Lettuce, Tomato Soup 234
Taco Soup 235
Vegetable Soup 236

Special Baked Green Beans 202
Spiced Pecans 36
Spinach Salad 157
Stir Fries 203
Strawberry Pecan Dessert 113
Strawberry White Chocolate Mousse 114
Stuffed Beef Rounds 225
Stuffed Cherry Tomatoes 37
Stuffed Green Peppers 71
Stuffed Mushrooms with Bacon 38
Stuffed Mushrooms with Parmesan Cheese 39
Sub Gum 213
Substitutions 248
Summer Salad 158
Szechuan Pork 214

T

Taco-Filled Peppers 72
Taco Salad 128
Taco Soup 235
Teriyaki Chicken Kabobs 85
Tips for Using This Cookbook 6-7
Toasted Amonds, Walnuts, Sesame Seeds 8
Tuna Casserole 176
Tuna Salad 129

V

Vanilla Silk Pie 115
Vegetable Soup 236
Vegetables: Net Carb Rankings 244

W

Whipped Cream 8
Wilted Cabbage and Sausage 215
Wilted Cabbage with Cheese 204
Wilted Lettuce Salad 159

Z

Zucchini Italian 205

Still Hungry?

Keep these items on hand and ready to eat:

- Celery Sticks with Peanut Butter
- Cheese Slices
- Cottage Cheese with Fresh Fruit
- Cottage Cheese with Tomatoes
- Crabmeat with Melted Butter
- Dill Pickles
- Apple Half with Cheese Slice
- Ham Slices
- Mixed Nuts
- Olives
- Pork Rinds with Vegetable Dip
- Ring Bologna
- Seasoned Sliced Almonds
- Shrimp Cocktail
- Smoked Almonds
- Summer Sausage
- Vegetables with Dip

Prepare these recipes from *Easy Low Carb Creations* to have on hand, ready to eat or reheat and eat:

- Bacon Wraps
- Chicken Drumettes
- Chocolate Peanut Pops
- Celery with Cheese Dip
- Frozen Pops
- Peanut Butter Cookies
- Pickle Pick-Ups
- Spiced Pecans
- Vegetables with Dill Dip
- Vegetables with Cheese Ball

For additional copies of *Easy Low Carb Creations*, contact the authors through the *Easy Low Carb Creations* web site at **www.easylowcarbcreations.com**
or
Dreams and Motivation Publishing, Inc.
135 W. State Road 124
Wabash, IN 46992
www.dreamsandmotivationpublishing.com